Laurent Gbagbo's Trial and the Indictment of the International Criminal Court

A Pan-African Victory

Gnaka Lagoké

Lincoln University

Series in Social Equality and Justice

www.vernonpress.com

In the Americas:	*In the rest of the world:*
Vernon Press	Vernon Press
1000 N West Street, Suite 1200	C/Sancti Espiritu 17,
Wilmington, Delaware, 19801	Malaga, 29006
United States	Spain

Series in Social Equality and Justice

Library of Congress Control Number: 2022950349

ISBN: 978-1-62273-873-1

I dedicate this book to Africa and its people, yearning for freedom, justice, and unity and who want to conquer the right to have the right to choose their own path and to freedom lovers, justice seekers, and human rights' advocates of the world whose voices have been sidelined and smothered regarding international justice.

Contents

Acknowledgments

This book is the result of a long and improbable journey of lectures, conferences, interviews, research, and social activism in the fight for freedom, justice, and truth in relation to the crisis in Ivory Coast and the ICC. In the course of that journey I have been enriched by numerous friends, foes, colleagues, and journalists I am indebted to. My primary expression of gratitude goes to the Great Architect, the Source of that collective energy and for the vision and grace He has bestowed upon me, which has been the driving engine of my journey.

I would like to honor the person through whom I came to this world: my mother Clémentine Guédé. She instilled in me from a young age the audacity to believe in the ability to materialize impossible things. I express my gratitude to my younger sister Marie who is like a guardian angel to me and whose emotional, material and financial support has never failed me.

I am indebted to the regents of my destiny, to the members of my cluster, visible and invisible, for their infallible commitment to my achievement. I thank Louise Kandakai for her insightful guidance and for her emotional and spiritual support. I have been the beneficiary of her wisdom.

I owe an unpayable debt to my significant other, Darlene De Graffinreidte, for her unconditional love, guidance, schooling, and multidimensional support of all my projects. She sustained me in a chapter of my struggling life. She was the pillar I could lean on to complete my PhD. She was the bedrock of the series of the Pan-African conferences my friends and I have launched since 2007; she was the cornerstone of my struggle for the sovereignty of Ivory Coast; and she is the pillar of my writing projects. I have been learning and benefitting from the insights, hindsight, foresight, and extensive knowledge of her soul of a master teacher. She contributed greatly to the completion of this project with her editorial and artistic skills and critical overview.

In the journey that led to this book, I attended and presented at several academic conferences. The first of the series was organized, surprisingly enough, in The Hague, the headquarters of the ICC, where Laurent Gbagbo was imprisoned. I owe a deep gratitude to Dr. Amber Murrey-Ndewa, Associate Professor at Oxford University (England), with whom I share a vision of a world of justice and freedom. She was the one who connected me to the organizers of the conference on ICC and Africa in The Hague, May 21–24, 2014. Also, I was privileged to speak in her class, on the same issue, when she was teaching at Clark University in Worcester, Massachusetts. In the line of the series of conference opportunities on the ICC, I would like to express my profound gratitude to Dr. Josephine Dawuni-Darpa, Associate Professor of political sciences at Howard University. Even though we do not share the same views on the issue of the ICC, she was the channel that connected me to the conference on ICC and Africa organized at Ghana Institute of Management and Public Administration (GIMPA) in Accra, March 16–18, 2016. It was at that gathering that I clashed with the chief prosecutor of the ICC, Fatou Bensouda, on her handling of the investigation in Ivory Coast. It was during that conference that I met Dr. David Hoile of the London-based Africa Research Centre, author of the book *Justice Denied*, with whom I have partnered since on ICC-related matters. He was the one who informed me about the ICC conference in Windhoek (Namibia)—June 12–15, 2016—that both of us attended and presented at. I owe then to Dr. David Hoile a deep gratitude for his guidance and his faith in a world of true justice. Moreover, I drew tremendous inspiration from his book.

I would like to also express my appreciation to Mrs. Jeanne Tilman, who invited me to share the stage with Dr. David Hoile at a public conference on the International Criminal Court that she put together in Amsterdam on September 28, 2018. Thanks to her invitation, I revamped the idea of the project of writing this book that Vernon Press accepted to publish. I have been introduced to that publishing house by Dr. Charles Quist-Adade, professor at Kwantlen Polytechnic University in Vancouver (Canada), whom I thank for his guidance and for putting me in contact with Vernon Press.

I am indebted to Habiba Toure, a Paris-based lawyer. When I needed it the most, she helped me locate the right court documents for this project. Furthermore, she provided some valuable information that enriched the content of this work. And above all, she was the only legal expert who took time out of her busy schedule to walk me through this journey, to help me undersand the judicial lexicon and explain to me what I could not understand. I would extend my gratitude to Demba Traore who connected me with her.

I would like to acknowledge the significant contributions of Mrs. Marie-Antoinette Singleton to this book. As companions in the struggle for the sovereignty of Ivory Coast, we have partnered, shared ideas, discussed, and strategized together. I also drew insights from a PowerPoint she put together in the early years of the post-electoral crisis of 2010-2011. I express my deepest thanks to Cynthia Kumassah whose timely and providential appearance, whose uplifting energy and whose editorial input contributed to the improvement of the work, in the final stage of this literary journey.

I would like to appreciate some of my compatriots, some of the members of my visible cluster, who dare to share with me a vision of a redeemed and united Africa that stands upon a unified and prosperous Ivory Coast. They have been true friends in some specific moments of my life, and I express to them my profound gratitude: Dr. Dagbo Gode Pierre; Sylla Falillou; Konin Kouadio; Gustave Assiri; Marc Nguessan; Marie Mactar Niang; Rachel Adjoumani; Dominique Kouadio;; JDK; Georges Duncan; Franck Ahoussi; Lea Boli; Dr. David Okou; Dr. Koffi Kouadio Becanty; Dr. Drissa Kone; Abraham Fadiga and his wife Caroline Patricia; Jean-Louis Pehe; Ange-David Baimey; Fabrice Leby; and Jean-Basile Nguetta. To the list of my compatriots, I add some friends of Ivory Coast and fellow Pan-Africanists, Eugene Pehoua and Kala Kinyama Richardson and Dr. Akil Khalfani who also helped me broaden my understanding of Pan-Africanism.

In the face of the imperial might of the international community, several social activists have provided the strategic support I needed, either in the name of internationalism or in the name of Pan-Africanism or in the name of both. I am indebted to them for their tremendous contributions to the struggle for the sovereignty of Ivory Coast: Maurice Carney (Director of the Friends of the Congo), Netfa Freeman (Institute for Policies Studies), Brian Becker, Heather Benno, Eugene Puryear, Sean Blackmon (Party for Socialism and Liberation/ Answer Coalition), Mary Alice Waters, Omari Musa, James Harris, Arlene Rubinstein (Socialist Workers Party), Wuyi Jacobs (Afrobeat Radio), Fahima Seck, and the Sankara family (Pascal, Paul, Pauline, and Lydie).

In the line of my professional stability, which greatly contributed to make this work possible, I express my gratitude to Dr. Mjiba Frehiwot, Dr. Zizwe Poe and his wife Mrs. Evelyn Davis-Poe, Sophia Sotileo; Dr. Patricia Joseph, Dr. Patricia Ramsey, Marion Amos Bernard, and Dr. Brenda Allen.

Dr. Mjiba Frehiwot is a friend and a vision partner. We both graduated from Howard University. Since our encounter, we built an unbreakable bond for the revival of Pan-Africanism. We have been teaming up, and with other friends and social activists, we have organized several Pan-African conferences, including some on the Ivory Coast crisis. She has been invaluable to me both for the vision and for my professional stability at Lincoln University. She was the one who recommended me to Dr. Zizwe Poe, Director of the Pan-Africana Studies Program at Lincoln University (Pennsylvania). Dr. Poe invested himself so that I could be hired in the Department of History, Political Science, Philosophy, Religion, and Pan-Africana Studies, certainly supported by the deities and ancestors namely Kwame Nkrumah, an alumnus of Lincoln University whom I claim and whose legacy I defend. He could count on the strategic support of Sophia Sotileo to whom I also owe a debt. But the hiring decision was made by Dr. Patricia Joseph, then Dean of Faculty. She was the hand that pulled me from the tunnel, at the darkest moment of my career, seconded by the former Vice-President in charge of Academic Affairs, Dr. Patricia Ramsey.

Once hired, I benefitted from the support and the mentorship of a number of persons at Lincoln University. I am grateful to Mrs. Evelyn Davis-Poe, who provided me with valuable support through the professor's assistant programs as a way to make me be an effective teacher.

I also express my gratitude to Marion Bernard Amos, Vice-President at Lincoln University in charge of Faculty Affairs, for her leadership, guidance, and friendship. She played a significant role at a particular juncture of my life, by making sure this book be published.

I extend my chief appreciation to Dr. Brenda Allen for her leadership and her commitment to elevate the name and the legacy of Lincoln University (Pennsylvania), which she has been presiding over since 2017, to new and higher heights. Since becoming president of the university, she has been unceasingly transforming Lincoln University (PA) into a fast-improving HBCU and a rewarding place to be.

Last but not least, I acknowledge the contributions of several journalists who, out of fairness, gave me the opportunity to express my vision of the new dispensation of Pan-Africanism, which stands upon the Ubuntu philosophy and my dissenting views—my lone voice on behalf of millions of voiceless, suppressed, and oppressed people of Africa and the world. They are affiliated with Democracy Now, Voice of America, Australian Broadcast Television, Russia Today, CCTV, TVC News, First Digital TV, Sputnik Radio, BBC, TRT, Afrobeat Radio, IvoirTV, Black Star News and Afrique Media.

Preface

A decade ago—following a controversial election after which both the then-incumbent president, Laurent Gbagbo, and his challenger, Alassane Ouattara, claimed victory—Ivory Coast entered a turbulent zone that led to an electoral stalemate.[1] The latter candidate was recognized as the lawful president by the electoral commission and by the international community. The former was declared the winner by the constitutional council, and his defiance provoked the wrath of the international community. French troops and the Ivory Coast–based UN forces entered the war, siding with the pro–Alassane Ouattara rebels who had occupied the northern part of the country for eight years, since 2002. Laurent Gbagbo was defeated militarily and captured on April 11, 2011. Alassane Ouattara became immediately the effective president of the country.

The electoral stalemate was a defining moment both for Ivory Coast, my country of origin, and for me. For most of the time Laurent Gbagbo was in power (2000–2010), I had had a certain amount of dissension with his administration and about some of his actions, policies, and decisions. Even though I have claimed part of his political legacy, I have also distanced myself from another part of the same political legacy. When the electoral stalemate erupted, I decided to defend what I thought was right and what I saw as the right side of history: to support the struggle for nationalism, sovereignty, and Pan-Africanism in Ivory Coast in what appears to be a revolution of its own kind linked to the global struggle for the redemption of Africa and its diaspora. And Laurent Gbagbo, despite his missteps and shortcomings, came to symbolize that new wave of Ivorian nationalism embedded in the revival of Pan-Africanism, as he meant to free Ivory Coast. I could not be a spectator to a tragedy and to a martyrdom of the Ivorian people, who—despite their different political ideologies, religions, and ethnic groups—constitute the humus of the African nation, as Ivory Coast, a multiethnic and multicultural nation is the microcosm of the United Nations of Africa. My heart of a Pan-Africanist enjoined me to tune the trumpet of justice. Like many I embarked on an improbable journey. All odds were against us, but I was convinced that we would win; Dr. Martin Luther King, Jr. said it appropriately: "The arc of the moral universe is very long, but it always bends towards justice." I gave media interviews, lectures, and conferences in universities, at community gatherings, and on social media about Ivory Coast's political, electoral, and military crisis.

---

[1] Ivory Coast and Côte d'Ivoire are used interchangeably throughout the book.

When Laurent Gbagbo was taken to The Hague, to the International Criminal Court (ICC), the issue of the International Court became part of the focus of my struggle and of my narrative, and I had to oppose the selective justice of the ICC. My detractors and some friends questioned the wisdom of my path. Even though I understood their concern and their assessment of the slim possibilities of victory, I knew that this battle was just and that I would be vindicated before the tribunal of history where the ICC's fate and condemnation would be sealed. I had to respond to this call, which is in line with the battle for the soul of Ivory Coast and Africa.

Laurent Gbagbo's trial became the legal battle of a series of episodes of a crisis that erupted in 2002. His imprisonment in a western country, a former colonial power, captured the imagination of many Pan-Africanists and reinforced the narrative of European neo-colonialism. They organized as they could to denounce the ICC as a court, seen as promoting a victor's justice and which is perceived as a tool in the hands of the most powerful nations, which only believe in the law of might is right. My commitment to true justice has made me oppose the instrumentalization of the court as a tool in the hands of the most powerful, even if I adhere to its spirit and to its noble mission. The struggle for justice cannot be segregated.

My commitment to true justice led me to several American universities and led me to take trips overseas, including to The Hague (Holland), May 24–25, 2014; to Accra (Ghana) March 17–18, 2016; and to Windhoek (Namibia) June 14–15, 2016. I have presented at academic conferences organized in these locations. In Accra—on Thursday, March 17, 2016, at Ghana Institute of Management and Public Administration (GIMPA)—I had an altercation with Fatou Bensouda, the chief prosecutor of the ICC, about her selective investigation in Ivory Coast. I decided to transform the paper on Laurent Gbagbo's trial before the court into a book, encouraged by events and friends. This work meets my professional and political goals, as I have been an agent of justice, freedom, and unity of Africa for decades. Embedded in the Pan-African vision I cherish, as a faculty member of Lincoln University in Pennsylvania (PA), it contributes also to the telling of the story of that university as it spotlights the contributions of two of its greatest alumni, two advocates of Pan-Africanism and champions of human rights: Kwame Nkrumah and Nnamdi Azikiwe.

In sum, the fight for true justice in Ivory Coast is the epitome of my struggle for justice and peace in the world. I have sided with the victims of human rights abuses across the globe, I have opposed various types of oppression, and I have shared the ideal of international justice. Decades ago, I happened to be in Germany for a mission which coincided with the 60th anniversary of the liberation of the concentration camp of Buchenwald. I visited that camp. I could feel the indignation of my soul at the sight of the crematories still full of the memories of the horrors of the holocaust engraved in the defaced human landscape. My imagination of the spectacle of the horrendous cruelties of the Nazis had made me understand the relevance and the imperative of international justice. This experience encrusted in me made me understand very quickly that in the case of the Ivorian crisis, Laurent Gbagbo's trial lacked the *prima facie* evidence.

Abstract

The International Criminal Court (ICC), created in 2002 to combat impunity, projects a sense of unfairness and stirs an unending debate. A trial before the court epitomizes the controversy surrounding the court, perceived as a neocolonialist tool in the hands of the most powerful nations. This research critically examines the trial of the former president of Ivory Coast, Laurent Gbagbo. The two-decade crisis in Ivory Coast was a series of armed, diplomatic, and political conflicts in which human rights were violated by all sides. Military confrontation resumed as a result of an electoral stalemate that followed a controversial presidential election in the fall of 2010. The most atrocious human rights abuse was perpetrated at the end of March 2011, by the rebel forces backed by the French and the United Nations troops: the massacre of Duékoué. In one day, hundreds of Laurent Gbagbo's followers were killed. However, the ICC undertook a selective prosecution against Gbagbo's camp.

After a trial of eight years, Laurent Gbagbo was finally acquitted. The news of his unanticipated acquittal shocked the world. Later, that decision was overturned and transformed into freedom with binding and coercive conditions by the Appeals Chamber, which had succumbed to political pressure. The former president of Ivory Coast spent months of confinement in Belgium until the Appeals Chamber rebutted the prosecutor's appeal against his release and confirmed his total acquittal and that of Blé Goudé. He eventually went back to Ivory Coast on June 17, 2021.

The trial of Laurent Gbagbo before the ICC, despite his acquittal (a tardy one), reflects a series of biases germane to international law and international justice, such as the victor's justice stance, the conflict between national law and international law, the question of sovereignty, and the issue of lawfare. The trial of Laurent Gbagbo, which was the hallmark of the selective international justice system embedded in unfairness, led to a historical landmark with his shocking acquittal which led to the indictment of the International Court whose fate has thus been sealed before history.

Introduction

The existence of an international arbitration institution has been a long-sought dream of justice lovers, human rights activists, and justice seekers across the globe. When the International Criminal Court (ICC) finally came to existence in 2002, it was the latest culmination of a long journey for the search and the quest of global justice in the field of international affairs. It vows to combat impunity, to bring justice to victims, and to bring victimizers to justice. Its birth was a major shift in international arbitration architecture.[1] It aims to enable "the values of global justice, human rights, and the rule of law."[2] The initial hopes it raised have waned, and it remains today at the center of an unending controversy. This research, which takes the Laurent Gbagbo's trial as a case study, critically examines the question of global human rights and the *modus operandi* of the International Criminal Court in world politics and in the field of international relations.

The idea of the existence of an international arbitration architecture was first expressed in contemporary history in 1872, after the Franco-Prussian War, by Gustave Moynier, resurfaced recurrently throughout history, during the trial of Leipzig after WWI, during the Nuremberg and Tokyo trials after WWII, and through the subsequent creations of special tribunals: Yugoslavia, Rwanda, and Sierra Leone.[3] This dream finally came to fruition with the creation of the International Criminal Court, whose constitutive document is the Treaty of Rome, adopted in 1998. While the idea of an international justice institution was welcomed, the way the business of the ICC is conducted nurtures suspicion, mistrust and distrust. Three world powers who have veto power at the United Nations (United States, China, and Russia) have not endorsed the court, and sóme even seek to undermine it. The other powers that enjoy the veto power at the United Nations Security Council (France and United Kingdom) support its existence, like the entire European Union, but have expressed some serious reservations regarding its functioning. In general, most powers use the court to advance their national security agendas to the

---

[1] Dawn Rothe and Christopher W. Mullins, *Symbolic Gestures and the Generation of Global Social Control* (Lanham: Lexington Books, 2006), 61.

[2] Dominic McGoldrick and Eric Donnelly, "Criminal Trials before International Tribunals: Legality and Legitimacy," in *The Permanent International Criminal Court, Legal and Policy Issues*, eds. Dominic McGoldrick et al. (Oxford: Hart Publishing, 2004), 42.

[3] Mark D. Kielsgard, *Reluctant Engagement: US Policy and the International Criminal Court* (Leiden: Martinus Nijhoff Publishers, 2010), 78.

detriment of the interests of true international justice and of the rights of weaker nations, mainly African. There are double-dealings and double standards on the part of both world powers and the ICC itself in the handling of international justice.

Most of the arrest warrants of the ICC were for Africans, and the twenty-seven cases of prosecution concerned African countries, including Ivory Coast, Sudan, the Democratic Republic of Congo, and Kenya. This research deals specifically with the court's relationship with Africa, mainly with Ivory Coast and the trial of its former president, Laurent Gbagbo.

After the electoral stalemate of 2010–2011, following the controversial presidential election in Ivory Coast, the then-incumbent president Laurent Gbagbo, who is known as a nationalist, was believed to have lost while he claimed victory. The international community recognized his challenger Alassane Ouattara as the legitimate president of the country. After failed negotiations, the international community, under the leadership of France and the United Nations, resorted to war against Ivory Coast, siding with the rebels to dislodge him. It was an escalation of violence in the context of the resumption of the war that erupted in 2002, which had led to the division of the country into two parts: the south controlled by Laurent Gbagbo and the north in the hands of the pro–Alassane Ouattara rebels.

The United Nations and France's troops bombed the positions of the army loyal to the former head of state of Ivory Coast, including the presidential palace where he found refuge. He was captured on April 11, 2011, and after seven months of custody in the once-rebel-controlled area in the north of the country, he was transferred to the ICC, where he was put on trial for several counts: namely crimes against humanity, alongside with his youth organization leader, Blé Goudé.[4] Later, the court also issued an arrest warrant for Gbagbo's wife, Simone Gbagbo, who spent seven years in prison in Ivory Coast.[5]

With the involvement of the ICC in the Ivorian crisis, the trial of Laurent Gbagbo became the legal battle of a series of episodes in a crisis that erupted in Ivory Coast in 2002. Thus, this research posits that the hallmark of the controversy of the ICC is the trial of Laurent Gbagbo. While several believed justice was being served, many others decried the selectivity of the court, which omitted the responsibility of Alassane Ouattara and his warlords, who brought

---

[4] The ICC confirmed the charges against Blé Goudé on Thursday, December 11, 2014.

[5] The ICC ordered Simone Gbagbo be handed over to it, on Thursday, December 11, 2014, rejecting Alassane Ouattara's regime's claims that it had taken the proper steps to try her in Ivory Coast.

a civil war to Ivory Coast in 2002, and who resorted to violence to dislodge Gbagbo in 2011. The former president of Ivory Coast was therefore singled out in a two-decade crisis in which all sides committed human rights violations. The single most atrocious human rights violation, the massacre of Duékoué (in the western part of the country) was perpetrated by the rebels during the electoral stalemate. Several hundreds of Laurent Gbagbo's followers were butchered, in one day, at the end of March 2011.

An increasing number of critics therefore denounce the one-sided prosecution and assert that the ICC is a neocolonialist institution in the hands of neocolonial forces that have been undermining Africa's quest for self-determination.[6] Its prosecutorial approach has been in collusion with the interests of foreign powers such as France, the former colonial power of the country, which has been on the side of Ouattara's forces and which has been pursuing a neocolonial agenda in its former African colonies, namely in Ivory Coast.

This research discusses the selective prosecutorial rationale and strategy of the ICC and the handling of the prosecutions in the Ivory Coast, and highlights significant issues related to the credibility of the International Criminal Court. The court denied Gbagbo the presumption of innocence, as his bail request was rejected thirteen times. He was eventually acquitted after eight years of trial in the context of a growing opposition against the court embedded in the revival of Pan-Africanism that rose against the court.

While answering the questions mentioned below, I will demonstrate that the forceful engagement of the ICC reinforces the general chorus of the court's critics, who see it as an extension of neo-colonialism: Is the ICC living up to its core functions to promote impartial justice and to undertake impartial investigation? How can the ICC prove its impartiality in Ivory Coast while its one-sided prosecution seems to reinforce the consolidation of the victor's justice? How can the ICC claim that it is not serving neocolonial interests while the consequences of its actions coincide with the plans of the neocolonial forces that initially opposed President Gbagbo?

This research aims at shedding light on factors at the basis of the controversy about the ICC, some inscribed in its founding document. It deconstructs the mainstream and the widespread Manichean view about the Ivorian crisis and Laurent Gbagbo's trial. In light of the historical background of this research, this study demonstrates that the ICC trial of Gbagbo does not serve the interests of

---

6 Raymond Koudou Kessié, "Pourquoi le Président Gbagbo doit etre Libéré," in *Le Président Laurent Gbagbo à la Cour pénale internationale: Justice ou imposture*, eds. Raymond Koudou Kessié and Hubert Oulaye (Paris: L'Harmattan, 2013), 224.

true justice and is at odds with the goal of nation building, peace, and reconciliation in a once war-torn country. This work is in contrast with the Eurocentric perspective of the trial.

The discussion in this book is conducted through two theoretical frameworks: the realist theory and Pan-Africanism. The *modus operandi* of France, the United Nations, the Western powers, and the ICC in the Ivorian crisis stands mostly on the realist theory, echoing the words of John Mearsheimer, who argues that "the sad fact is that international politics has always been a ruthless and dangerous business, and it is likely to remain that way."[7] He states that great powers are never satisfied with the power they have, and therefore they strive to increase it or to control their spheres of influence or expand them.[8] The neocolonial aspect can be interpreted both through the lens of the realist theory and through Pan-Africanism.

With regard to Pan-Africanism, it is imperative to note that it is this movement that seeks to unify Africa and its peoples—and that advocates values such as unity, common purpose, oneness, solidarity, and pride among Africans and peoples of Africans descent.[9] This theory will be used to explain the reaction of a community of justice seekers and freedom lovers who see the fate of Laurent Gbagbo as the epitome of the African collective memory filled with recurrent tragedies from slavery to neo-colonialism. For them, the trial is a remembrance of the misfortunes of the African leadership and of the pogrom of the African people. Therefore, it will be demonstrated how this trial captures the imagination of Africa and its people and contributes to the revival of Pan-Africanism.

The historical context is also a favorable opportunity to shed light on this study. Recent political developments that have transpired in the United States, in Sudan, and in the Russian invasion of Ukraine pique interest in this book. A book on the ICC in a context marked by an ongoing war between the United States and the court, the military overthrow of Omar al-Bashir, former president of Sudan, who has been a target of the ICC after a people's movement, and the numerous call for justice against the Russian president Vladimir Putin since the Russian invasion of Ukraine on February 24, 2022 sharpened the curiosity of the court stakeholders and many readers. Besides the unpredictable and suspenseful trial of the former Ivorian president, these three events

---

[7] John J. Mearsheimer, *The Tragedy of Great Power Politics* (New York: W.W. Norton & Company, 2003), 2.

[8] John J. Mearsheimer, *The Tragedy of Great Power Politics*, 2-3.

[9] P. Olisanwuche Esedebe, *Pan-Africanism: The Idea and Movement 1776–1963*, 2nd ed. (Washington, DC: Howard University Press, 1994), 5.

heightened the hotly debated issue of international justice's ability to deliver justice.

This research is significant in many ways. The book contributes to the plurality of discourses about international justice, about the relationship between the ICC and Africa, and about the trial of Laurent Gbagbo. It is a distinctive and singular work that will greatly contribute to enriching the debate about the ICC and Africa. It will be one of the very first in English to discuss at length the Ivory Coast crisis and Laurent Gbagbo's trial in relation to international justice, Pan-Africanism, and neo-colonialism. It is important to underline that there has been a blackout of that trial in the United States and in the English-speaking world. Consequently, many scholars and people are uninformed about it. Most books published on the role of the International Criminal Court in the Ivory Coast crisis are in French. These pioneer books gave a thorough and expansive analysis of Gbagbo's trial and denounced the prosecutorial approach of the ICC in collusion with neocolonial interests, but they could not link such insightful analysis to the discussion on Pan-Africanism and to the history of international justice as this work does.

This book will therefore fill a vacuum. It provides to the readers an update about the intricacies of a trial that is both the hallmark of the controversy surrounding the ICC and a landmark in its outcome in the history of international justice. Laurent Gbagbo is the first former head of state to be brought before the court; he was then the first former head of state to be acquitted, leaving many of his detractors in disbelief and shock.

This study intersects with social sciences and humanities, thus being a contribution that is likely to be of interest to a wide range of people. The research draws from primary and secondary data, relevant books, scholarly articles, and newspaper articles. Part of the study is an eyewitness account of the Ivory Coast crisis. This research is enriched with firsthand information, thanks to my background in journalism. Court documents produced by judges and various chambers, the prosecutor, and Gbagbo's legal defense provided an insightful source of information that enrich the study. The ICC videos of the trial which was broadcasted live are a useful wealth of information as well.

This study proceeds in five major parts. The first part deals with the historical account of the crisis, which highlights the specific features of the Ivorian crisis. Therefore, it is entitled "Anatomy of a conflict." It is composed of five subparts: ethnicity, violence, electoral stalemate, neocolonial aspect of the crisis, and the Pan-African dimension of the Ivorian crisis. The historical account of the crisis lays the ground to help better understand the question of the ICC (un)fairness.

The second chapter, entitled "International justice and the International Criminal Court," discusses the dual journey of international justice and of the notion of human rights that led to the creation of the ICC. In addition, this chapter stresses the double-dealings of the ICC and its sponsors (the West) and engages a debate about Africa and the court. The third chapter focuses on how the ICC dealt with the Ivory Coast crisis. It is entitled "The ICC and Ivory Coast: justice, peace, and neo-colonialism." This section of the book highlights a set of the Laurent Gbagbo trial's incongruities, thus highlighting the role of the international criminal court in Ivory Coast as a reflection of Western neo-colonialism. The fourth chapter, entitled "Laurent Gbagbo's trial, testimonies, acquittal, and the decision" gives a summative account of the testimonies of the prosecutor's witnesses. It will be demonstrated that they contributed to the weakening of the case as several key testimonies led to the acquittal of the former president of Ivory Coast. The last chapter, "The decision, the prosecutor's appeal, and the Appeals Chamber's judgement," contains a summary of the oral decision of the Pre-Trial Chamber that decided to acquit Laurent Gbagbo and Blé Goudé in mid-January 2019. This chapter also includes the appeal of the prosecutor against the acquittal and the Appeals Chamber's total acquittal of the accused. In sum, in this work, the trial of Laurent Gbagbo has served as a case study to demonstrate that the court has failed to live up to its core functions and its main missions, which are about ending impunity and investigating fairly. This research is definitively an unsavory tale and an unflattering assessment of the ICC.

Chapter 1

Anatomy of a conflict

This section of the book brings to light the historical truth about the responsibilities of various actors and the complexities and intricacies of the crisis whose anatomy encompasses the following distinct features: ethnicity, the electoral stalemate, violence, the neocolonial aspect, and the Pan-African dimension. But first is a brief historical overview.

Historical overview of Ivory Coast

The crisis the Ivory Coast has been enduring for over a quarter of a century has its roots in the colonial history of the country and in the post-independence era marked by the adoption of one-party rule. As the main goal of this research is to buttress the corrosive role of the ICC in relation to the Ivorian crisis, it is important to give a historical background of Ivory Coast politics that encompasses an account of the crisis.

Ivory Coast: independence and democracy

Ivory Coast, located in the western region of Africa, is the largest producer of cocoa and has the most important economy in one of the regional economic communities of Africa, the West African Economic Monetary Union (WAEMU), which comprises most of the former French colonies of West Africa. The country is home to twenty-nine million people, including a great number of foreigners. Less than a decade after the Berlin Conference (1884–1885), which partitioned Africa, in 1893 the French established the colony of Ivory Coast and ruled it as one of its West African colonies regrouped within French West Africa. The other French colonial federation was French Equatorial Africa.[1]

Since the early years of colonial rule, Ivory Coast attracted migrants from other colonies who were looking for jobs and who worked in the cocoa and coffee farms. This pattern greatly impacted its social demographics and explains why today Ivory Coast is a microcosm of the United States of Africa, a melting pot, a multiethnic and multicultural nation. This contextual environment adds to the convolutions of Laurent Gbagbo's trial and to the

---

[1] Alice Ellenbogen, *La Succession d'Houphouët-Boigny: Entre tribalisme et démocratie* (Paris: L'Harmattan, 2002), 19.

controversial involvement of the International Criminal Court (ICC) in the Ivorian crisis, which cannot be explained solely from an ethnocentric perspective.

The country became independent in 1960 under the leadership of its first president, Félix Houphouët-Boigny, of the Baoulé ethnic group, which is a part of the larger Akan group. The first president of Ivory Coast was the undisputed leader for freedom of the French colonies in Black francophone Africa. Following the Brazzaville conference of 1944, the existence of unions and political parties was allowed, and colonial Ivory Coast functioned in the context of a colonial guided democracy.

Félix Houphouët-Boigny, with friends and peers, put together three political instruments that he led and that helped him in his career and in the struggle against the French colonial rule: The *Syndicat Agricole Agricole* (SAA), the farmers' union created in 1944; the *Rassemblement Démocratique Africain* (RDA); and the *Parti Démocratique de Côte d'Ivoire* (PDCI) created in 1946.[2] The RDA was a vast coalition of progressive and democratic forces of the French colonial federations in Africa. The PDCI was a member of the RDA and was the leading political formation for the independence of Ivory Coast.[3]

Félix Houphouët-Boigny's political stances later evolved to be in collusion with the French colonial authorities after 1951, to the point that he was in favor of all the reforms whose objective was to create the Franco-African Community, a form of a federal empire, which would be led by France and which would comprise its Sub-Saharan African colonies in 1958.[4] His position contrasted with those of other leaders who advocated Pan-Africanism, such as Kwame Nkrumah of Ghana and Sékou Touré of Guinea.

During his tenure in power, Houphouët-Boigny's rule stood upon three pillars: a benevolent dictatorship through a one-party system, the myth of the superiority of the Akans (mainly the Baoulés), and the alliance between the Akans and the northerners, predominantly Muslim. Questioned about his succession, forgetting that Ivory Coast was a republic and not an Akan kingdom, Houphouët-Boigny said more than once: "You never know the successor of an Akan leader in his lifetime."[5] And this idea of power being the exclusive property of the Akans or the Baoulés was widely shared by the executives of the ruling ethnic group. The model of a one-party system, which

---

[2] Ellenbogen, *La Succession d'Houphouët-Boigny*, 31-32.

[3] Ellenbogen, *La Succession d'Houphouët-Boigny*, 24.

[4] Ellenbogen, *La Succession d'Houphouët-Boigny*, 46.

[5] Tessy Bakari-Akin, *Côte d'Ivoire: une succession impossible?* (Paris: L'Harmattan, 1991), 51.

was praised and adopted by the fathers of African independence, has been, among other things, one of the causes of poor development, coups d'état, civil wars, and embezzlement of public funds. Ivory Coast did not escape that fate. It has had a bad transition from the one-party rule era to the return to a multiparty system, or from formal democracy to effective democracy. The provision of Article 7 of the Constitution of 1960 recognized the freedom of association, including the freedom to create political parties.[6] There was a constitutionally guaranteed formal democracy that could not be translated into reality in a one-party context, as dissenting voices were silenced, and leaders of conflicting opinions were either ostracized, imprisoned, or assassinated. The *Parti Démocratique de Côte d'Ivoire* (PDCI), which evolved in a multiparty context during colonization, later became a unified party in the aftermath of independence, after it brought other political denominations into its ranks through coercion. Houphouët-Boigny reigned as a benevolent dictator for thirty-three years, from 1960 to 1993.

An attempt by Kragbé Gnagbé to create an opposition political party, the *Parti Nationaliste* (PANA), led to violent repression and a massacre in 1970 of the Guébiés (a subgroup of the Bétés, Laurent Gbagbo's ethnic group) located in the center west of the country. Kragbé Gnagbé was eventually murdered. Various attempts intended to contribute to the democratization of the political space were unsuccessful until the late 1980s.[7] During the first two decades of Ivory Coast independence, the country experienced relative economic prosperity that eventually was plagued by the huge yoke of France and by internal problems, such as nepotism, money embezzlement, and strong social divides. The environment was ripe for a successful struggle for freedom and justice.

Since the 1980s, Ivory Coast has experienced some serious economic challenges that led to the implementation of everlasting structural adjustment programs. The university professors' union, the *Syndicat National pour la Recherche et l'Enseignement Superieur* (SYNARES), was the main pocket of resistance. By the year 1982, after a strike by that organization for better wages, a political figure personalized the struggle of the voiceless: history professor Laurent Gbagbo. He had already opposed some actions of the government and he had been sent–in the early 1970's–to prison to a military base in Séguéla in the northern part of the country. After the 1982 strike, fearing for his life, he went to exile to France, where he spent almost six years. During his presence in

---

[6] CIV. Const. of 1960 Art. VII.

[7] Magali Chelpi-den Hamer, *Militarized youths in Western Côte d'Ivoire: Local Processes of mobilization, demobilization, and related humanitarian interventions (2002-2007)* (Leiden: African Studies Centre, 2007), 56.

France, he campaigned ardently to get his message across Europe and Africa. While most of revolutionaries opted for an armed struggle to overthrow corrupt one-party system regimes in Africa, he chose a more pacific path, which was enshrined in the following words that he coined as "the peaceful transition to democracy."

The return to democracy in the context of the post-independence era coincided with a general movement of democratization on the continent of Africa and in the world. A popular discontent was rising in the country due to growing poverty. The end of the 1980s symbolized a democratic awakening and a mobilization for individual and collective freedoms. In Ivory Coast, in 1989, Félix Houphouët-Boigny contemplated the idea of reducing the salaries of the civil servants as a drastic measure to resolve the economic crisis. He organized one of his traditional national councils, which was a regular platform that occasionally brought together most of the representatives of the country to discuss the state of the nation or to discuss burning and pressing issues. Most of the representatives rejected the idea of salary cuts. During that gathering, the SYNARES requested a multiparty system. Félix Houphouët-Boigny did not heed the concerns of a portion of the national council. His stubbornness gave birth to a social uprising, which coincided with a shift in world politics marked by the fall of the Berlin Wall, the de-Sovietization of Eastern Europe, the fall of the Soviet Union, and the wind of democratization in the world.

People were rising up and demanding more freedom. Corazon Aquino, symbol of the popular will for reform in the Philippines, came to power in February 1986 after defeating the dictatorship of Ferdinand Marcos, becoming the first woman president of the country. The Berlin Wall fell in October 1989, marking the merger of the two Germanys (East and West), which were separated for more than forty years after the end of World War II. The Romanian dictator Ceausescu lost power in December 1989 after a popular uprising. Eastern Europe was prone to convulsions of change sparked by the revolt in Poland under the leadership of Solidarity leader Lech Walesa. From Africa, the Free Nelson Mandela Movement rose and spread across the globe and contributed to ending apartheid. That movement mobilized and galvanized an impressive number of people of all races, all religions, and all ideologies, including renowned artists. In an international environment marked by this wind of justice and freedom, Nelson Mandela was released on February 11, 1990, after twenty-seven years in prison. This event was certainly the mobilizing factor for the African masses in their quest to end the single-party system in order to have more freedom. In this era, several justice seekers and freedom lovers encouraged the idea of the existence of an international court.

Transition to democracy and the Pandora's Box

Through a people's movement, Ivorians struggled to tear down the one-party system, which fell on April 30, 1990. It all began as a student movement on February 19, 1990. This student revolt, once organized, spread progressively and surreptitiously into Ivorian society. The youth, unions, and political parties (unofficial and non-authorized) joined hands to conquer some freedoms and to protect the wages of the civil servants. This mass movement consolidated democratic values in the country.[8] On April 30, the government of Ivory Coast allowed the legalization of political parties. Article 7 of the constitution, which guaranteed the formal existence of political parties, was thus activated.[9]

Unions spread, newspapers mushroomed, and public debate spaces flourished. Students created another organization different from the state-controlled movement, *Mouvement des Etudiants et Elèves de Côte d'Ivoire* (MEECI), which had been in force since 1969.[10] The newly founded organization, backed by the university professors' union and by the opposition political parties, was called *Fédération Estudiantine et Scolaire de Côte d'Ivoire* (FESCI).[11] The once leader of the rebellion, Guillaume Soro, who was once the speaker of the house under Alassane Ouattara and prime minister under both Alassane Ouattara and Laurent Gbagbo, and Blé Goudé, the former president's youth leader who faced trial with him at the ICC, were both prominent leaders of FESCI.

The general election of 1990 gave legitimacy to the opposition, as Laurent Gbagbo ran for president against Félix Houphouët-Boigny. He seized the opportunity to campaign also for strict respect of Article 5 of the 1960 Constitution, which stated that the right to vote in general elections should be strictly for Ivorians. Up until 1990, foreigners were authorized to vote in all the elections in Ivory Coast.[12] During the 1990 presidential election campaign, the former ruling party labeled the rising political figure, the leader of the opposition, as an enemy of the Baoulés and of the foreigners. It managed to distribute Ivory Coast national identity cards to the latter so they could participate in the elections. The leader of the opposition obtained 18% of the votes,[13] and his party secured ten seats in the parliament.

---

[8] Mamadou Koulibaly, *Sur la Route de la Liberté* (Abidjan: Presses des Universités de Côte d'Ivoire, 2004), 50.

[9] Ellenbogen, *La Succesion d'Houphouët-Boigny*, 71.

[10] Ellenbogen, *La Succesion d'Houphouët-Boigny*, 51.

[11] Christian Bouquet, *Géopolitique de la Côte d'Ivoire* 2nd edition (Paris: Armand Collin, 2008), 237.

[12] Mamadou Koulibaly, *Sur la Route de la Liberté*, 52.

[13] Koulibaly, *Sur la Route de la Liberté*, 52.

In line with his ethnocentric understanding of politics, and certainly not satisfied with the demands for democratization, President Félix Houphouët-Boigny did not take proper and adequate steps to channel the passions and the tribal ardor that were repressed and contained within the single party. The Ivorian constitution adopted in 1960 was modified several times to finally consecrate a monarchical type of succession, which saw the accession to power of Henri Konan Bédié in its new version of November 6, 1990. Article 11, changed to an older version, designated the president of the national assembly, Henry Konan Bédié, of Baoulé origin, as the constitutional successor in case of the sitting president's death.[14] The position of prime minister (Article 12) with an extensive delegation of powers in case of the absence of the president from the national territory (Article 24) was created.[15]

Alassane Ouattara, who first led an interministerial committee in the second part of the year 1990, was appointed prime minister with the main mission to resolve the economic challenges of the country. Soon after, credible voices decried his being prime minister, not because they doubted his abilities as a manager but because they questioned his Ivorian citizenship and his attachment to the land of Ivory Coast. He had citizenship of Upper Volta (now Burkina Faso), the origin of his parents, even though it was believed that he had been born in Ivory Coast. This led to a concept called *Ivoirité* which claimed to promote Ivorian cultural distinctiveness and preserve the country from intruders.

Besides Félix Houphouët-Boigny, the Ivorian political spectrum was dominated from then on by the following political figures: Henri Konan Bédié, speaker of the house; Alassane Ouattara, prime minister; Laurent Gbagbo, leader of the opposition; and General Robert Guéi, chief of the army, who revealed himself through a set of repressions on behalf of the ruling party. A political crisis occurred in 1992, involving the players who had dominated the political life of the country for over thirty years. It is called February 18, named after the date of the incident when the opposition protests were cracked down on by Alassane Ouattara, while he was prime minister and supported by Henri Konan Bédié, speaker of the house. Félix Houphouët-Boigny was in Europe for an extended period.

The army had undertaken a punitive expedition against students during the night of September 17–18, 1991. The alleged crimes committed that night against the students—rapes, beatings, torture—were confirmed by the national investigation commission put in place under the pressure of the Ivorian

---

[14] Ellenbogen, *La Succesion d'Houphouët-Boigny*, 79-80. See also CIV. Const. of 1990.

[15] Ellenbogen, *La Succesion d'Houphouët-Boigny*, 81.

masses. The commission, led by Judge Camille Oguié, requested that the perpetrators be punished and sanctioned, including the minister of security, and the chief of the army, General Robert Guéi. Félix Houphouët-Boigny refused to sanction them, arguing that he could not turn his own knife against himself. It was in that environment that the leader of the student union FESCI, Martial Ahipeaud, who was ideologically close to the opposition, was arrested. The leader of *Front Populaire Ivoirien* (FPI), Laurent Gbagbo, decided to launch a series of protests for the conclusions of the commission to be respected, which culminated in the February 18, 1992 demonstration.[16]

That day, the protesters endured violent repression. The whole state apparatus of Ivory Coast—the army, the police, the gendarmerie, all the services of intelligence, and the government-instrumentalized thugs (called *loubards* in Ivorian French)—attacked the demonstrators who were asking for more freedom. The leader of the opposition, his wife Simone Gbagbo; his son Michel Gbagbo and several other protesters, after being beaten severely, were jailed. Hundreds of people were deprived of their rights of movement and association and freedom of speech and of the press.[17] During a press conference Alassane Ouattara even accused Laurent Gbagbo of destroying public buildings and property with a cudgel. The then leader of the opposition spent almost six months in prison, with his wife, his son, and most of the leadership of his political party.

February 18, 1992 occurred in a moment of exacerbated crisis and tension on economic, social, and political fronts. The new Prime Minister, Alassane Ouattara, nurtured by neoliberalism, undertook measures such as privatization and budget cuts on social programs (employment, education, health, etc.) that increased the opposition against the regime. He suppressed the students' buses and authorized a double-standard or double-speed salary for teachers. The teachers hired after 1991 were receiving half the salary of their colleagues who were already in the workforce prior to that year. He installed a residency card (*carte de séjour*) to identify foreigners living in Ivory Coast. This latter act exacerbated social fracture and disintegrated the national and social fabric. The state police, committed to enforcing the measure, became the victimizer of many residents of Ivory Coast, as some were harassed or beaten in the streets. Some Ivorians were mistakenly also harassed for having names believed to be those of foreigners. People in long Muslim dresses, called

---

16 K. Martial Frindéthié, *From Lumumba to Gbagbo: Africa in the Eddy of the Euro-American Quest for Exceptionalism* (Jefferson, NC: McFarland & Company Publishers, 2016), 93.

17 Judith Rueff, *Côte d'Ivoire: Le feu au pré carré* (Paris: Editions AutrementFrontieres, 2004), 20.

boubous, were often victim of humiliation due to police brutality. Relatively peaceful cohabitation was now under threat. This administrative harassment continued under Laurent Gbagbo, who suppressed the card in 2008.

The frequent trips to Europe for treatment of Félix Houphouët-Boigny in his latter years created a vacancy in the power structure and caused a more ferocious and fierce battle for his succession between Henri Konan Bédié and Alassane Ouattara. At his death in 1993, Ouattara attempted to retain executive power, ignoring Article 11 of the constitution. Henry Konan Bédié was eventually able to assume power, with the backing of the PDCI and the army led by General Robert Guéi.[18] He could not stop the implosion of the ruling political party and the disintegration of the country.

A splinter from the PDCI-RDA, the *Rassemblement des Républicains* (RDR), whose main constituency was the northerners, was created on behalf of Alassane Dramane Ouattara, who assumed its presidency in 1999, upon returning from the International Monetary Fund (IMF), where he served for five years. The opposition parties, the RDR and the FPI, now united in a coalition called Republican Front, actively boycotted the 1995 presidential election, denouncing the lack of transparency in the electoral process. Henri Konan Bédié won, but the social fracture of the nation led to a failed and foiled coup d'état in 1995. He was eventually overthrown by a military coup on December 24, 1999, which led to a transition government headed by General Robert Guéi. Alassane Ouattara's nationality issue haunted the transition, and the country became more divided. His candidacy was rejected for dubious nationality along with that of former president Henri Konan Bédié. The two remaining main contenders were Laurent Gbagbo and General Guéi, who faced off on October 22, 2000.

The former won and became president only after a popular bloody uprising had forced the latter, who had proclaimed himself the winner earlier, to relinquish power. Laurent Gbagbo, now in power, was accused of not trying to stop the concept of *Ivoirité*. Soldiers close to Alassane Ouattara, who had deserted the army and found refuge in Burkina Faso, attempted to overthrow him first on January 7–8, 2001, and then on September 19, 2002. The latter foiled coup turned into a brief civil war, which resulted in a geographical division of the country for most of the time Laurent Gbagbo was in power. The rebels who named their military-political organization *Mouvement Patriotique de Côte d'Ivoire* (MPCI) controlled 60% of the territory and the two zones were separated by a buffer zone, which was controlled by the French troops named

---

[18] Gnaka Lagoké, "Le Film de la Démission d'Alassane Ouattara," *Le Nouvel Horizon* no. 171 (December 24, 1993): 4.

Licorne. One year later, the United Nations was called on as a mediator by President Laurent and established a mission in Ivory Coast.[19]

Several grassroots movements, self-defense groups, and paramilitary groups, such as the *Groupement Patriotique pour la Paix* (GPP), and the Front for the Liberation of the Great West, the *Front de Libération du Grand Ouest* (FLGO) based in the western part of the region and led by Maho Glofiehi mushroomed and vowed to protect the regime of Laurent Gbagbo and the institutions of the republic. Also public spaces for public debates called agoras and *parlements* which were in force since the era of Houphouët-Boigny multiplied. They served as places of mass political education. With the war, the militant ardor intensified. The grassroots organizations and self-defense groups based in Abidjan were known as *Galaxie Patriotique* or the Young Patriots. Their undisputable leader was Blé Goudé, founder of *Congrès Panafricain des Jeunes Patriotes* (COJEP).[20] Recurrently and regularly, they organized mass movements and rallies to oppose the rebellion and its leaders, France, and the United Nations mission accused of neo-colonialism. Several peace agreements attempted to resolve the crisis: Accra I, Accra II, Accra III (2002–2004); the French-sponsored Marcoussis Agreement in January 2003; Pretoria I and Pretoria II in 2005 and 2006; and the Ouagadougou Agreement in 2007. All urged the rebels to disarm[21], and the Pretoria Agreements brokered under the leadership of the then South African president Thabo Mbeki allowed Alassane Ouattara to be reintegrated into the political arena. He could finally run for president in 2010, and this election led to a deeper crisis and to the militaristic involvement of France and the United Nations. The next section will further dissect the ethnocentric characteristics of the conflict.

Ethnicity: Ivoirité versus Charter of the North

Ivory Coast has repeatedly and subsequently endured a series of crises related to the questions of identity and ethnicity that endangered its stability and its territorial integrity: the opposition between *Cotivoiriens*[22] and foreigners during colonial times, the Sanwi War in the sixties, the Guébié crisis in 1970, the two contrasting ethnocentric ideologies that rose almost at the same time in

---

[19] Magali Chelpi-den Hamer, *Militarized youths in Western Côte d'Ivoire: Local Processes of mobilization, demobilization, and related humanitarian interventions (2002-2007)* (Leiden: African Studies Centre, 2007), 67-68.

[20] This movement was transformed into a political party in 2015 with a different content which is Congrès Panafricain pour la Justice et l'Égalité des Peuples.

[21] Magali Chelpi-den Hamer, *Militarized youths in Western Côte d'Ivoire*, 78-79, 174.

[22] Ivorians used to be called *Cotivoiriens*.

the early '90s, *Ivoirité* for the Akans and the Charter of the North for the Northerners within the ruling party. These last two ideologies led to the still unfolding military and political crisis.

The seeds of ethnic and identity politics had been planted since the early years of independent Ivory Coast under the first president, Félix Houphouët-Boigny, who was the first to construct the myth of the superiority of the Baoulés within the larger Akan group. He reversed the ethnic hierarchy made by the European settlers, who ranked the major groups in descending order as follows: the Mandé descendants of Soundjata Kéita, the Akans composed mostly of Baoulés and Agnis, and the Kru group. In the reconstruction of this same hierarchy by Houphouët, the Akans (with preeminence given to the Baoulés) supplanted the Mandés to take the top place in the hierarchy. The Krus, for their part, always remained at the bottom of the ladder of the hierarchy.[23] The rule of the first president of Ivory Coast stood upon the discriminating principle of Baoulé ethnic superiority and the effective and progressive union of all Akans, coupled with the alliance he built with prominent figures of other ethnic groups: with the patriarch Gon Coulibaly from the Senoufo tribe predominantly located in the northern part of the country. It is worth mentioning that the praxis of *Ivoirité* is wrongly believed to be the sole cause of the conflict in Ivory Coast, particularly in relation to ethnocentric politics preceding the theoretical and ideological formulation of the concept.

In the latter years of Houphouët-Boigny, while Alassane Ouattara was Prime Minister, another ethnocentric ideology was articulated: the ideology for the northerners commonly known as the Charter of the North. The Reggae singer Alpha Blondy, in a pamphlet believed to be one of the founding documents of the Charter of the North, listed a string of grievances of the Dioulas[24] and launched an appeal for secession once the first Ivorian president dies. He wrote:

> We do not want to be part of the Republic of Ivory Coast anymore after Houphouët. We are tired of being treated as foreigners in a country that we consider ours. When a Dioula or an Ivorian citizen belonging to one or another of the ethnic groups mentioned above [he gave a list of most of the ethnic groups that belong to the larger Dioula group] enters a room to sign a state civil document, he or she is accused of being Malian, Senegalese or Burkinabe or Guinean; and this applies to high-ranking

---

[23] Harris Memel-Fotê, "Un Mythe Politique des Akan en Côte d'Ivoire: le sens de l'Etat," in *Mondes Akan: Identité et Pouvoir en Afrique Occidentale*, eds. Pierluigi Valsecchi and Fabio Viti (Paris: L'Harmattan, 1999), 23–24.

[24] This is a term that designates people who are from the northern part of Ivory Coast and who are predominantly Muslim.

officials in the country, and, case in point, many are criticizing President Houphouët for having appointed a Burkinabe as Prime Minister, alluding to Alassane Ouattara.[25]

Alassane Ouattara's presence ignited the question of citizenship,[26] the division between the Akans and the Dioulas, and later the fracture of the nation. He was supposedly born in Ivory Coast to foreign parents from Upper Volta. He was taken by one of his uncles to Upper Volta, where he studied and then carried out his university studies as a national Voltaic in the United States. He later returned to Ivory Coast in 1990 to assume political positions after holding important positions at the Central Bank of West African States whose acronym in French is BCEAO which stands for the *Banque Centrale des États de l'Afrique de l'Ouest* and at the International Monetary Fund (IMF). He was decorated in Ivory Coast in 1982 as a citizen of Upper Volta.[27] He was appointed as the Director of the African Department at the IMF in 1984, as a citizen of Upper Volta.[28] Despite such evidence, Ouattara denied he had ever been a Burkina Faso citizen or that he had ever switched citizenship. He claimed that he only had a passport of Upper Volta and that he had always been an Ivorian.[29]

The Dioulas saw him as the messiah and the savior they had been waiting for and through whom they could have access to state power. They were convinced that their turn had arrived and that they deserved to assume state power after serving as "crutches" to the Baoulés' rule. This Akan-Northerners alliance started to crack in the early years of the return to democracy. Interviewed about the Charter of the North movement, Alassane Ouattara, while prime minister, did not condemn this separatist movement. Many saw his answer as an endorsement of a movement through which he could satisfy his political and presidential ambition.

Ouattara's rise on the Ivorian political scene frightened the ruling Akan elite, who committed to stopping him. They constructed the concept of *Ivoirité*, defined as a cultural and political phenomenon that encapsulates the history, the sovereignty, the cultural particularism, and the singular identity of Ivory Coast. Henri Konan Bédié, who vowed to refound a new Ivory Coast upon taking power under the "white mantle of *Ivoirité*," defined it as "a unifying

---

[25] Yacouba Konaté, "Le Destin Tragique d'Alassane Ouattara," in *Côte d'Ivoire l'Année Terrible 1999–2000*, eds. Marc Le Pape and Claudine Vidal (Paris: Karthala, 2003), 301–2.

[26] Ellenbogen, *La Succession d'Houphouët-Boigny*, 73–74.

[27] Fraternité Matin, December 27, 1982, p.3.

[28] Jeune Afrique No 112, December 1984, p. 66.

[29] Alassane Ouattara expressed that position during the National Reconciliation Forum which took place in Ivory Coast from October 9 to December 18, 2001.

concept, the foundation on which the Ivorian nation must rest. *Ivoirité* is first an identification framework emphasizing the specific values of the Ivorian society, but it is also a framework for integrating the first ethnic components who gave birth to Ivory Coast and it integrates all the external contributions that have come to blend in the mold of a shared destiny."[30]

However, it conveyed an ideology of protectionism of the Ivorian nationality against the dispossession of Ivory Coast land and resources by non-Ivorians.[31] It was an ideological tool conceived to halt Alassane Ouattara from running for president, thus denying the northerners the right to have access to state power.[32] Its understanding differed from its definition. Some of its theoreticians opposed two sets of Ivorians, those of multilineage fiber and the Ivorians of circumstance.[33] The people from the south would represent the former, and people from the north would represent the latter. The country has never been able to resolve this contention.

The fierce battle between Alassane Ouattara and Henri Konan Bédié led to the overthrow of the latter on December 24, 1999. General Guéi, accused of a failed coup d'état in 1995, was chosen by the mutineers to lead a military transition. During the transition, the issue of the citizenship of the presidential candidate in the election exacerbated the division of the Ivorian nation. Soldiers close to Alassane Ouattara, many from the northern part of the country, after failing to change the course of the 2000 military transition—by attempting to overthrow General Guéi through two unsuccessful mutinies, July 10–11 and September 18–19—withdrew to Burkina Faso and later attempted to overthrow Laurent Gbagbo, waging a civil war against him.

One of the major contributions of the military transition was the adoption of a constitution intended to create a space for a greater and participative political and electoral democracy and transparency in the management of public affairs. All the stakeholders were involved and took part in the discussions, which took place through a consultative and constitutive assembly. The creation of an independent electoral commission, whose main goal was to oversee and to organize the electoral process, was adopted. The voting age was

---

[30] Henri Konan Bédié gave that definition in a speech he delivered on the 10th congress of his party, the PDCI, on August 26, 1995.

[31] Jean Noel Loucou, "De l'Ivoirité," in *L'Ivoirité ou l'esprit du nouveau contrat social du Président Henri Konan Bédié*, ed. Saliou Touré (Abidjan: Presses Universitaires de Côte d'Ivoire, 1996), 20.

[32] Christian Bouquet, *Géopolitique de Côte d'Ivoire*, 2nd ed. (Paris: Armand Colin, 2008), 26.

[33] These two expressions were used for the first time in Ivory Coast political discourse by the former ruling party officials in the early 1990s.

lowered from twenty-one to eighteen years, and the constitution established a single ballot system for the assertion of universal suffrage. Another important contribution was the abolition of the death penalty in Ivory Coast. The process of the adoption of the 2000 Constitution was inclusive.

On July 23, 2000, the majority of Ivorians voted yes (86.53%) against the no (13.47%) votes during the referendum whose turnout was 56%. The constitution supposed to usher a new era of more peace, democracy, and development became the ground for greater instability. The very Article 35, which appeared to set Ivory Coast on the path of a stronger democracy, contained the seeds of conflict. On the one hand, that article limited presidential terms to two mandates of five years' maximum each, established that any presidential candidate should not be older than seventy-five, and provided that in case of a vacancy of the presidency, the speaker of the house should assume executive power with the main goal of organizing a presidential election.[34] On the other hand, Article 35 also took over the provisions of the 1994 electoral code, which eliminated Alassane Ouattara from the race for the presidential election. It stipulated that a candidate in a presidential election in Ivory Coast should not have switched citizenship and should be an Ivorian citizen, born from a father and mother who should be born Ivorians.[35]

Voices denounced such provisions of the constitution, arguing that it was xenophobic in a country of immigration. Those who supported it counterattacked and claimed that it was necessary to protect the nation from being taken over by foreigners. Even though Alassane Ouattara was visibly the target of this disposition in the constitution, he called on his supporters to vote Yes. Many of them boycotted the referendum. General Guéi, who had promised to "sweep the country" and leave power to the civilians, did not stick to his word, decided to run for president, and eliminated some candidates, among whom were two heavyweights, Henri Konan Bédié and Alassane Ouattara, the latter for dubious nationality. Many of Laurent Gbagbo's detractors accused him of having outsmarted and outmaneuvered General Guéi with the intent and the objective that he would reject Alassane Ouattara and others' candidacies so he (Gbagbo) would be the only one to stand against him and defeat him. The election was held amid the indifference of the supporters of those whose candidacies were rejected.

At the end of the voting process, both General Robert Guéi and Laurent Gbagbo claimed victory. The latter called on Ivorians to take to the streets to stop the former's "imposture." Under the pressure of the street, in the face of

---

[34] Mamadou Koulibaly, *Sur la Route de la Liberté*, 58-60.

[35] CIV. Const. of 2000.

strong and effective popular demonstrations and after the killing of hundreds, General Guéi fell from power, and Laurent Gbagbo became the effective president on October 26, 2000.[36]

Alassane Ouattara threw his supporters into the streets, thus adding to the escalation of violence and to the bloodshed. A charnel house of around fifty people, supposedly discovered by Alassane Ouattara's close aides who claimed it was mainly composed of Muslims, made the headlines of newspapers across the globe. A campaign about the so-called genocide of the Muslims or Dioulas haunted Laurent Gbagbo's rule. Pressure mounted to request Alassane Ouattara's reintegration in Ivorian politics.

Laurent Gbagbo, failing to stay above the fray, made declarations and comments that further divided the country. He once called Alassane Ouattara a vagabond of nationality who is not worthy of being president of Ivory Coast.[37] He repeated these lines of attacks against Alassane Ouattara during the presidential election campaign even when the latter was not on the ballot. During the National Reconciliation Forum (October 9-December 18, 2001) he convened himself and supposed to heal the wounds of the Ivorian nation and to help build a reconciled Ivory Coast, Laurent Gbagbo spoke three times: in his capacity of president, he delivered the opening and the closing remarks, and as a citizen-witness. During his address as a witness, in a show of force doubled with jubilation, he made a blunder that Ouattara took advantage of to destabilize him. He had declared:

> We have adopted this constitution to resolve three problems: the limitation of presidential term, article 11, and the nationality of Alassane Ouattara. The limitation of term addresses the issue of longevity in power, as Houphouët had ruled and remained in power indefinitely. The constitution also addresses the issue of a monarchal mode of succession to the presidency. This concerns Bédié. The provision about the nationality of a candidate to the presidency has been inserted in article 35 because of Alassane Ouattara.[38]

As a response, Alassane Ouattara declared during the forum and thereafter that the constitution was made to bar him from running for president. The National Reconciliation Forum, which was an opportunity for a national and collective catharsis, turned out to be a failure. Most of the people who spoke at the forum complained about the discrimination and violence of which they

---

[36] Frindéthié, *From Lumumba to Gbagbo,* 102-103.

[37] Konaté, "Le Destin d'Alassane Ouattara," 275.

[38] Kouamé Nguessan, "Le Forum pour la réconciliation nationale. 9 octobre–18 décembre 2001," in *Côte d'Ivoire: L'Année Terrible,* 344.

had been victim. None of them took responsibility for their actions in the crisis.[39]

The advocates of the Charter of the North shelled a string of complaints against the rest of Ivory Coast that was supposedly responsible for the martyrdom and the pogrom of the northerners. Based on this logic, they continuously launched their call for secession or for a war, which was justified in their eyes. Religion was used as a mobilizing tool for the Ivorian Muslims and as a divisive instrument for the partition of the country. In France, during a conference he gave in 1999, Alassane Ouattara stated that people did not want him to be president because he was a Muslim. It was a rallying cry repeated in chorus by Muslim leaders now in open opposition against the predominantly Christian south and considered *ivoiritaire*. Upon his accession to power after April 11, 2011, Alassane Ouattara launched an intensive and expansive ethnic catch-up campaign, making a massive appointment of northerners to positions of responsibility in the administration, arguing that they rightfully deserved to be appointed since they represented 40% of the population and because they were excluded from appointments during the reign of Gbagbo.[40]

The state of Ivory Coast under all of its presidents (Félix Houphouët-Boigny, Henri Konan Bédié, Robert Guéi, Laurent Gbagbo, and Alassane Ouattara) failed to build a real national unity in the truest sense of the concept. These leaders have respectively used identity politics at times either to attain power or to maintain it. A divided nation with unresolved issues, with old deep-seated rivalries, mixed with ethnocentric divisions, led to an explosive cocktail during the 2010 election.

The 2010 electoral stalemate

Leaning on the constitution, which stipulated that elections could not be held if the country was divided, the Laurent Gbagbo regime resisted calls to hold an election in 2005 and instead organized public hearings for tens of thousands of Ivorians who did not have their ID cards. The purpose of those hearings was to deliver identity papers to those who would meet the criteria so that their names could appear on the electoral lists. In 2006, a first wave of court hearings escalated into deadly clashes between supporters of President Laurent Gbagbo and the opposition. The former suspected foreigners of wanting to take advantage of the opportunity to have Ivorian IDs. The idea that the electoral list

---

[39] Nguessan, "Le Forum pour la réconciliation nationale," 339.

[40] Vincent Hugueux, "Côte d'Ivoire: Ouattara veut 'protéger' les minorités," *L'Express*, January 25, 2012, http://www.lexpress.fr/actualite/monde/afrique/cote-d-ivoire-ouattara-veut-proteger-les-minorites_1075076.html.

was thought to be full of many intruders and new voters was predominant. The former Ivorian president finally succumbed to the pressure and accepted the organization of the election in the fall of 2010. This resulted in an electoral stalemate with the involvement of international partners: namely France and the United Nations.

The long-awaited election, the United Nations mission, the Electoral Commission, and the Constitutional Council

The election came with a sense of relief for the international community, whose patience had run out. But it was a moment of uncertainty with a lot of controversies for Ivory Coast concerning several aspects of the electoral process. For the purpose of clarity, it is important to give a brief historical overview of the involvement of the United Nations in the Ivorian crisis.

It was at the request of former President Gbagbo that the United Nations set foot on Ivorian soil as a mediator after the failed coup d'état of 2002, which turned into a short civil war. The first UN mission in Ivory Coast, called *Mission des Nations Unies en Côte d'Ivoire* (MINUCI), was established through resolution 1479 on May 13, 2003. Its main goal was to implement the Linas-Marcoussis Agreement and oversee a ceasefire within its six-month mandate. This was later followed by UN Operations in Côte d'Ivoire (UNOCI)[41], which supervised the 2010 election and certified the results. It was put into place on February 27, 2004.[42]

Since then, Ivory Coast was de facto under embargo as it lost a portion of its sovereignty. In 2005, which was an election year, the presidential election could not be organized. Gbagbo was de facto president of the country because of a provision of the 2000 Constitution that stated that the president in power be in power if the election could not take place. This was how the UN took a series of resolutions to recognize him as the rightful president of Ivory Coast. The UN Resolution 1633 (adopted on October 21, 2005) extended President Gbagbo's term in office by a maximum of one year. The same resolution recommended the appointment of a new prime minister with stronger executive powers, a road map for disarmament, supervision of the identification process, evaluation and monitoring of the peace process, and the organization of elections by an international working group.

The former governor of the West African States Central Bank, Charles Konan Banny, became prime minister with the backing of the international

---

[41] UNOCI and ONUCI are interchangeably used throughout the book. ONUCI is the French of UNOCI.

[42] Magali Chelpi-den Hamer, *Militarized youths in Western Côte d'Ivoire*, 76.

community. His appointment led to a tug-of-war between him and Gbagbo. One year later, on October 17, 2006, the African Union and the UN Security Council extended President Gbagbo's mandate by one year, in the hope that the road map for peace could be implemented during that time.

In the list of several peace agreements, one—the Ouagadougou Political Agreement, signed on March 4, 2007—is worthy of attention. Driven by the desire to get rid of Charles Konan Banny, Gbagbo decided to establish direct negotiations with the leader of the rebellion, Guillaume Soro, and opted to place them under the aegis of Burkina Faso's president, Blaise Compaoré, the very person who sheltered the rebels and supported them and trained them. Upon the signing of the Ouagadougou Political Agreement, Guillaume Soro was appointed prime minister in place of Charles Konan Banny. On January 15, 2008, Resolution 1795 requested UNOCI to support the full implementation of the Ouagadougou Political Agreement and recalled that the special representative of the Secretary-General, the chief mission of the UN representation, shall certify all stages of the electoral process of the presidential election, which should be open, free, fair, and transparent.

The last UN resolution, Resolution 1975, before the fall of Gbagbo was adopted on March 30, 2011. It claimed to "protect the civilians," but its objective was to authorize a neocolonial war against Ivory Coast. It is worth mentioning that France was the country that drafted most of the resolutions proposed to the Security Council during the crisis in Ivory Coast. Francophone African countries have given up their sovereign rights to France in the field of foreign affairs.[43]

One of the contentions of the electoral stalemate concerned the body legally allowed to proclaim the results. Two domestic institutions embroiled in a standoff in this regard were the Independent Electoral Commission and the Constitutional Council. It is important to explain the internal functioning of the electoral commission in which various stakeholders did not have equal representation. The regional results were to be compiled and sent to the 31 members of the central commission in Abidjan. Only 22 could deliberate on electoral issues. As a result, decisions were to be taken by consensus, according to the recommendations of the Pretoria Agreement.

The regional results were to be announced by the spokesperson of the Electoral Commission on national TV. Regarding the proclamation of national provisional results, the responsibility fell on the president of the commission, who had a three-day deadline to proclaim them on national TV as well. After failure to comply with the deadline, the Constitutional Council had to take over

---

43 Frindéthié, *From Lumumba to Gbagbo*, 141.

the matter of the proclamation of the election results, as it had in the case of the November 28 runoff. According to Article 94 of the 2000 Constitution, the Constitutional Council controls the regularity of the electoral process and is the only body allowed to announce the results of presidential elections. The Electoral Commission and the Constitutional Council proclaimed divergent results, thus leading the country into an electoral stalemate.

The 2010 electoral stalemate: who won the election?

The first round of the long-awaited election finally took place on October 28, 2010. The rebels were still holding onto their weapons, despite several peace agreement resolutions that urged them to disarm. The forceful involvement of the international community, the accusations of fraud, and the unending debate about who really won the election contributed to heighten the electoral stalemate. The runoff—which took place on November 28, 2010—resulted in a deeper conflict. Regardless of the outcome of the elections, as it opposed two rivals who embodied quasi-irreconcilable positions between the south and the north in a divided country, Ivory Coast would have experienced a post-electoral crisis anyway.[44]

For the first round, Laurent Gbagbo was in the lead with 38% of the vote, followed by Alassane Ouattara with 32%, and Henri Konan Bédié in third place with 25%. The turnout was 83%. As soon as the results of the first round of the election were announced, some credible sources hinted that Henri Konan Bédié's actual rank was number two and not number three. He announced very quickly that he would submit a request for annulment involving nearly 600,000 votes. There were around 300,000 vote's difference between him and Alassane Ouattara. Surprisingly, the appeal was not filed on time. The former president, Laurent Gbagbo, who probably thought that he was in a more favorable configuration to face Alassane Ouattara in the second round, certainly because of the nationality issue, did not dispute the results of the first round.

The Electoral Commission failed to respect the deadline of December 1, and the following day, on national TV, the Constitutional Council's president, Paul Yao N'Dré, announced that its institution was the only lawful institution authorized to proclaim the results. That day, in the early hours of the afternoon, in violation of the rules and regulations of the electoral commission, the president of this institution, Youssouf Bakayoko, was accompanied by Phillip Carter III and Jean-Marc Simon, respectively the US and French ambassadors, to Alassane Ouattara's campaign headquarters at the Golf Hotel. There, without the presence of the other members of the Electoral Commission, he proclaimed

---

[44] Daniel Chirot, "The Debacle in Côte d'Ivoire," *Journal of Democracy* 17, no. 2 (2006): 75.

on international televisions that Alassane Ouattara had won the election with 54% of the votes against 46% for the incumbent president Gbagbo.[45] The turnout announced for the runoff was 81%, despite the reports of media and certain observers who thought it could not exceed 70%.[46] The United Nations Mission in Ivory Coast certified the results and declared Alassane Ouattara the winner of the elections.

On Friday, December 3, Yao N'Dré rejected the Electoral Commission's results, claiming that they were null and void, and proclaimed his own results pursuant Article 94 of the constitution that was in force: Laurent Gbagbo was the winner with 51.45% of the vote against 48.55% for Alassane Ouattara. He discounted votes from several regions for alleged fraud, all from Alassane Ouattara's strongholds, Bouaké, Korhogo, Ferkessedougou, Katiola, Boundiali, and Dabakala, and even added one to the list of invalidated regions, Séguéla, where there was no report of complaints about alleged fraud.[47] The same day, Alassane Ouattara, in a letter, requested to be sworn in by the president of the Constitutional Council.

On Saturday, December 4, at 1:00 p.m., Laurent Gbagbo was sworn in pursuant Article 39 of the constitution, which required the oath ceremony to take place within 48 hours after the proclamation of the results. Hours later, Alassane Ouattara sent a written oath to the Constitutional Council president and informed him he had just taken the oath at the Golf Hotel, his headquarters. The European powers and the United States led the chorus of condemnations of Gbagbo and asked for his resignation. Several mediators from various countries and institutions attempted to reconcile the positions of the two main antagonists. Gbagbo's proposition to recount the votes, supported by Thabo Mbeki (former president of South Africa), Jerry John Rawlings (former president of Ghana), and José Eduardo Dos Santos (then sitting president of Angola) was rejected by the UN and the international community on the basis that it would not be fair to Alassane Ouattara.[48] Ouattara was thus seen as the legitimate winner, recognized as such by several other bodies, such as the African Union, the Economic Community of West African States (ECOWAS), and the European Union of a duly organized and transparent election.

---

[45] Frindéthié, *From Lumumba to Gbagbo*, 134.

[46] United Nations Operation in Côte d'Ivoire Communiqué 937, November 29, 2011.

[47] Philippe Assalé, *Reconstruire les forces de défense et de sécurité en Côte d'Ivoire: Contribution citoyenne* (Paris: L'Harmattan, 2011), 54.

[48] Frindéthié, *From Lumumba to Gbagbo*, 142.

In light of the conflicting stances about the results of the election, it is imperative to ask a fundamental question that looms large: "Who won the election?" This question became the chorus of the pro-Gbagbo groups and later was asked by several observers who decided to go beyond the dominant discourse about the outcome of the 2010 presidential election in Ivory Coast. In order to give adequate answers to the above-mentioned question, which helps shed new light on the outcome of the election, it is important to look at the results of the first round, the certification of the election by the UNOCI, and the turnout of the second round.

Henri Konan Bédié recalled the incident about the flipping of the results of the first round in October 2013 at a congress of his party, the PDCI: "The rank I occupied in the 2010 election was not mine…but you'll agree with me that the dice were already stacked."[49] The French ambassador Jean-Marc Simon's words added to suspicion regarding the results of the first round. Before leaving office, he declared after a visit to Henri Konan Bédié in 2012: "All appreciated his attitude quite worthy of democratic praise after the first round in which he agreed not to be present in the second round and to provide unfailing support for the one that the Ivorians then designated, President Alassane Ouattara."[50] Also, the certification of the results by the United Nations Mission in Ivory Coast was problematic.

UNOCI certified the election while its representatives were present in only 721 polling stations out of a total of 20,073, which represented only 3.6% of the polling stations. Laurent Bigot revealed that the United Nations Special Representative in Ivory Coast, Choi Young-Jin, confessed that his teams had reviewed all the minutes but they could only concretely guarantee the authenticity of a small portion of them.[51]

Even though it could be a challenge to tell who really won the election, it is less difficult to doubt the results that announced Alassane Ouattara the winner. This statement stands upon the conflicting reports of the turnout of voters for the runoff. The United Nations Mission in Ivory Coast (ONUCI) Communique 937 revealed that the turnout of the runoff would be lower compared to the number of voters for the first round, which was 83%, but would vary between 60 and 70%.[52] The French news organization *France 24* quoted the Electoral

---

[49] Laurent Bigot, "Côte d'Ivoire: mais qui a gagné la présidentielle de 2010?" *Le Monde*, May 19, 2016, https://www.lemonde.fr/afrique/article/2016/05/27/cote-d-ivoire-mais-qui-a-gagne-la-presidentielle-de-2010_4927642_3212.html.

[50] Bigot, "Mais qui a gagné?"

[51] Bigot, "Mais qui a gagné?"

[52] United Nations Operation in Côte d'Ivoire Communiqué 937, November 29, 2011.

Commission report that it was 70%, right after the closing of the polls.[53] Later on, the UN and the international community agreed with the turnout number of (81%) for the runoff, which was announced as the official result—certainly fixed with the complicity of the international players. Laurent Gbagbo refused to concede and clung to power even though his proposition about the recount of the votes was rejected by the United Nations. Alassane Ouattara, designated winner of the election, as expected, also refused a recount of the votes and advocated the use of force to dislodge a defiant Laurent Gbagbo from the presidential palace and to end the electoral stalemate.

The debate about military intervention

The UN Security Council issued a couple of general declarations, echoed by leaders of the West—the French and the American presidents—urging the incumbent president of Ivory Coast to step down. The pressure was barely bearable. There was an atmosphere of an end of regime. Assailed from various parts, assaulted by diverse players of the international community, isolated in Africa, Laurent Gbagbo's regime started to experience increased cracks at all levels—at the grassroots and military levels. An air and a sense of surrender coupled with a spirit of betrayal started to take over his close aides. He was threatened to be taken to the International Criminal Court. His regime was under increasing pressure, with a series of military and economic threats and sanctions including the freezing of assets of Ivorian officials and an ultimatum. Most international banks subsidiaries in the country ceased to operate in observance of the French and UN-imposed sanctions which included an embargo on food and medicine. This led to a humanitarian crisis mainly because of shortage of medicine used in Ivory Coast which is mostly imported from Europe.[54]

Under economic sanctions, up against the wall, the former Ivorian president ordered Ivorian officials to use the funds available in the Ivorian local branch of the BCEAO during the post-election crisis of 2010–2011 for the management of state affairs. He was accused of committing a hold-up. He nationalized the foreign banks on February 17, 2011.[55] He also started the process of creating an Ivorian currency, thus attempting to leave the monetary union which binds France to its former colonies in Africa: the CFA (*Communauté Financière*

---

[53] Guillaume Guguen, "Les électeurs suspendus à la publication des résultats," *France 24,* December 3, 2010, http://www.france24.com/fr/20101129-cote-ivoire-election-presidentielle-taux-participation-second-tour-cei-gbagbo-ouattara.

[54] Frindéthié, *From Lumumba to Gbagbo,* 136-137.

[55] Frindéthié, *From Lumumba to Gbagbo,* 136.

Française) Franc Zone. The process of creating an Ivorian currency would mean the implosion of the West African Economic and Monetary Union of which Ivory Coast represented 40%.[56]

The CFA zone countries (fifteen) are bound to a monetary and financial agreement with France which requires they deposit the bulk of their foreign reserves (at least 50%) in the French Public Treasury. This undermines the monetary, financial, economic, and political sovereignty of francophone African countries that use the CFA, which is pegged to the Euro (until 1991 to the French franc). Ivory Coast is the largest cocoa producer and represents 40% of the West African Economic and Monetary Union (WAEMU). The Ivorian crisis thus reopened the debate about the relevance of the CFA Franc currency, which started in the early years of the independence of West African countries with Togo then led by its first president, Sylvanus Olympio.

The Togo case was a tragic experience that certainly traumatized African leaders to the point that many have not questioned the irrelevance of the CFA Franc. Togo, under the leadership of Sylvanus Olympio with the assistance of a Vietnamese consultant, clearly expressed its desire to launch its own currency, and the French leadership could not sway the desire of its leaders. The project was led by the then minister of finance, Hospice Coco. After tense and difficult negotiations, France eventually accepted the principle of the Togolese currency but urged the leaders not to divulge the project, which was conducted in secrecy. France and Togo agreed that the newly independent African country would create its currency soon after the signing of a treaty planned to take place mid-January 1963, in Paris. On the night of January 12–13, 1963 Sylvanus Olympio was assassinated in a French-backed bloody coup d'état. The president who replaced him, Nicolas Grunitzky, immediately affirmed that he was not in favor of the creation of a Togolese currency.[57] The intention of Laurent Gbagbo regime to create an Ivorian currency might have been an aggravating determining factor that infuriated his adversaries who did not tolerate his impertinence, as it was seen as a declaration of war by France. And France retaliated. It organized the international community and pushed for a military intervention to take a defiant Gbagbo out of power.

---

[56] On December 21, 2019, the French president, Emmanuel Macron, and the Ivorian president, Alassane Ouattara, announced that the CFA Franc would be replaced and renamed ECO. This move was a reaction to the Anti-CFA Franc Campaign, which had galvanized African grassroots movements.

[57] Célestin Monga and Jean-Claude Tchathouang, *Sortir du Piège Monétaire* (Paris: Economica, 1996), 25–26.

During the campaign to wage a war to dislodge him, the international media and the international community accused his regime of having put a blockade against the Golf Hotel with the intent to starve its occupants to death. Alassane Ouattara and hundreds of close aids, civilians and soldiers had found refuge in the Golf Hotel. The international community, under the leadership of France and the United Nations, initially maneuvered unsuccessfully to push the African Union, and/or the ECOWAS, to put together a force to intervene militarily in Ivory Coast. The Ghanaian government led by president Atta Mills, whose territory was supposedly chosen to welcome the Economic Community of West African Monitoring Group (ECOMOG) forces, the military branch of ECOWAS, issued a declaration stating that it would not provide any soldiers to a West African military contingent if the option of a military intervention was to be executed.[58]

Raila Odinga, former prime minister of Kenya; Goodluck Jonathan, president of Nigeria; and Blaise Compaoré, from Burkina Faso, were among the advocates of a military option to resolve the crisis. These forceful and militaristic intentions, supported by some in Africa and echoed by Ouattara's camp, caused an outcry in Africa and around the world. Dissenting voices opposed the idea of a military intervention. Thabo Mbeki and Jerry John Rawlings, former presidents of South Africa and Ghana respectively, and then-sitting presidents, such as those of Cape Verde, Gambia, Angola, and Guinea-Bissau, were in favor of a peaceful, political, and diplomatic resolution of the crisis. Former Ghanaian president Captain Jerry John Rawlings reiterated his call for extreme restraint in the management of the Ivorian crisis. In a statement issued on Thursday, December 23, 2010, three days after he called for restraint and maturity by all stakeholders in the crisis, President Rawlings said the situation in Ivory Coast was not a "simple electoral dispute but a web of ethnic and political complexities that should be handled with tact and diplomacy rather than the open hints of forceful intervention."[59]

The former Ghanaian president argued that military intervention was groundless, could not bring sustainable peace to the country, and would exacerbate ethnic and political divisions, as he warned against a "full-scale war with horrific consequences."[60] He added that "the two men at the center of the

---

[58] Francis Kokutse, "Ghana President Says 'no' to Troops in Ivory Coast," *The San Diego Union Tribune*, January 7, 2011, https://www.sandiegouniontribune.com/sdut-ghana-president-says-no-to-troops-in-ivory-coast-2011jan07-story.html.

[59] Peter Clottey, "Gbagbo Aide Hails Call for 'Restraint' in Ivory Coast Crisis," VOA News, December 27, 2010, https://www.voanews.com/a/gbagbo-aide-hails-call-for-restraint-in-ivory-coast-crisis—112576964/157108.html.

[60] Clottey, "Gbagbo Aide Hails Call for 'Restraint'."

dispute have both indicated their preparedness to see a recount or further verification of the results by neutral observers. Is there any hidden motive in refusing to take up the challenge being offered by the two parties?"[61] On the other hand, the United Nations Secretary-General, Ban Ki Moon, who weighed in on the debate, refused the recount. The intransigeance of antagonist players eventually led to the resumption of violence that will be highlighted in the following section.

Violence

The failure to build a multiethnic Ivory Coast and the desire to impose the will of one group—be it an ethnic group, a coalition of ethnic groups, or political parties—over others led to the use of violence as a means to resolve the disputes. The resumption of the conflict after the 2010 election was another episode of the civil war, with the same players who had been having antagonistic interactions since 1990 and who clashed recurrently in a post independent Ivory Coast in 1992, 2000, 2002, 2004, 2010–2011, and up to now.

Coup d'état of 2002

The coup d'état that overthrew Bédié in 1999 opened a Pandora's box of violence in Ivory Coast with a series of coup d'état attempts and recurrent armed conflicts. Laurent Gbagbo was—on September 19, 2002—in Europe on an international trip,[62] when soldiers under the leadership of Ibrahim Coulibaly, aka IB, trained in Burkina Faso with the initial funding of Alassane Ouattara and with the financial support of Libya under Kadhafi, attempted to overthrow him.[63]

Prior to the 2002 attempt, they had sought to take him out of power on January 7–8, 2001.[64] Internal disagreements among the rebels contributed to the rise of Guillaume Soro, a former Ivorian student union leader, as the leader of the rebellion.[65] In 2002 the rebels committed massive human rights violations, including genocide, rape, and extrajudicial killings. The rebels split

---

[61] Clottey, "Gbagbo Aide Hails Call for 'Restraint'."

[62] Stephen Smith et al., "Le Vrai Visage de la Rebellion," *Le Monde*, October 11, 2002, https://www.lemonde.fr/archives/article/2002/10/11/cote-d-ivoire-le-visage-de-la-rebellion_4260860_1819218.html.

[63] Fanny Pigeaud, *France Côte d'Ivoire: Une Histoire Tronquée* (Paris: Vents d'ailleurs, 2015), 32.

[64] Magali Chelpi-den Hamer, *Militarized youths in Western Côte d'Ivoire*, 64.

[65] Guillaume Soro, *Pourquoi je suis devenu un rebelle: La Côte d'Ivoire au bord du gouffre* (Paris: Hachette Littérature, 2005).

the country into two. They governed and managed the northern part of the country for eight years, while Gbagbo held on to the south. In that environment of war, human rights violations were committed in the two geographical regions separated by a buffer zone composed of the French forces and the UN troops.[66] In the south controlled by Gbagbo, Ouattara's supporters have been in a permanent logic of armed insurrection and civil uprising since 2002.

A major moment of the military confrontation was the year 2004. Two major incidents occurred that year: a crushing by Gbagbo's forces of a pro-Ouattara demonstration on March 25, 2004 leading to the death of more than one hundred people,[67] and the launching of a military expedition by Gbagbo to free the northern part of the country from the occupation of the rebel forces. The military offensive was called "Operation Dignity." This led to the military involvement of France against the regime of Gbagbo and to the South African diplomatic mediation to resolve the Ivorian crisis. France allegedly sought to overthrow President Gbagbo who could maintain his power thanks to a popular mobilization of his supporters. This will be elaborated upon in the section related to the neocolonial aspect of the crisis.

Post-electoral violence 2010-2011

The military intervention per se against the Ivorian regime led by Laurent Gbagbo, under the auspices of the United Nations and the French Force Licorne occurred in two major phases: the attack by Ouattara's troops who were given the green light to do so by the UN and France against Gbagbo's forces and the Western military intervention by French troops and UN forces.

During the post-electoral crisis, the international media and some of the representatives of European powers profusely reported that peaceful demonstrators were harassed and killed by Gbagbo's regime. There was violence coming from all sides of the spectrum and the electoral crisis was heightened by the armed struggle between various players.

For the sake of clarity, it is important to recall that from 2002 to 2007, 60% of Ivory Coast territory was in the hands of the rebels who had made the second most populous city of the country, Bouaké, their headquarters. The incumbent president Laurent Gbagbo was controlling the economic and political poles of the country, Yamoussokro the political capital and Abidjan, the biggest harbor of the country and the economic capital home to eight million people and San-

---

[66] Amnesty International, "Côte d'Ivoire: A Succession of Unpunished Crimes," February 27, 2003. https://www.amnesty.org/en/wp-content/uploads/2021/06/afr310072003en.pdf.
[67] United Nations Security Council Report of May 13, 2004.

pedro, the second harbor of the country. Even though the country was reunited since 2007 following the Ouagadougou Agreement signed that year the rebels were in quasi control of the positions they had occupied since 2002, noting that they had not disarmed, in violation of the above-mentioned Ouagadougou Agreement and of the preceding ones. When the electoral stalemate started, violence resumed more in the contested zones held by the regime of Laurent Gbagbo. The forces of Alassane Ouattara undertook a military operation in the interior of the country to gain control of as many contested zones as they could. They sought to conquer the western part of the country and the economic capital, Abidjan, the heart of the economic and political power of Ivory Coast. These regions became the most disputed battlefields.

Several groups representing the Laurent Gbagbo's regime felt they were called upon to protect the zones they were holding onto as they did in 2002 and 2004. These groups were comprised of the security forces, the Young Patriots, the self-defense groups, mercenaries mainly coming from Liberia. Their main goal was to defeat once for all the pro-Ouattara's forces who were composed of the rebels initially reunited in the MPCI, once called the *Forces Armées des Forces Nouvelles* (FAFN) and which were renamed the *Forces Républicaines de Côte d'Ivoire* (FRCI) by Alassane Ouattara on March 17 2011, the traditional hunters called the dozos, other mercenaires from neighboring countries and the Invisible Commando which was operating in one of the most populous district of Abidjan, Abobo, a stronghold of Alassane Ouattara. The UN Nations troops, the blue helmets (10,000 in number) and the French soldiers of the Licorne Force constituted the international legion of fighters who later sided with the pro-Ouattara's forces.

Within Abidjan, Yopougon (Laurent Gbagbo's stronghold) and Abobo (Alassane Ouattara's stronghold), Cocody, Plateau, and Treichville were the primary major battlefields. The forces of Laurent Gbagbo wanted to make sure Abidjan would not fall to Alassane Ouattara forces who decided to do a guerilla warfare in the economic capital which started in Abobo. Abidjan was put under a curfew by Laurent Gbagbo that his security forces tried to reinforce. Prominent leaders including Laurent Gbagbo himself, Simone Gbagbo and Blé Goudé (appointed minister of Youth) multiplied meetings, rallies and speeches in order to mobilise their supporters and troops. They denounced the neo-colonial agenda of the west and insisted that the incumbent president was the true winner of the elections.

The self-defense groups erected roadblocks as vigilantes to search vehicles and people as they sought to unmask intruders and infiltrators notably Alassane Ouattara active supporters and fighters or representatives of the United Nations mission in Ivory Coast who, alongside the French troops, were providing strategic and military support to the pro-Alassane Ouattara's rebels.

Human rights abuses were committed by all sides. But the international media and human rights organizations echoing the position of the west magnified the crimes committed by the forces of the ruling coalition.

The pro-gbagbo groups were accused of having committed human rights violations against constituencies, sympathisers, and properties affiliated with the opposition namely Alassane Ouattara. Beatings, arbitrary arrests, attacks on opposition leaders offices, extrajudicial killings and rapes were alleged crimes pro-Gbagbo forces were accused of in regions they were holding onto namely Abidjan. One of such killings is described in the following lines to Amnesty International by an eyewitness :

> The night of 5-6 December [2010] a large group of security forces supporting Gbagbo came to our home, some in uniforms and others in plain clothes; we did not open and from the window we saw seven cargos [army or police vehicles]. When we thought they had gone, we opened the door and me and my brother, Fofana Youssouf, went out but more forces were still there and started shooting. We rushed back into the courtyard and at that point my brother was hit. He died shortly after.[68]

Incidents occurred around some specific events such as the protests planned respectively on Thursday, December 16 and Friday, December 17, 2010 by Alassane Ouattara's camp in order to increase the pressure on Laurent Gbagbo. The proclaimed goals of the mid December rallies whose itinerary would lead the "protestors" to the national radio and television were to install Soro Guillaume, leader of the rebellion who became Laurent Gbagbo's Prime Minister after the Ouagadougou Agreement signed in 2007 and who just switched side to rally Alassane Ouattara of whom he said was the legitimate winner of the election. The alleged objective was to carry out an insurrection accompanied by an armed struggle in a context of urban guerrilla warfare. There were pro-Alassane Ouattara soldiers and mercenaries carrying weapons in broad day light among unarmed demonstrators. Violence and firing from both sides ensued causing the killing of police officers loyal to Gbagbo and the death of several civilians among the demonstrators.[69]

---

[68] Amnesty International, "They Looked at His Identity Card and Shot Him: Six Months of Post-Electoral Violence " May 2011, p. 16, https://www.amnesty.org/fr/wp-content/uploads/2021/06/afr310022011en.pdf.

[69] RTI, "Côte d'Ivoire: Document RTI sur la marche du 16/12/2010 et les combats qui ont suivi," YouTube video, December 31, 2010, https://www.youtube.com/watch?v=Hy3a j3zUniw.

There were reports that the systematic attacks on some people were done according to identity and religious lines. Several human rights organizations and international media gave echo to news and reports of crimes committed against northerners and citizens of neighboring countries such as Mali, Burkina Faso, Guinea and Senegal. Blé Goudé, leader of the Young Patriots gave an ultimatum perceived as a serious threat on December 29, 2011 to Alassane Ouattara to leave the Golf Hotel where the latter found refuge, protected by hundreds of his security forces in arms and surrounded by supporters, partners and political allies. He asked his supporters to go bare hands on January 1, 2011 to the Golf Hotel, if Alassane Ouattara was still there by then, in order to dislodge him.[70] He could never execute his ultimatum. In a speech which supposedly added fuel to the fire that he pronounced on February 25, 2011 at Yopougon Bar, the leader of the Young Patriots, Blé Goudé called for more vigilance in order to catch and neutralize all foreigners and all those who did not belong to the respective communities they were protecting, as they were defending the capital and protecting Laurent Gbagbo's regime.

Human rights organizations and the international community stakeholders viewed that speech as an aggravating factor of the escalation of tension and violence and of the commission of human rights abuses in Abidjan. Roadblocks mushromed througout Abidjan and the vigilantes have arrested, beaten, and killed according to human rights groups. Members of the pro-Gbagbo militiamen were believed to have resorted to a method of execution called Article 125. The number 125 refers to the addition of 100 CFA Francs[71] and 25 CFA Francs, the former is the price of petrol and the latter is the price of a box of matches. The victim was put in a tire and set on fire. An eye witness of such a killing method (Article 125) gave the following account of a crime committed on February 27, 2011, two days after Blé Goudé speech:

> One of the Young Patriots said he did not know him and they said: 'He's a Dioula, therefore he is from Burkina Faso, therefore he is a rebel'. They stripped him and beat him up. During this time, the man was looking around at us because we, market traders, knew him, but we were afraid to speak up for him. We felt bad about it, especially because they killed this brother of ours right in front of us. The Young Patriots put a tyre round his neck, poured petrol over his body and set fire to him. The

---

[70] AFP, "Blé Goudé Appelle à Libérer » le QG de Ouattara », https://www.youtube.com/watch?v=Bma1962DYhg, Tuesday, July 5, 2022 at 11:15 AM.

[71] A dollar was 500 CFA Francs before the current inflation; 100 CFA was roughly 25 cents or a quarter.

victim's nickname was Tchédjan (which means 'the big man' in dioula).[72]

Human Rights Watch also reported that it recorded 34 deaths, 14 of them by way of article 125 in the days that followed the speech given by Blé Goudé on February 25, 2011.[73] Human rights organizations also reported that Laurent Gbagbo's forces have shelled repeatedly densely populated areas in Abobo. One of the targets was a populous market place in Abobo. It was shelled on March 17, 2011 causing several casualties: 20 people lost their lives and 60 were wounded.[74] Two weeks before, a few days before the UN International Women's Day a women rally was organized and was crushed causing the death of women. This incident caused an uproar of the international community who decided of a military intervention to protect civilians and dislodge Laurent Gbagbo.

With regard to Alassane Ouattara forces, they launched their military expedition along 3 regions, the east, the west, and the central west as they moved towards Abidjan, the great prize to conquer. On their way, they committed crimes such rapes, extrajudicial killings as they burned down villages, and farms. The western region of the country fell to Alassane Ouattara's forces at the end of March 2011. His troops opened the biggest prison in Abidjan on March 31 to set free the inmates, thus adding to the insecurity in the country. The urban guerilla of pro-Alassane Ouattara's forces was initiated by several groups namely the Invisible Commando. The Gbagbo camp decreed a ban on the overflight of Abidjan by the UN and French planes and helicopters. The latter did not respect the measure because they did not recognize any longer the authtority of Laurent Gbagbo seen as the ex-president of the country and because their mandate came from the United Nations Security Council.

The UN Chief closed his eyes on the activities of the Invisible Commando. Ibrahim Coulibaly (IB)—the very man who organized and launched the coup d'état attempt of 2002 and who was outmaneuvered and outsmarted by Guillaume Soro, who became the leader of the rebellion—was the chief of the group instrumental in adding to the tragedy during the post-electoral conflict. There was a fallout between him and Alassane Ouattara. He was suspected of pursuing his own agenda after he fell from grace.

---

[72] Amnesty International, "They Looked at His Card and They Shot Him Dead", May 2011, p. 25.

[73] Human Rights Watch, "They Killed them like it was Nothing", October 2011, p. 44, https://www.hrw.org/sites/default/files/reports/cdi1011webwcover_0.pdf.

[74] Amnesty International, "They Looked at His Card and They Shot Him Dead", p. 20.

IB would reemerge during the electoral stalemate as the leader of the unidentified armed group called the Invisible Commando, which took possession of the Abobo district, Alassane Ouattara's stronghold in Abidjan. The military attacks of the Invisible Commando contributed to the escalation of violence. The *New York Times*, certainly driven by the intention to exculpate Alassane Ouattara's responsibility in the violence, denied his ties with the Invisible Commando: "It is unclear what connections, if any, the 'invisible commando' has with the Ouattara camp. At least one independent newspaper here has published statements purporting to come from the shadowy forces, denying such ties."[75] Fanny Pigeaud, French journalist and author, who dedicated a book on the truncated history of the relations between France and Ivory Coast, gave more details about the origin of the Invisible Commando and its activities during the electoral stalemate:

> An urban guerrilla war started in December in Abobo, a densely populated district of Abidjan with a population of 1.5 million inhabitants. These are elements of Ibrahim Coulibaly, aka IB, who are the initiators: they settled in the Ivorian economic capital after escaping the massacres of 2003–2004 ordered by Soro against them. Their group will later be called "Invisible Commando" by the media. Their organization is not new: they have tried several times, since 2004, to make coups d'état. Since January 2006, they have tried to attack the Akouédo military camp. At the end of 2007, they were the ones, with military accomplices [in the national army], who were behind "Noel in Abidjan," an abortive coup attempt. Since then, they have been on standby.[76]

In an interview given to RFI on March 14, 2011, Choi Young-Jin, the UN Chief Mission in Ivory Coast gave an assessment of the political situation and of the development of the war. He announced that there were 400 people killed after 100 days of stalemate, He also added that Laurent Gbagbo forces have lost control of most of the country but it was the responsibility of the Gbagbo regime to protect civilians. The failure for the ruling regime to honor its responsibilities to protect the civilians was an opportunity and a duty for his mission to gather incriminating evidence to procecute the Laurent Gbagbo camp.[77] There were news that the Golf Hotel which was deprived of water and

---

[75] Adam Nossiter, "Women Said to be Killed at Ivory Coast Protest," *The New York Times*, March 4, 2011, https://www.nytimes.com/2011/03/04/world/africa/04ivory-coast.html.

[76] Pigeaud, *France Côte d'Ivoire*, 221.

[77] RFI, Interview de Choi sur RFI, "La Majorité des Militaires ne sont pas prêts à Combattre pour Gbagbo," March 3, 2011, https://www.connectionivoirienne.net/2011/

electricity (restored by the Licorne Force) was attacked on April 9, 2011. All fingers were pointed at Gbagbo but his security forces did not claim the attack.[78] The rumors of the attack on the Golf Hotel surfaced during a military intervention which had started on April 4, 2011 against Laurent Gbagbo's regime led by an international force composed of the French and the UN troops.

Post-electoral violence and Western military intervention

The western military intervention to dislodge Laurent Gbagbo divided the African community. In his book, *Côte d'Ivoire: Le Coup d'État*, Charles Onana published letters and exchanges between Blaise Compaoré (former president of Burkina Faso), Goodluck Jonathan (former president of Nigeria and then president of ECOWAS), and Nicolas Sarkozy (former president of France) about the best way to resolve the Ivorian crisis. The former president of Burkina Faso wrote a letter to the French president to ask him to use his power to have the United Nations pass a resolution that would allow a French-UN military intervention in Ivory Coast. He added that he and Goodluck Jonathan were ready to put their troops and those of ECOWAS at the disposal of an international military expedition. On February 25, Sarkozy wrote to Goodluck Jonathan and assured him that he was taking the proper measures and steps that would help oust Gbagbo. In that letter the French president recommended that an emissary should be sent to Jacob Zuma (former president of South Africa), who would have the mission to explain the crisis to him, because in the opinion of the French leader, the South African president did not understand the Ivorian crisis.[79] Charles Onana, interviewed in a documentary produced by Nicoletta Fagiolo, summarized the project of his book in the following assessment:

> These letters are evidence that we were no longer in a post-electoral crisis. Since the beginning, the goal was to overthrow a regime. They had to find the right moment, the right pretext, and the right arguments in order to bring regime change in Ivory Coast. The right moment was the election. The right pretext was the actual vote even if the conditions were not met, the country was still divided into two parts. The right argument was that Gbagbo was not the winner but the loser of the election. All the ingredients were put together so that people would not

---

03/14/interview-choi-sur-rfi-la-majorite-des-militaires-ne-sont-pas-prets-a-combattre-pour-gbagbo/.

[78] RFI, "Choi Young-jin: L'ONUCI est toujours en contact avec Laurent Gbagbo" April 4, 2011, https://www.rfi.fr/fr/afrique/20110411-yong-jin-choi.

[79] Charles Onana, *Côte d'Ivoire: Le Coup d'État* (Paris: Editions Duboiris, 2011), 335–340.

oppose the idea and the principle of the coup d'état. The press bought into it. No one dared to ask to investigate the outcome of the election.[80]

During the electoral stalemate, violent incidents led to the forceful involvement of the United Nations in the crisis. The most important one was the all-women march in Abobo held on March 3, 2011 by Alassane Ouattara's supporters around International Women's Day, which is celebrated each year on March 8. The news spread that seven women were killed by the security forces of the incumbent president. A chorus of condemnation from Brussels to Paris, from London to Washington, was the epitome of the international community's conviction that the crime was perpetrated by the incumbent leader's security forces: "But on Thursday, Mr. Gbagbo's forces responded to the demonstration in the tense Abobo neighborhood by shooting into the marching crowd of hundreds of women, two witnesses said. Six were killed instantly in the machine-gun fire, others were wounded, and the marchers dispersed in a panic, the witnesses said. Amateur video taken on the spot appeared to confirm their account."[81]

For the international community, Laurent Gbagbo has just crossed the Rubicon and made it clear that he must go. The words of Philip J. Crowley, State Department spokesman, on Twitter highlighted such a position: "The moral bankruptcy of Laurent Gbagbo is evident as his security forces killed women protesters and his country runs out of resources."[82] Several supporters of the former president of Ivory Coast were quick to expose the video arguing that the content of the video was staged or was photoshopped. As for the images, they seemed to show it was staged since one of the women supposedly killed got up before she was ordered to lie down again.

The Abobo march and the images of women believed to have been massacred by Laurent Gbagbo accelerated the process of his international marginalization and ostracism and subsequently led to the adoption of UN resolution 1975, voted on March 30, 2011, under the mantle of which France entered the war for the benefit of his rival. The United Nations claimed that that resolution was aimed at protecting civilians against the atrocities committed by Gbagbo's regime. The UN resolution was the legal basis for the military assault of the French and the UN forces against Laurent Gbagbo's army.

---

[80] Nicoletta Fagiolo, "Laurent Gbagbo, The Right to Difference, part 1," YouTube video, September 14, 2014, https://www.youtube.com/watch?v=xwDLCb2UkXE.

[81] Nossiter, "Women Said to be Killed."

[82] Nossiter, "Women Said to be Killed."

Certainly emboldened by the UN resolution and benefitting from the military support of the UN and the French troops Ouattara's forces became irresistible while moving toward Abidjan, burning farms, houses in cities and villages, beating, raping, and killing whomever would stand in their way. The hallmark of their military expedition in the countryside is known by the name of the city (Duékoué) where it occurred, the Massacre of Duékoué, which was a real genocide. The city was torn by interethnic killings, which turned into a deadly retaliation by Alassane Ouattara's forces at the end of March 2011. Hundreds of the Guéré group, an ethnic constituency close to Gbagbo, were killed in one day. Even an eyewitness posted as a journalist in Duékoué who disputed the numbers argued that he could count 266 bodies. Bodies were also found in wells.[83] The bodies were collected and were buried by the UN troops who were stationed less than a mile away and who did not prevent the tragedy.[84]

The military involvement of France and the UN raised the question of the ethics of the intervention. The humanitarian intervention doctrine (combined with the responsibility to protect) suggests the use of the right of a foreign military intervention in a state unable or unwilling to assure the safety and the protection of its own citizens.[85] Maite Nkoana-Mashabane, the South African Minister of Foreign Affairs, openly said that she did not vote for a resolution for war in Ivory Coast: "I do not remember giving a mandate to anyone for an air raid on Ivory Coast. We do not necessarily support what we did not vote for."[86]

The UN- and French-led attack on the city of Abidjan started on April 4, 2011. Their helicopters started bombing Ivory Coast military bases (Agban, Akouedo I & II) from 1:00 p.m. GMT. The stockpile and the military arsenal of a military camp caught fire. Hospitals, military barracks, the presidential palace, national TV, and residences were bombed. Witnesses reported that the UN and French helicopters also shot at a large number of civilians lining up in a shopping center to get food. Several witnesses reported that the French helicopters carried and dropped Alassane Ouattara's forces, to whom they had been giving strategic support. The UN and French bombing of military bases served only one purpose, to destroy the power of the Ivorian national army, thus giving a

---

[83] Saint-Tra Bi, *Duékoué: La vérité interdite* (Abidjan: Nouvelles Editions Balafons, 2019), 102. Pigeaud, *France Côte d'Ivoire*, 244–245.

[84] Bi, *Duékoué*, 125–127.

[85] Hector Olasolo, *The Role of the International Criminal Court in Preventing Atrocity Crimes through Timely Intervention* (The Hague: Eleven International Publishing, 2011), 7.

[86] Raymond Koudou Kessié, "Quand le Président Gbagbo Porte sa Croix," in *Le Président Laurent Gbagbo à la Cour Pénale Internationale*, 58.

comparative advantage to Alassane Ouattara's forces, who had been unsuccessful in taking control of Abidjan for months.

After one week of bombing, Laurent Gbagbo was finally captured on April 11, 2011, in what is seen as a coup d'état.[87] His wife, Simone Gbagbo; his son Michel Gbagbo; and hundreds of people were also arrested. Pictures and videos of them with bloody faces and with some wearing only underwear were taken and circulated on social media and around the world, in the age of the information technology revolution. Thousands of lives were lost in a four-month-long electoral stalemate.[88] Laurent Gbagbo was presented as being the sole responsible party of the Ivorian tragedy. Some in the western world were bold enough to refer to Alassane Ouattara's share in the crisis and in the political violence in Ivory Coast: "Though he emerged in the Western media as the good versus Gbagbo's evil, Ouattara, too, has been accused of having blood on his hands."[89]

Laurent Gbagbo was initially taken to a prison in Korhogo, in the northern part of the country, in the rebels' stronghold and later to the International Criminal Court prison in the Netherlands on November 30, 2011. His wife Simone Gbagbo was taken to another city of the northern part of the country, Odienne. Days after the fall of Gbagbo, Alassane Ouattara's forces have been exclusively accused of various types of crimes: namely extrajudicial killings, expedited prosecution, and mass murder. Ouattara's Dozos attacked—on July 20, 2012—the Nahibly camp of displaced people, causing deaths and an uproar of the backers of the regime.[90] Hundreds of Ivorians had their accounts frozen for more than five years. Hundreds more spent years in prison without trial. The houses of several hundred officials were besieged by Ouattara's warlords. Migrants from neighboring countries took over the farms of displaced and exiled Ivorians. On August 6, 2018, under external and internal pressure, Alassane Ouattara resolved to free hundreds of political prisoners, including Simone Gbagbo. Despite such a gesture, which decreased the tension, Alassane Ouattara did not create a space for true reconciliation.

---

[87] Onana, *Côte d'Ivoire: Le Coup d'État.*

[88] Even though there is not any evidence to demonstrate it, the number of 3,000 deaths announced by the international community can be disputed.

[89] Moni Basu, "Ouattara versus Gbagbo: Good versus evil?" CNN, April 12, 2011, http://www.cnn.com/2011/WORLD/africa/04/12/ivory.coast.atrocities/index.html.

[90] Several human rights organizations have written reports on the attack of the Nahibly camp. An important report to read is that of Amnesty International, "It Looks Like Nothing Happened Here: Still No Justice One Year after Nahibly Camp Attack," July 29, 2013. https://www.amnesty.org/en/documents/AFR31/009/2013/en/.

Moreover, the series of mutinies by his own warlords and soldiers against his regime over unpaid financial bonuses promised to them before the military offensive against the former Ivorian president convinced skeptics about his alleged involvement in the formation of the rebellion, a claim he denied for years. Several contingents of armed groups (a group of 8,400, the Special Forces composed of more than 2,000 elements, and 6,500 demobilized respectively) took to the streets, firing in the air, blocking the main arteries of cities across the country. They all wanted a bonus of $20,000 for each soldier.[91] The mutinies heightened the tension in the country. Many observers feared a coup d'état. Several mutineers have affirmed on public international media that they were recruited to fight for Alassane Ouattara, and they deserved to be paid for their work. The complacency of the International Criminal Court, which did not feel compelled to take such affirmations into account in its quest for truth and justice in Ivory Coast, and the complicit silence of the West reinforce the neocolonial aspect of the crisis.

The neo-colonial aspect of the Ivorian crisis

The hallmark of French neo-colonialism, also known as *Françafrique* in Ivory Coast, besides control over economic life and the French military presence in the country, has been its involvement in the crisis. And the neocolonial aspect of the crisis encompasses the role of France and Western powers, the involvement of the United Nations, and the role of the International Criminal Court.

Neo-colonialism is perceived as "the most incisive indictment of the Euro-American Grand Imperialist project."[92] It has been thoroughly articulated by Kwame Nkrumah, first president of Ghana, in his book *Neo-Colonialism: The Last Stage of Imperialism* (1965). For the sake of this conversation, it is imperative to recall how he defines the phenomenon:

> The essence of neo-colonialism is that the State which is subject to it is, in theory, independent and has all the outward trappings of international sovereignty. In reality its economic system and thus its political policy is directed from outside. The methods and form of this direction can take various shapes. For example, in an extreme case the troops of the imperial power may garrison the territory of the neo-

---

[91] "Ivory Coast Mutiny: Government announces deal with soldiers," BBC, May 15, 2017, https://www.bbc.com/news/world-africa-39920149.

[92] Charles Quist-Adade, "From Neo-Colonialism to Neoliberal Globalization: Lessons from Nkrumah's Neo-Colonialism: The Last Stage of Imperialism," in *Re-Engaging the African Diasporas: Pan-Africanism in the Age of Globalization*, eds. Charles Quist-Adade and Wendy Royal (London: Cambridge Scholars Publishing, 2016), 104.

colonial State and control the government of it. More often, however, neo-colonialist control is exercised through economic or monetary means. The neo-colonial State may be obliged to take the manufactured products of the imperialist power to the exclusion of competing products from elsewhere. Control over government policy in the neo-colonial State may be secured by payments towards the cost of running the State, by the provision of civil servants in positions where they can dictate policy, and by monetary control over foreign exchange through the imposition of a banking system controlled by the imperial power.[93]

The Gold Coast, renamed Ghana, was the first Sub-Saharan African country to win its independence on March 6, 1957, and became the beacon of hope and a symbol of the possibility of freedom for Africans and people of African descent. It set the pace for the decolonization of Africa and reignited the Pan-African struggle on the continent of Africa and across the globe. Several African countries (17 in 1960) gained their right to self-governance and self-determination, including Ivory Coast. Most of the newly independent countries were confronted with a new system called neo-colonialism, described above by Kwame Nkrumah.

Since 1958, France has used a set of schemes to maintain its grip over its former African colonies and over Africa, from the political binding to the signing of military agreements and of economic and commercial treaties and to the use of coups d'état to take out of power regimes believed to be anti-French. The French war hero General de Gaulle, who returned to power in 1958, was instrumental in establishing the Franco-African Community that year with the adoption of a constitution that regulated the life of France and its colonies. The draft of the constitution was submitted to French citizens and to French colonial subjects. Only Sékou Touré of Guinea opposed it, with a no to France on September 28, 1958. The colonial power reacted with wrath and ostracized him.[94]

The wind of independence that led to the independence of Ghana in West Africa shook up the Franco-African Community, particularly after the defiance of Sékou Touré. France could no longer maintain its grip on its African colonies. Applying divide-and-conquer politics, it disintegrated its colonial federations. When it could no longer maintain its newly invented empire, it gave independence to the member territories one after the other. It managed to maintain its colonies in a colonial pact through several commercial,

---

[93] Kwame Nkrumah, *Neo-Colonialism: The Last Stage of Imperialism* (London: Thomas Nelson & Sons, 1965), 3.

[94] Aristide R. Zolberg, *One Party Government in the Ivory Coast* (Princeton: Princeton University Press, 1964), 230-231.

development, and military agreements. This ensured its domination over them. France enjoys preferential treatment from its former African colonies. De Gaulle put into place a special Department of African Affairs, led by Jacques Foccart, who was the perpetrator and orchestrator of coups d'état in Africa against nationalist leaders who wanted to distance themselves from France's sphere of influence. Dictators loyal to France were endorsed.

The debate about the acceleration of the decolonization and the unity of Africa was raging, giving rise to competing and conflicting positions. In the height of the debate about Pan-Africanism, the former president of Ivory Coast Félix Houphouët-Boigny advocated a stronger bond between African countries and France and Europe.[95] He used the words *Françafrique* and *Eurafrique* to oppose them to Pan-Africanism. The word *Françafrique* became popular thanks to the publication of the pioneering and seminal book La *Françafrique, le plus long scandale de la République*.[96]

Françafrique is a multifaceted web of relationships through which France maintains its dominance over its former colonies. That web of relationships encompasses the diplomatic, political, cultural, economic, financial, and monetary dimensions through agencies in various sectors: military, banking system, business deals, and French corporations. A leader who does not fit in this is quelled or destroyed or combated. Those who comply have all the support of France. There is a perennial battle in francophone countries between those who seek more freedom and those who want to advance *Françafrique*.

After sixty years of independence, Ivory Coast remains a captive space in the hands of the French despite its administrative and political independence. Gary Busch depicts the hegemonic influence of France over Ivory Coast and its role during the Ivorian crisis in his pamphlet "The French, the UN and Ivory Coast":

> To this day the French Treasury continues to control the Ivory Coast currency, its capital reserves and its trade and investment policies. The French Army continues to control the rebel mob of half-trained soldiers and 'Dozos' which make up the Ouattara Army, its equipment, its training and its deployment. The French business community dominates almost every aspect of the national economy, even the oil industry and the cocoa industry where it shares its presence with a limited number of overseas companies. Other than those they maintain

---

95 Félix Houphouët-Boigny, *Anthologie des Discours, 1946–1978* (Abidjan: CEDA, 1978), 176.

96 Francois-Xavier Verschave, *La Françafrique, le plus long scandale de la République* (Paris: Editions Stock, 1998).

a monopoly in transport, water, electricity and ports and control most of the international commerce in Ivory Coast products and imports. There are hundreds of French administrators standing alongside Ivorian civil servants, "guiding" their decisions.[97]

Bruno Charbonneau gives a more frightening depiction of how strong the French grip on Ivory Coast is:

> At the dawn of the twenty-first century, France Telecom had acquired 51% of Citelcom, and Orange was the largest mobile phone provider in Côte d'Ivoire, the Bolloré Group owned 67% of Sitrail who ran the railroad between Abidjan and Ouagadougou and had a near monopoly position in the transport sector (Saga) and tobacco (SITAB). Air France held 51% of Air Ivoire, Bouygues, through its subsidiary Saur had acquired the concession for the electric company Ciprel and 25% of the Compagnie d'Electricité Ivoirienne, and controlled the national water company, Sodeci; Total and ELF had 25% of the SIR (Ivorian Society for oil refining), the banking sector was divided between BNP, Crédit Lyonnais and Société Générale.[98]

Scholars, pundits, and analysts who do not take this factual evidence of the French presence in the Ivory Coast's politics fail to have a comprehensive analysis of the Ivorian crisis. The neocolonial aspect of the Ivorian Crisis can be analyzed through five major actions: the refusal by France to give military support to Gbagbo's army to quell the rebel forces in 2002; the backing by France of an agreement that legitimized the rebellion, the Marcoussis Agreement; the French diplomatic effort to isolate and weaken the regime of Gbagbo (through sanctions and the UN resolutions); the neocolonial wars against Gbagbo's regime in 2004 and 2011; and the involvement of France in the ICC prosecution of the former head of state of Ivory Coast.

Nonactivation of the traditional military agreement

After the coup d'état attempt of 2002, the former Ivorian president asked France to help him stop the rebellion, in the name of the agreements that bind the two countries since the independence of Ivory Coast. The former colonizer, according to the accord, ought to protect the integrity of the Ivorian territory in the context of a foreign attack. The leaders of France argued that Ivory Coast

---

[97] Gary K. Busch, "The French, the UN and Ivory Coast," Academia, accessed February 26, 2022, https://www.academia.edu/5096960/The_French_the_UN_and_the_Ivory_Coast.

[98] Bruno Charbonneau, *France and the New Imperialism: Security Policy in Sub-Saharan Africa* (Farnham: Ashgate Publishing, 2008), 155.

was not under a foreign attack but was rather facing a mutiny or an internal conflict.[99]

The rebels came with mercenaries from Burkina Faso, which was their base and where they trained. The French authorities put pressure on Gbagbo not to accept any help from Obasanjo of Nigeria, which was the first country to decide to rescue him. When the rebels retreated to the central and the northern parts of the country, the French created a buffer zone between the northern-controlled rebel region and the south under the control of Gbagbo, thus consecrating the partition of the country for eight years.

Marcoussis Agreement and the legitimization of the rebellion by France

On January 24, 2003, a French-sponsored agreement, named after the French city where it took place, became the cornerstone of the peace process: the Marcoussis Agreement. It was signed by the Ivorian political parties and the rebels. Representatives of the Ivorian security forces and of the Ivorian government were not invited.

Even though the agreement acknowledged respect for the Ivorian Constitution, the integrity of Ivory Coast territory, and Laurent Gbagbo as president of the country, its conclusions made of constitutional, legislative, and regulatory recommendations somehow violated the Ivorian Constitution, undermined the president's authority, legitimized the rebellion, and consecrated the partition of the country into two. It imposed the appointment of a new prime minister with extensive powers over Gbagbo in a power-sharing scheme.[100] The agreement declared that a provision of the constitution that was voted for by 86% of Ivorians in 2000, about the citizenship of a candidate to the presidency should be changed as a solution to Alassane Ouattara's nationality-eligibility problem. The meeting also recommended the naturalization of thousands of people called the *apatrides*, believed to having been "deprived" of their Ivorian nationality, according to the claims of the rebels groups. The *apatrides* constitute a category of people born in Ivory Coast before 1972 from foreigners and who naturally deserved Ivorian citizenship but did not claim it. It must be pointed out that the rebels acted in bad faith because during the one-party system the government allowed foreigners to vote and therefore could not prevent the *apatrides* from claiming their duly deserved Ivorian nationality.

---

[99] Bertin Kadet, *La Politique de défense et de sécurité de la Côte d'Ivoire* (Paris: L'Harmattan, 2011), 17-18.

[100] Charles Maisonneuve, *Le Bourbier Ivoirien* (Toulouse: Editions Privat, 2005), 91.

Ivory Coast adopted *jus soli* (the right of soil) in 1961, which was replaced in 1972 by *jus sanguinis* (the right of blood). According to the provisions of the former, it sufficed to be born in the country to be Ivorian. The latter enshrined the primacy of the right of blood to the detriment of the right of soil. The Marcoussis Agreement acknowledged that the Ivorian citizenship code that combined *jus sanguinis* and *jus soli* with a broad provision for naturalization was a good legal framework but called on executive officials to hamper administrative harassment caused by police forces against foreigners.[101]

The Ivorian rebels forces were renamed *Forces Nouvelles* (New Forces). That name was given to the rebellion by the very man who was mediating on behalf of France, Pierre Mazeaud. He refused to see them as rebels and thought of them as the representatives of a new movement or force that would bring a new order to Ivory Coast.[102] The Marcoussis Agreement mentioned also the issue of the alleged death squads supposedly committing extrajudicial killings on behalf of Gbagbo's regime in the southern part of the country. But it did not denounce the crimes committed by the rebels groups, namely the killing of the gendarmes, a corps in the Ivorian security forces.

The Conference of Heads of State, which took place in the Kleber Conference Center in Paris, suggested the creation of an Abidjan-based monitoring committee to foster the implementation of the Marcoussis Agreement. It was to be made up of a number of stakeholders representing the United Nations, the International Francophone Organization, the European Union, the Commission of the African Union, the Executive Secretariat of ECOWAS, the IMF and the World Bank, the G8 countries, and France. In Ivory Coast, street protests by the former president's loyal supporters denounced the Marcoussis Agreement as an expression of neo-colonialism. Most of the members of the monitoring committee paid allegiance to France over Ivory Coast and were definitively inclined to follow any road map set up by France. Eventually French forces were used to attempt another coup d'état in November 2004 during the military expedition to free the north called "Operation Dignity."[103]

Operation Dignity and neocolonial military intervention

Ivory Coast experienced two neocolonial wars, in the first week of November 2004 and in the first quarter of 2011. This segment focuses on the 2004 war, as the Western military intervention has already been discussed in the section "Electoral Stalemate." In the fall of 2004, Laurent Gbagbo decided to free the

---

[101] Magali Chelpi-den Hamer, *Militarized youths in Côte d'Ivoire*, 70-71.

[102] Maisonneuve, *Le Bourbier Ivoirien*, 90.

[103] Fanny Pigeaud, *France Côte d'Ivoire: Une histoire tronquée*, 66.

northern part of the country from the occupation of the rebels. The military expedition, "Operation Dignity," was launched in the first week of November 2004, led by Philippe Mangou, who would later be appointed head of the army.

The then president of France, Jacques Chirac, opposed the idea and vehemently asked President Gbagbo not to embark on such an expedition, which could lead to some unforeseen consequences. Gbagbo was adamant to conduct the military expedition. It was believed that he was advised to make it quick and to avoid collateral damage.

On November 4, 2004, two Sukhoi 25 planes piloted by Belarussian mercenaries launched airstrikes on the rebels' positions in the rebel stronghold, Bouaké. The third day of the aerial attack was sanctioned by an "accidental" bombing of French positions based in the Descartes high school in Bouaké: nine French soldiers and an American humanitarian worker were killed. At first Laurent Gbagbo did not believe that the Belarussian pilots had killed the French soldiers, because he had not ordered such an action, which would be considered folly. When he found out that the news of their death was confirmed, then he knew he was caught in a trap. France retaliated. For French officials and journalists, there was only one person responsible: the former president of Ivory Coast who authorized Operation Dignity.

The French president ordered the destruction of the Ivorian planes on the ground. French troops and more than thirty tanks moved toward the Ivorian presidential palace. This triggered massive street protests by Gbagbo's supporters, who saw this movement as a maneuver to overthrow their leader, thus denouncing French neo-colonialism. The standoff lasted three days, marked by looting and the departure from Ivory Coast of hundreds of French citizens. The French troops shot at unarmed Ivorians: sixty-nine people, including children, were killed, and more than one thousand people were wounded. There is a need to shed new light on the events of November 2004. This undertaking boils down to the following question: Who ordered the bombing of the French positions? The key to this enigma is revealed in what happened to the Belarussians.

After landing the two Sukhoi 25 planes in Yamoussoukro—which the French later destroyed on the ground—the pilots were arrested. After four days in French custody, they were handed over to French special police officers. Later they were found in Togo, where they were arrested and released again under the order of French authorities. Exfiltrated from Togo by the French special police officers, they vanished. They could not be interrogated, and the investigation was stalled. France evoked a top-secret matter to oppose the Belarusian mercenaries being interrogated. French military officials such as General Poncet, the former head of Licorne, the French peace-keeping forces in Ivory Coast, later said that Laurent Gbagbo was not the one who ordered the bombing of the Descartes high school and of the French positions.[104] France rallied the UN Security Council to vote the resolution 1572 in order to put an arm embargo on Ivory Coast on November 14, 2004.[105]

On May 22, 2019, the French Court of Justice of the Republic of France, the French judicial institution that has jurisdiction to judge crimes or offenses committed by members of the government in the exercise of their functions, concluded that three former ministers under president Jacques Chirac, Michèle Alliot-Marie (who was minister of defense at that time), and Dominique de Villepin and Michel Barnier, respective Ministers of Foreign Affairs, should not be prosecuted and therefore escaped an investigation into their role in the bombing of the French military camp in Bouaké in 2004. This decision angered Jean Balan, legal representative of the Bouaké victims' families, who announced that the families would continue the fight to clarify the circumstances of the tragedy:

> It is a decision contrary to justice which arouses my deep anger because it goes against the record of investigation which lasted 15 years and it is contrary to the conclusions of the judges of instruction. We are prevented by an *oukase* from discovering the truth...We want to know where the order to bomb came from and why this order to bomb the French camp. It is known from the record that it does not come from Gbagbo.[106]

France's 2004 disproportionate retaliation led to the involvement of South Africa in the Ivorian crisis as a mediator for a peaceful settlement of the conflict. This involvement constituted an important step in the revival of the Pan-African movement in connection with the Ivorian crisis. The 2011 French military intervention was seen as the continuation of the military confrontation between France and the Laurent Gbagbo regime. After the capture of the Ivorian president, France used its power to get him tried before the International Criminal Court.

The involvement of France in the ICC prosecution of Laurent Gbagbo

After legitimizing the rebellion, which it supported strategically and militarily, after waging a war against Laurent Gbagbo, France assisted the ICC Office of the Prosecutor in building a case against him. The French authorities led by

---

[104] Onana, *Côte d'Ivoire: Le Coup d'État*, 207–232.

[105] Fanny Pigeaud, *France Côte d'Ivoire: Une histoire tronquée*, 69.

[106] "Bombardement de Bouaké: les proches des victimes en colère face à l'abandon des poursuites," *France 24*, May 29, 2019, https://www.france24.com/fr/20190529-bombar dement-bouake-2004-colere-victimes-abandon-poursuites-jean-balan.

Nicolas Sarkozy himself repeatedly threatened the former Ivorian leader with prosecution by the ICC. This will be elaborated in Chapter 2. The electoral stalemate had become a favorable historical moment for the momentous momentum of the Pan-African nature of the Ivory Coast crisis.

The Pan-African dimension of the Ivory Coast crisis

In this section, I give a brief overview of the Pan-African movement, and I demonstrate how the Ivorian crisis contributed to the revival of Pan-Africanism and how the Pan-African community was divided in two groups around conflicting views about Laurent Gbagbo's Pan-Africanist credentials.

The Ivory Coast crisis and the revival of Pan-Africanism

This section of the book begins with a brief overview of the history of Pan-Africanism, after which I intend to discuss the Pan-African dimension of the Ivorian crisis. Pan-Africanism is a movement of resistance, solidarity, unity, and empowerment of Africans and peoples of African descent united in a common destiny. It stresses the commonality of experience of people of African heritage, regardless of their geographic location, in the face of racism, slavery, colonialism, apartheid, neo-colonialism, and globalization. Pan-Africanism, a social, cultural, spiritual, political, and economic movement of renaissance of Africans and peoples of African descent remains a clarion call of Black nationalists who seek to reconnect themselves with their fatherland. As an ideology, a theory, and praxis, which encompasses several dimensions and disciplines, it is advocated and espoused by policy makers, political leaders, activists, and academicians.

The word "Pan-Africanism" was first used in 1900 by Henry Sylvester Williams, who organized the first Pan-African Conference that year. Later, the movement became instrumental in helping defeat colonialism in Africa. The two world wars which took place in 1914-1918 and 1939-1945 respectively accelerated the end of colonialism in Asia, in the Middle East, in Latin America and in Africa. They also contributed to consolidating Pan-Africanism. Africa under colonization was involved in both wars and its soil served as a battlefield. Two ideologies provoked these two wars. The rise of nationalism, which also inspired the Pan-African movement, was to lead to the First World War while fascism, born after the economic crisis of 1929, led to the Second World War.

Two figures involved in the fight for racial justice in the United States, and who have greatly contributed to the progress of the Pan-African cause, have stood out, at times, in conflict with each other: W.E.B du Bois and Marcus Garvey. Dubois was the one who articulated and theorized the ideology of Pan-Africanism. He was the organizer of five Pan-African Congresses in 1919, 1921,

1923, 1927, and 1945. He transcended the notion of Pan-negroism that he had coined in 1898 to become an advocate of Pan-Africanism that could embrace other races even though the focus was on blacks.

Marcus Garvey, founder of the Universal Negro Improvement Association (UNIA) movement left his homeland, Jamaica, to migrate to the USA. He was against miscegenation and wanted the separation of races. He was also the champion of the Back to Africa Movement in the twentieth century. He had been able to acquire a boat, the Black Star Line. The hagiographers of the Pan-African movement recognize him for having popularized it among the masses. His conventions which he organized in the 1920s in Harlem, the capital of the literary movement "The Harlem Renaissance" sometimes accompanied by musical concerts, mobilized tens of thousands of blacks.

Kwame Nkrumah, influenced by the ideas of Marcus Garvey and co-organizer of the Manchester Congress of 1945 under the leadership of W.E.B. Dubois, was the one who helped establish the Pan-African movement on the African continent and who allowed a liberated and now independent state (Ghana) to be its vector thus taking the Pan-African movement to the level of a state.

The Manchester Congress, organized in 1945, focused on the decolonization of Africa. It was a reaction of Pan-Africanists of the world to the invasion of Ethiopia, the unconquered, by fascist Italy led by Mussolini in 1935. It was presided by W. E. B. Du Bois, and its chief architect was George Padmore, aided by Kwame Nkrumah. The latter is credited with having brought the movement to Africa when he became the "Leader of Government Business" of the Gold Coast in 1951. The Pan-African movement was ignited when Ghana became independent. In 1957 it was the first to be independent in Black Africa and was therefore rightfully viewed as the beacon of hope, freedom, and unity of African nationalists[107] and of people of African descent—Black Americans who were fighting against the Jim Crow laws.

Kwame Nkrumah, once the leader of Ghana, supported liberation movements on the African continent. Ghana became the hub of Pan-Africanism, the space for reflection, and the starting point for Africa's liberation actions. It was in that spirit that he organized the 1958 conferences and the series of the All-African People's Conferences. The Conference of Independent African States was organized from April 15–22, 1958 in Accra and brought together representatives of the eight African independent countries—Ethiopia, Tunisia, Sudan, Egypt,

---

[107] Vincent Bakpetu Thompson, *Africa and Unity: The Evolution of Pan-Africanism* (New York: Humanities Press, 1969), 124.

Morocco, Libya, Liberia, and Ghana. The goal was to coordinate efforts and strategies for the decolonization of the continent of Africa.[108]

Months later, Accra hosted again another Pan-African gathering but of the representatives of political parties, unions, youth, women, and journalists with the same purpose: the independence and the unity of Africa. The chief architect of the All-African People Conference of December 1958 was George Padmore, then advisor to Kwame Nkrumah. For nearly a week, from December 8–13, 1958, nearly 300 delegates representing more than 30 countries debated the strategy of struggle for independence and the modes of attaining freedom. Most of the delegates such as Patrice Lumumba of Congo, Julius Nyerere (Tanganyka), Frantz Fanon (on behalf of the Algerian National Liberation Front), Tom Mboya (Kenya) met for the first time and shared their respective experiences of the struggle. They came out of this conference more motivated and committed to the independence of Africa.[109] Two years later, 17 African countries became independent. Even countries like Ivory Coast, who wanted to stay in the Franco-African community, had to accept independence.

After the independence of several African countries in 1960, the continent became more divided along ideological and methodological lines in the context of the cold War. Two major groups emerged: The Casablanca Group, or the Revolutionary Group, and that of the moderates known as the Monrovia Group. The Organization of African Unity, which came into being on May 25, 1963, was a compromise between these two groups. It was above all the triumph of the position of the members of the Monrovia Group, who were advocates of capitalism and who preferred a gradualist approach to the unification of Africa. The Casablanca Group was dominated by leaders, advocates of socialism, who were in favor of immediate unification of Africa.[110]

With the creation of the Organization of African Unity (OAU), Pan-Africanism reached the heights of the continent. The OAU vowed to fight for the total independence of Africa and for the economic integration of Africa. Several other African territories were still under colonial rule (the Portuguese colonies, southern African territories, and South Africa under apartheid). The Organization of African Unity (OAU) renamed the African Union (AU) in 2001 promoted regional economic integration and oversaw the creation of regional economic communities and conceived continental plans such as the Lagos

---

[108] Zizwe Poe, *Kwame Nkrumah's Contribution to Pan-Africanism: An Afrocentric Analysis* (Los Angeles: University Press of Sankore, 2010), 109.

[109] Thompson, *Africa and Unity*, 129–133.

[110] P. Olisanwuche Esedebe, *Pan-Africanism: The Idea and Movement 1776–1963*, 184-185.

Plan of Action, the Treaty of Abuja, the New Economic Partnership for Africa's Development (NEPAD), and the African Continental Free Trade Area (AfCFTA).

That continental body, the AU, which represents the interests of Africa in various fields of international relations, international development, and in criminal matters, had to clash with the ICC about the way the court handled its rationale of prosecution. After the creation of the Organization of African Unity, Pan-Africanism entered a deep period of apathy following the overthrow and physical elimination of nationalists and Pan-Africanists, only to resurrect in the late 1980s thanks to the rise to power of Thomas Sankara (Burkina Faso) and to the Free Nelson Mandela Movement. Kadafhi, former leader of Libya, became the greatest heir of Pan-Africanism in his latter years. Pan-African ideals have also been a central part of the Ivorian political crisis, even if some dispute Laurent Gbagbo's Pan-Africanist credentials. As a nationalist who defended values—such as freedom, justice, and the dignity of Africa—Laurent Gbagbo's resistance had Pan-Africanist implications. He survived a French-led coup during Operation Dignity. This course of events, his fate, and his trial have captured the imagination of a number of Pan-Africanists. The Ivorian crisis therefore contributed to the revival of Pan-Africanism.

The Pan-African dimension of the Ivorian crisis can be divided into three parts: the involvement of South Africa as mediator in 2004, Pan-African sentiment since 2010–2011, and the Pan-African resistance against the ICC during the former president's trial. In this section I will address only the first two parts. I discuss the third one in the section related to the trial per se.

The involvement of South Africa in the Ivorian crisis provided a political solution to the issue of Ouattara's nationality and also revived the debate about the reawakening of Pan-Africanism. Former South African president Thabo Mbeki was the architect of the Pretoria Agreements, the major provisions of which were the modification of the Independent Electoral Commission, which opened its membership to the rebels' representatives, and the invitation of the United Nations so it could be involved in the election process. An amendment to Article 35 of the 2000 Constitution was also requested. Thabo Mbeki asked Laurent Gbagbo to use the powers conferred on him as the president in Article 48 of the 2000 Ivory Coast Constitution to allow Alassane Ouattara to run for president in the name of peace.[111]

In addition, the Pretoria Agreement was a step forward in the resolution of the Ivorian crisis and a landmark and a hallmark of African solidarity, in the spirit of Pan-Africanism. The ANC leaders, indebted to the African solidarity which was instrumental in the dismantling of apartheid, articulated a clear

---

[111] Christian Bouquet, *Géopolitique de la Côte d'Ivoire*, 125. See also CIV. Const of 2000.

vision for Africa and a clear idea of the historical mission of South Africa toward Africa. This vision was coined by Thabo Mbeki as "The African Renaissance."[112] It is another variant of Pan-Africanism, which aims at promoting democracy and good governance in Africa, helping build a prosperous integrated Africa, and requesting that Africa own the conflict-resolution processes. The involvement of South Africa in the Ivorian crisis prompted tension between that country and France, the former colonial master of Ivory Coast. The testimony of Thabo Mbeki about the tragic events of November 2004 stresses the opposition of France to the African Union mandate given to South Africa to play the role of mediator in the Ivorian crisis. Thabo Mbeki declared:

> The French have taken over Abidjan. They were in control of the airport. They were in control of the road from the airport to the city. They were in control of the bridges. They were in control of the Hotel Ivoire. And they were deciding of what should happen. They did not want us to come. And we said that we have an appointment with the president of the Republic and that we have an obligation to honor that appointment. And, because we have been asked by the continent to mediate. We told the French we were coming in order to meet President Gbagbo on the day that was agreed. And we would land and Abidjan would have to be open, and we would drive into the city. And they said they have agreed that we should come. And we went. There was a threat of confrontation between the French soldiers and people who were demonstrating outside the hotel to prevent those troops from attacking the president. We discussed with President Gbagbo that many people could be killed. And President Gbagbo said they were ready to send some people to persuade the people who were demonstrating to leave. And in return French troops should leave the Hotel Ivoire and occupy another hotel further away from the presidential palace. That requires I should speak to then president of France, President Jacques Chirac to make that suggestion. I did speak to him. And we agreed to that while I was in Abidjan. Of course, I went back to President Gbagbo and I said that I spoke to President Chirac and that we agreed that they [French soldiers] would evacuate the hotel. Before that the Ivorian demonstrators should proceed to leave. That was agreed. At that point we left. This was before we left Abidjan to South Africa. So, then, we left with that agreement to go the airport, only to get the report that in fact the French had opened fire on the Ivorian demonstrators there and killed people.[113]

Since then, the conflict in Ivory Coast captured the imagination of the global African community and instigated and contributed to the renewal of the Pan-

---

[112] Thabo Mbeki, "Prologue," in *African Renaissance*, ed. Malegapuru William Makgoba (Cape Town: Tafelberg Publishers, 1999).

[113] RTI, YouTube video, accessed June 10, 2013, https://www.youtube.com/watch?v=d3zO4euzF7Q#t=98.

African consciousness, which was consolidated by other historical movements and events. One can mention the Rhodes Must Fall Movement and the Fees Must Fall Movement in South Africa, the wave of economic justice led by the Economic Freedom Fighters in Southern Africa, the people's movements that ousted Abdoulaye Wade in Senegal (2012) and Blaise Compaoré in Burkina Faso (2014), the growing campaign for reparations, the Black Lives Matter Movement and the Anti–CFA Franc Campaign.

In 2016, the president of Senegal, Macky Sall, made a statement about the positive aspects of the CFA Franc. His assertion sparked the reaction of several activists who called for a movement of indignation against the CFA Franc. This took the form of simultaneous conferences in Africa and in Europe.[114] The movement rightfully called "Anti-CFA Campaign" could be traced back to a dimension of the Ivorian crisis. Despite such evidence, several scholars, activists, and Pan-Africanists attempted to deny the Pan-Africanist dimension of the Ivorian crisis.

Dissenting African voices: prodemocracy versus anti-neocolonialists

It is important to underline that the members of the Pan-African community have had dissenting positions, which can be divided into two schools of thought: the anti-neocolonialists and the prodemocracy schools of thought.

The anti-neocolonialists

This school of thought, anti-neocolonialism, opposed Western military intervention in Ivory Coast and saw it as a neocolonial war as it was perpetrated by Ivory Coast's former colonial master, France, alongside a militarized UN. The advocates of that school of thought refuted the grounds on which the Westerners decided to go in and use force against the army of Ivory Coast. In their view, the sovereignty and the integrity of Ivory Coast should not have been violated on fallacious grounds to protect civilians. Here, suffice it to mention Jerry John Rawlings, former president of Ghana, and the former president of South Africa, Thabo Mbeki. The latter published an article, "What the World Got Wrong in Côte d'Ivoire" in *Foreign Policy*. In that article, he vehemently denounced the West, the UN, and the African Union for failing Ivory Coast. He also called for the reform of the UN system which is all but democratic and perpetuates the interests of the most powerful. The following excerpt summarizes the spirit and the letter of his opinion piece:

---

[114] Fanny Pigeaud and Ndongo Samba Sylla, *L'arme Invisible de la Françafrique: Une histoire du Franc CFA* (Paris: La Découverte, 2018), 188-191.

It will now be difficult for the United Nations to convince Africa and the rest of the developing world that it is not a mere instrument in the hands of the world's major powers...We can only hope that Laurent and Simone Gbagbo and the Ivorian people do not continue to suffer as abused and humiliated victims of a global system which, in its interests, while shouting loudly about universal human rights, only seeks to perpetuate the domination of the many by the few who dispose of preponderant political, economic, military and media power.[115]

Other Pan-Africanists disagreed with that perspective and claimed that democracy was endangered by the actions of former Ivorian president Laurent Gbagbo who was using the Pan-African rethoric to garner support and cling to power. They represent the prodemocracy school.

The prodemocracy school

The prodemocracy school believes that the 2010 presidential election in Ivory Coast fulfilled its goal, which was to put an end to the crisis in that country. Its proponents affirmed that the process was well conducted and that the results announced by the electoral commission certified by the UN were true. They share the idea that the will of the Ivorian people was respected and that Alassane Ouattara was the legitimate winner of the election. They invite Africans to elevate the standards in relation to good governance, democratic practices, and good leadership.

An election organized in a divided country with two opposing military forces, particularly with the rebels controlling their half of the territory where they imposed their rule, could not be considered a credible election. The advocates of the prodemocracy school could not take into account in their analysis of the crisis that it exists a deterministic relationship between the political context and the electoral contest. As they defended their position, they invited their opponents to go beyond anti-imperialist views and stick to the outcome of the election. In his charge against Gbagbo, one of proponents of the prodemocracy school, Nii Akuetteh accused as follows:

They should have appreciated that inclusive democracy lies at the heart of the Pan-Africanism of Dubois, Nkrumah, Nyerere and Lumumba. And that appreciation should have admonished these friends thus: You cannot embrace *Ivoirité*, you cannot viciously discriminate against fellow Ivorians simply for being Muslim, and you cannot kill and expel African immigrants; you cannot do all that and still call yourself a Pan-Africanist. Personally, forgiving these friends for the sacrilege of calling

---

115 Thabo Mbeki, "What the World Got Wrong in Côte d'Ivoire," *Foreign Policy*, April 29, 2011, http://foreignpolicy.com/2011/04/29/what-the-world-got-wrong-in-cote-divoire.

President Gbagbo 'today's Lumumba' is going to be very hard for me—though not impossible.[116]

Nii Akuetteh was reacting to a call for a conference my friends and I organized in Washington, DC, on February 12, 2011, which analyzed Gbagbo's fate in light of the humiliating spectacle of Lumumba's arrest on April 11, 2011, which was reminiscent of the way Lumumba was arrested fifty years ago. As far as I am concerned, I had not yet sought to present Gbagbo as a staunch Pan-Africanist. Even though Laurent Gbagbo's Pan-Africanist credentials can be disputed, not for the false arguments mentioned above by Nii Akuetteh, his nationalist resistance against neo-colonialism contributed to reinvigorate African nationalism and Pan-Africanism.

The reality is that there are striking similarities and patterns that exist between both leaders, Lumumba and Gbagbo, and between the Zaire (now Democratic Republic of Congo) crisis of 1961 and the Ivorian crisis of 2011. The guest speaker invited at the February conference to give a lecture on the comparative study of Congo and Ivory Coast respectively under Lumumba and Gbagbo regarding the role of the United Nations transformed the lecture into a book under the title *From Lumumba to Gbagbo: Africa in the Eddy of the Euro-American Exceptionalism.* He sums up the crux of his discussion in the following words: "In fact though 50 years apart, Ivorian president Gbagbo and Congolese Prime Minister Lumumba fates in the hands of the Euro-American imperial force are so strikingly similar that they deserve mention as case studies of the West continuous endeavors to undermine total independence in Africa."[117]

The first similarity is the division of their respective countries due to ethnic-driven secession. The second is the detrimental role played by European powers and the UN backing the rebels. The third is the endorsement by the UN of their removal from power and their arrests. The fourth is the public ignominious humiliation after their respective captures. And they have been displayed as trophies of neocolonial wars. The rest is a difference of degree, not a difference of nature and essence, as the fates of Gbagbo and Lumumba have strong commonalities.

Another proponent of the prodemocracy school of thought was Horace Campbell, political scientist and renowned Pan-African scholar and activist for

---

[116] Nii Akuetteh, "Democracy and Africa's Top Priorities. Minimizing Conflict. Alleviating Poverty. Defending Sovereignty and Resources: What Has Democracy Got to Do with Any of These?" 3rd Annual Fr. Bill Dyer Lecture, Africa Faith & Justice Network, Washington, DC, November 4, 2011, 10.

[117] Frindéthié, *From Lumumba to Gbagbo,* 198.

whom it was about democracy and nothing else. The premises of his stance are summed up in the following lines from an article entitled "Gbagbo and the Ivorian Test: Moving beyond Anti-imperialist Rhetoric," published in January 2011, that sound like a court sentence or a prosecutorial charge:

> Our task is to lay out some of the democratic questions in the current struggles in the Côte d'Ivoire. The post-election stalemate in Côte d'Ivoire once again sharpens the demand by African peoples for democratic African societies devoid of leaders who have turned tools of anti-imperialism into tools for the oppression of their own people. From Zimbabwe to Uganda, Kenya, Ethiopia, and Ivory Coast, the peoples of Africa have grown impatient with leaders who were anti-imperialist heroes but once they entrenched themselves in power, they did not only become allies of the imperialists they had fought against, they become obstacles to the aspirations of their peoples, who yearn for freedom of movement, freedom of religious expression, gender equality, citizenship, peace, and human dignity. We advocate for a paradigm in which the aspirations and will of the people supersede the selfish interests of leaders and their imperialist accomplices; a paradigm in which neither the likes of Laurent Gbagbo nor Alassane Ouattara would have the free rein to betray the mandate and aspirations of the people. This paradigm cannot be guaranteed by the manipulation of anti-imperialist sentiment against the democratic aspirations of citizens as we are currently witnessing in Côte d'Ivoire.[118]

In his sententious article Horace Campbell sided with the narrative put forth by the international community, which was not driven neither by a humanitarian cause nor by the pursuit of a democratic agenda in Ivory Coast but by a neocolonial project. He attributed the root cause of the crisis solely to *Ivoirité* and did not mention the Charter of the North. He agreed with the narrative that Alassane Ouattara won and refused to have a second look at the controversy about the turnout during the runoff of the presidential election. Campbell would just say that Alassane Ouattara is not an angel, nor a messiah, but he does not present any information that shows that Ouattara Alassane has his share of responsibility in the crisis that could not be reduced to just an electoral dispute. By the time Horace Campbell published his article in January 2011, Alassane Ouattara's forces, including the Invisible Commando, were already in action and were already engaged with the troops loyal to Gbagbo in an armed conflict before the full-blown war. He who saw Kadhafi as an obstacle to African unity when the former Libyan leader suggested the breakup of the Nigerian

---

[118] Horace Campbell, "Côte d'Ivoire: Gbagbo and the Ivorian Test - Moving beyond Anti-Imperialist Rhetoric," Rasta Livewire, January 17, 2011, https://www.africaresource.com/rasta/articles/cote-divoire-gbagbo-and-the-ivorian-test-moving-beyond-anti-imperialist-rhetoric.

federation between Christians and Muslims and yet opposed the North Atlantic Treaty Organization (NATO) intervention in Libya[119] could not be consequential regarding the Ivorian crisis.

Both Nii and Campbell—as they sought to demonize Gbagbo, the victimizer and the source of all evils—presented Ouattara as an innocent and the victim, excused imperialism, espoused its rhetoric, sided with the Western discourse, failed to discuss or even mention the disastrous role played by France, and the selective prosecutorial strategy of the ICC in the Ivory Coast crisis. The ICC's choice to incriminate the former president, to investigate his alleged crimes exclusively and exculpate those of Alassane Ouattara and those of France caused an uproar among Africans and many justice and freedom stakeholders in the world. Hence rose a debate about the controversial role of the ICC in the Ivory Coast crisis, which needs to be conducted within a global conversation on the journey to international justice.

---

[119] Horace Campbell, *Global NATO and the Catastrophic Failure in Libya* (New York: Monthly Review Press, 2013), 10.

Chapter 2

International justice and the
International Criminal Court

This chapter discusses a confluence of streams of aspirations that resulted in the formation of the International Criminal Court: the attainment of freedoms, civil rights, and human rights and the quest for the creation of an international justice court to prevent human rights abuses. The idea of human rights precedes that of the creation of an international court.

Human rights: the journey of a concept

During the Renaissance period, when slavery was in force, some Europeans have had divergent views about that system. One of such was the controversial Spaniard Fray Bartolomé de las Casas. He petitioned in 1515 the Spanish Crown to stop the violation of the Indians' rights and pleaded that the latter be treated as people endowed with soul who therefore deserved better treatment. After being a slaver, he experienced an epiphany, underwent a double conversion: that of a new man eager to defend the rights of the Indians and that of a man who became a priest and who preached the gospel to the Indians. He once advocated the enslavement of non-catholics such as Africans and Muslims and later drifted away from that stance.[1] He has been hailed as one of the pioneers of international law. However, the conversation about the codification of human rights in documents takes us back to England.

Md Kamruzzaman and Sashi Katto Das seminal article "The Evaluation of Human Rights: An Overview in Historical Perspective" provides elements of information for the historical panorama about human rights. Thomas Paine is credited to have been the first to use the concept of "human rights" when he was translating the French Declaration of the Right of the Man and of the Citizen into English. Human rights are inherent, inalienable, and universal. Before their presentation of the concept of human rights in historical perspective, they have shown a spectrum of these human rights. The basic human rights are the rights to freedom, health, wealth, and to the pursuit of happiness. All human beings are entitled to these rights irrespective of their

---

[1] Bartolomé de Las Casas, *A Brief Account of the Destruction of the Indies* (London: R. Hewson, 1689).

origin, religion, race, class, gender, and sexual orientation. These rights have permeated various sectors of the society from the political and economic spheres to the cultural space. Hence the multiple types of rights: civil rights, political rights, economic rights, social rights, and cultural rights. These are enshrined in several universal declarations of human rights and countries' constitutions. The definition of human rights has not always been expansive and comprehensive, as historical events, political regimes, and systems of exploitation have denied these rights to various people and regions in different parts of the world.[2]

In Europe, during the middle ages, the English Magna Carta of 1215 was credited to be one of the first to contain references to the notion of individual and human liberties. It was an agreement between King John of England and a group of barons who revolted against him because he had increased the taxes they were paying. That agreement, whose original version lasted for ten weeks, covered issues of taxation, feudal rights, and justice. It established a set of legal boundaries and limitations on the power of the king. Two articles highlight the essence of the Charter:

> Article 39: No free man shall be seized, imprisoned, dispossessed, outlawed, exiled or ruined in any way, nor in any way proceeded against, except by the lawful judgement of his peers and the law of the land.

> Article 40: To no one will we sell, to no one will we refuse of delay right or justice.[3]

David Carpenter in "Magna Carta 1215: its social and historical context" highlights the journey of the gradual significance of he Magna Carta in British history and in world history. The Magna Carta was believed to be a document about the rights of the aristocrats. The notion of free men it referred to was about the nobles or the barons. It excluded the majority of the population composed of peasants and did not guarantee women's rights. King John called on the Pope to invalidate it. The refusal of the king to abide by the spirit and the letter of the Magna Carta led to another rebellion by the nobles who eventually ousted him from power, after they sided with the French who eventually won the war against England in 1216.

---

[2] Md Kamruzzaman and Sashi Katto Das, "The Evaluation of Human Rights: An Overview in Historical Perspective," *American Journal of Service Science and Management* 3, no. 2 (2016): 5.

[3] Md Kamruzzaman and Sashi Katto Das, "The Evaluation of Human Rights: An Overview in Historical Perspective," *American Journal of Service Science and Management* 3, no. 2 (2016): 8.

Several recurrent references were made to the Magna Carta throughout centuries, through which the document has gained gradual ascendency and credence in society and in the collective memory of the British. The Magna Carta, revised subsequently throughout years soon acquired a reputation whose repercussions transcended its original vocation, which was sectarian, limited, and exclusionist. The British parliament started requiring that the members of the political elite take their oath on it in 1341. The idea of the inviolability of human rights took ground during the renaissance period sparked by the humanism movement.

As far as the journey of the Magna Carta was concerned, it gradually became the pillar, the building block, and the cornerstone of Great Britain's fundamental laws and rights, namely the Petition of Rights, adopted in 1628 in the middle of the Thirty Years' War (1618-1648), the British Bill of Rights (1689) signed into law right after the Glorious Revolution (1688); and it later inspired the founding documents of the creation of the United States of America (the Declaration of Independence, the American Constitution, and the American Bill of Rights).[4]

In the seventeenth century, during the age of Reformation, the Petition of Rights, adopted on June 7, 1628, in the middle of the Thirty Years' War (1618-1648), was a milestone in the journey of the notion of human rights. It sought to protect the rights of individuals and those of the members of the parliament from the intrusion of the monarchical power in England. Its Article 1 states: "No person should be required to pay a tax or benevolence without parliamentary approval."[5] At the end of the Thirty-Year Wars, the Treaty of Westphalia signed in 1648 became another milestone in the quest for individual freedoms. That treaty established the sovereign territorial integrity of several European countries and religious tolerance.

The Glorious Revolution of 1688 resulted in a constitutional monarchy in Britain, and it was a major transitional shift from monarchy to democracy. The Bill of Rights as a by-product of the Glorious Revolution enacted a set of laws that limited the power of the king and established the transfer of the sovereign rights from the king to the people. Members of the parliament's rights were consolidated. They could enjoy freedom of speech and the interference of the king in the affairs of the parliament was reduced.[6]

---

[4] David Carpenter, "Magna Carta 1215: its social and historical context" in *Magna Carta: History, context and influence*, ed. Lawrence Goldman (London: Institute of Research Institute, 2018), 20-22.

[5] Kamruzzaman and Das, "The Evaluation of Human Rights," 9.

[6] Kamruzzaman and Das, "The Evaluation of Human Rights," 9.

The Industrial Revolution, which started in the second half of the eighteenth century in England and which spread throughout Western Europe and the United States of America, was conducive to other expressions of freedom: nationalism, liberalism, and feminism, just to mention a few. The last defines the rights of women and the equality of the sexes. The struggle for the emancipation of women includes their right to vote, to be elected, and to own property.

The Universal Declaration of Human Rights (UDHR) of 1948, adopted in the aftermath of World War II by the newly created United Nations, became the moral compass of mankind. It echoes the Magna Carta, stands upon such documents as the American Declaration of Independence (1776) of the American Revolution and the Declaration of the Rights of Man and of the Citizen (August 26, 1789) of the French Revolution. The notion of human rights was enshrined in these documents.

The American Revolution, based on the premise and the promise of democracy, was also a guarantor of aristocrats' rights as slavery was not abolished, Native Americans' rights were denied, and women's rights were ignored. However, the following statement of the US Declaration of Independence reverberated across the globe: "We hold these truths to be self-evident, that all men are created equal, that they are endowed by their creator with certain unalienable rights that among these are life, liberty, and the pursuit of happiness." This was reiterated by the first clause of the French Declaration of the Rights of Man and of the Citizen: "Men are born and remain free and equal in rights." The two other important contributions of the French Revolution besides this Declaration were as follows: the proclamation of the abolition of privileges (August 4, 1789) and the decree of the Constitutive Assembly of May 15, 1791, which established equal rights between Whites and Blacks.

The French Revolution, inspired by the American Revolution, created the space for the slave revolt in Saint-Domingue (later renamed Haiti) and led to the Haitian Revolution (1791–1804), which resulted in the creation of a state controlled by former slaves. The Haitian Revolution represented a powerful symbol for black slaves in the Americas and in the United States. It was for them a symbol of freedom, a reminder of the possibility of fulfilling the promises never made by the American Revolution, a new dawn of hope for blacks still slaves in the United States of America.[7] The process of black liberty in the Americas was marked by the flight of slaves, the underground railroads, the

---

[7] C.L.R. James, *The Black Jacobins: Toussaint L'Ouverture and the San Domingo Revolution,* 2nd ed. (New York: Vintage Books, 1989).

continuous slave revolts, and a massive campaign against slavery, through the abolitionist movement, which mobilized several generations of freedom lovers and justice seekers.

The issue of slavery, sidelined during the American Revolution, later haunted the American nation. A civil war (1861–1865) was fought between the industrial North and the agrarian South, which clung to slavery. Three legal decisions were taken around the American Civil War and symbolized hope for equality for blacks in America. They were the Thirteenth, Fourteenth, and Fifteenth Amendments, passed in 1865, 1868, and 1870 respectively. Their goals were to end slavery, to grant citizenship to blacks, and to grant blacks the right to vote.[8] But the Reconstruction era (1865–1877) ended with the compromise of 1877 which followed the controversial American election of 1876 which opposed Rutherford Hayes (Republican Party) and Samuel Tilden (Democratic party). The federal government removed troops from the South, leaving Blacks at the mercy of the South which was engaged in the reclaiming of its redemption based on the continuation of white supremacy. Racist groups put into place a system of erosion of Blacks' rights through the black codes, the Jim Crow laws, lynchings, killings, and the destruction of the properties, farms, and businesses of blacks. It took a second revolution, that of the golden age of the Civil Rights Movement (1953–1968) to make effective the rights of the Blacks in America. The ultimate victory of that long journey for human rights was the Voting Rights Act of 1965 which gave the power to the federal government to suppress the poll tax, the literacy tests, to enforce black voter registration and the black vote under the supervision of voter examiners appointed by the Attorney General.[9]

The Voting Rights Acts was signed on August 6, 1965 by the then American president Lyndon B. Johnson. The March on Selma that took place on March 7, 1965 ended with the beating of civil rights activists and the killing of one white civil right activist. That incident prompted the timely and appropriate reaction of President Lyndon B. Johnson. He delivered before the Congress on March 15, 1965 a historic speech "The American Promise". He urged the Congress to vote on a bill in order to end the Jim Crow electoral practices. For the American president Lyndon B. Johnson, it was a defining moment to uproot the remnants of segregation and to tackle the shackles of injustice and racism in the United States of America. He started his speech with the following words: "I speak

---

[8] Bruce J. Dierenfield, *The Civil Rights Movement* Revised edition (London and New York: Routledge, 2013), 9.

[9] Dewey W. Grantham, *The United States since 1945: The Ordeal of Power* (New York: McGraw-Hill Book Company, 1976), 216.

tonight for the dignity of man and the destiny of democracy."[10] He reminded the duly elected officials reunited in the Congress of their historical responsibility to live up to the promises of the American nation and American democracy. He recalled the right to basic human rights of Black Americans, repeating the famous creed of the American society enshrined in the American Declaration of independence "All men are created equal." He correlated the premises of the American Revolution, the promises of the Civil War, the goals of the Civil Rights Movement, and the rationale of the March in Selma. While he expressed his faith in the victory of the American people over racism by using what was the anthem of the Civil Rights Movement 'We Shall overcome" he praised the resilience and determination of Black Americans whose struggle contributed to perfecting the American union and the American democracy: "The real hero of this struggle is the American Negro. His actions and protests, his courage to risk safety and even to risk his life, have awakened the conscience of this Nation. His demonstrations have been designed to call attention to injustice, designed to provoke change, designed to stir reform."[11] He then dismissed the arguments of those who used state's rights or national rights to perpetuate segregation. He argued therefore that "There is no state's rights or national rights. There is only the struggle for human rights."[12] Steven L.B. Jensen called the political action of the American president "human rights diplomacy."[13] The words of the American president were widely circulated and had a profonde echo and impact beyond the American borders. A copy of the speech was sent to every African Ambassador to the United States of America on May 8, 1965.[14] That year, under the leadership of the United States, now emboldened after righting the wrongs of its society, the United Nations passed the International Convention on the Elimination of All Forms of Racial Discrimination on December 21, 1965. Almost three weeks before the adoption of that convention, the UN adopted the right to petition on December 2, 1965. Let it be recalled that the right to petition was blocked over and over by powers of the world which were the agents of colonialism and apartheid since the creation of the United Nations.

During the Industrial Revolution, the Communist Manifesto, published in 1848, became the foundational document for the protection of the rights of

---

[10] Steven L. B. Jensen, *The Making of International Human Rights: The 1960s, Decolonization and the Reconstruction of Global Values* (Cambridge: Cambridge University Press, 2016), 115.

[11] Jensen, *The Making of International Human Rights*, 115.

[12] Jensen, *The Making of International Human Rights*, 115.

[13] Jensen, *The Making of International Human Rights*, 115.

[14] Jensen, *The Making of International Human Rights*, 117.

workers and inspired revolutions such as the Bolshevik Revolution in Russia in 1917, the Chinese Revolution in 1949, the Cuban Revolution in 1959, and the creation of left-leaning political parties and unions in the world. The double quest for the acknowledgement of human rights and for the creation of an international criminal court expressed in the nineteenth century after the Franco-Prussian War in 1872 and at the 1899 Hague Convention was consolidated around the two World Wars in light of the massive human rights violations they caused. Two institutions were created after WWI (1914–1918) and WWII (1939–1945) respectively to promote peace, to prevent war, to protect human rights, and to hold human rights abusers accountable: The League of Nations and the United Nations, both preceded by two declarations whose central idea was the imperative of self-determination: Woodrow Wilson's 14 Points and the Atlantic Charter of 1941. The Atlantic Charter was a declaration issued by Franklin Delano Roosevelt, the US president, and Winston Churchill, the British Prime Minister. The latter had a restrictive understanding of the Atlantic Charter. He did not see its application to the colonies as his country was adamant to continue its colonial project. Even though the Atlantic Charter did not contain the words "human rights," it was seen as an important stepping stone and the backbone of the itemization of human rights.[15]

The weariness and the worriedness of wartime gradually abated with the end of WWII, which created a space for the establishment of several other institutions and projects for peace and prosperity, even though several regions of the world were still under colonial rule. The Marshall Plan helped rebuild Western Europe. The General Agreement on Trade and Tariffs (GATT), renamed the World Trade Organization (WTO) in 1995; the International Monetary Fund (IMF); and the World Bank were created. Of greater importance, the United Nations was created as the greatest instrument of peace. The naming « United Nations » was not fortuitous. During the course of WWII, the leaders of the allied forces have recurrently used the name « United Nations » when they referred to countries which were fighting against Nazi-Germany and its allies. When the idea to set up a commission to investigate and prosecute WWII atrocities, cruelties and crimes committed by the Germans, the name « United Nations » was applied to the commission eventually called the United Nations War Crimes Commission (UNWCC). That London-based institution operated from 1943-1948. The name « United Nations » would be given to the universal

---

[15] Steven L. B. Jensen, *The Making of International Human Rights: The 1960s, Decolonization and the Reconstruction of Global Values* (Cambridge: Cambridge University Press, 2016), 23.

organization or international body created on October 24, 1945, to promote peace and preserve war: the Organization of the United Nations.[16]

The forgotten history of the UNWCC received exhausted treatment by Dan Plesch, in *Human Rights after Hitler: The Lost History of Prosecuting the Axis War.* He vowed to contribute to the restoration of the historical memory of a part of the international prosecution and arbitration. He uncovered and highlighted the tremendous contribution of the UNWCC in the history of prosecution in his archival work. Contrary to the widespread idea accepted by leading scholars in the field of international justice which stipulates that rape was first recognized as a crime against humanity during the establishment of the International Criminal Tribunal of Yugoslavia (ICTY), Plesch revealed that the United Nations War Crimes Commission (UNWCC) was the first to include rape as a sex based and gender violence among the crimes during the prosecution of thousands of trials that that institution oversaw, supervised and supported from 1943-1948.[17]

He deconstructed the narrative about the Nuremberg and the Tokyo trials recorded in history as landmarks of international justice and which represent building blocks for subsequent trials. Plesch argued that even though the Nuremberg and the Tokyo trials were seen as the bedrocks of international prosecution, trials and tribunals, legal scholars should be mindful of the fact that the world's historical memory is far much bigger than the trials and the conviction of a small number of high officials who appeared in Nuremberg and Tokyo courts. That commission could gather 36,000 charges, organized 2,000 trials and convicted thousands of defendants. While Nuremberg and Tokyo only dealt with 50 cases.[18] Cold war politics and logic explained why countless accounts of war cruelties committed by the Nazis echoed by unsung heroes of justice sank into oblivion for decades. For President Truman, communist Soviet Union was the number one enemy, once Germany was defeated. Instructions were given for the archives of the UNWCC to be placed under seal. Thousands of Nazis who could probably be brought before justice were set free in order to help rebuild Germany. This approach to post-WWII politics obscured an important part of the international justice history. The UNWCC was a prelude to the Commission on Human Rights which drafted the Universal Declaration

---

[16] UNWCC, *History of the United Nations War Crimes Commission and the Development of the Laws of War* (London: Her Majesty's Stationery Office, 1948).

[17] Dan Plesch, *Human Rights after Hitler: The Lost History of Prosecuting the Axis War* (Washington: Georgetown University Press, 2017), 11.

[18] Plesch, *Human Rights after Hitler: The Lost History of Prosecuting the Axis War*, 5.

of Human Rights but it was also the anticipated scheme for the creation of the Organisation of the United Nations.

The Universal Declaration of Human Rights (UDHR) was adopted on December 10, 1948, after it was drafted by the United Nations Commission on Human Rights chaired by Eleanor Roosevelt, wife of Franklin Delano Roosevelt, the American president who led the United States of America during both the Great Depression and World War II. But the mind and the brain behind the UDHR was René Cassin. The document on human rights was initially called Draft International Declaration on Human Rights. It was renamed upon his suggestion Universal Declaration on Human Rights.[19] He was a Jewish-French jurist, a war veteran who suffered injuries during WWI and who championed for the end of conflicts during the interwar period. He had to exile to England after the capitulation of the government of Vichy led by Petain following the invasion of France by the German troops when WWII erupted. He joined the Free France movement established by General de Gaulle to fight for the liberation of France from the German occupation. René Cassin won the Nobel Peace Prize in 1968 for his work which led to the creation of the United Nations and for the adoption of the international human rights bill.[20]

The UDHR as a universal human rights document was a product of a collective effort of various nations of the world, unlike the previous documents, which were the aspirations of specific nations (the United States and France) and which were regional (Western Hemisphere and Western Europe). Eleanor Roosevelt summed up the spirit and letter of the UDHR in the following words:

> We stand today at the threshold of a great event both in the life of the United Nations and in the life of mankind. This Universal Declaration of Human Rights may well become the international Magna Carta of all men everywhere. We hope its proclamation by the General Assembly will be an event comparable to the proclamation of the Declaration of the Rights of Man by the French people in 1789, the adoption of the Bill of Rights by the people of the United States, and the adoption of comparable declarations at different times in other countries.[21]

However, the Commission of Human Rights established in 1947 did not give a positive answer to calls from colonies to investigate the human rights abuses perpetrated by European powers in these regions. Even though the United States was in the driving seat pushing for the prosecution of Nazis, it opposed

---

[19] Jensen, *The Making of International Human Rights*, 18.

[20] Plesch, *Human Rights after Hitler: The Lost History of Prosecuting the Axis War*, 55-56.

[21] Mary Ann Glendon, *A World Made New: Eleanor Roosevelt and the Universal Declaration of Human Rights* (New York: Random House, 2001), 166.

the idea of international courts with universal jurisdiction. Allowing such an understanding of international justice in the aftermath of WWII meant that that jurisdiction could delve in American domestic affairs marked by segregation laws and lynching. In other words, these international courts with the power to interfere in domestic affairs of countries could feel qualified to prosecute lynching which was in force in the United States of America. Dan Plesch denounced that contradiction in a self-explanatory and appealing title of a chapter in his book "Crimes against Humanity: The "Freedom to Lynch" and the Indictments of Hitler.[22]   Several stakeholders seized the opportunity at the United Nations to expose the duplicity of the Europeans engaged in the colonial project and who were advancing a limited and restrictive implementation of the notion of human rights. The Europeans surely did not want the UN to be a platform to discuss segregation in the United States, Apartheid in South Africa, or the massive human rights abuses in the British, French, Spanish, Belgian, American, Italian, and Portuguese colonies. The struggle for the decolonization process in Asia, Africa, the Middle East, and Latin America gave a thorough and larger meaning to the notion of human rights and liberties, as former colonial subjects, in their quest to achieve the right to self-determination also could claim the rights to be called humans.

The existence of a global platform (the United Nations) created avenues for the acceleration of decolonization and the recognition of human rights for previously colonized people, who consequently contributed to the consolidation of the universalization of the concept of human rights.[23] Several constitutions of newly independent countries drew from the UDHR, while the UN was turned into a space where systems like colonialism and apartheid were scorned and denounced. The debate about the link between decolonization and human rights divided scholars. For some, the question of human rights was distinct from the issue of decolonization. Christian Reus-Smit argued in his book *Individual Rights and the Making of the International System* that: "if decolonization was about rights, it was about collective rights not individual rights and that the international codification of human rights was a Western project."[24] In the same vein, Samuel Moyn published a book, *The Last Utopia: Human Rights in History,* to defend the purity of the human rights concept and movement, to distinguish it from the decolonization process, and to argue that anticolonialism was not a human rights movement. Even though he

---

[22] Plesch, *Human Rights after Hitler: The Lost History of Prosecuting the Axis War,* 158.
[23] Ali A. Mazrui, *Towards a Pax Africana: A Study of Ideology and Ambition* (Chicago and London: The University of Chicago Press, 1967), 129.
[24] Christian Reus-Smit, *Individual Rights and the Making of the International System* (Cambridge: Cambridge University Press, 2013), 152.

acknowledged the significance of the existence of the UN and the adoption of the UDHR as instruments and tools for a more humane new international order, Moyn contended that the rhetoric of rights was still a peripheral discourse in the aftermath of WWII.[25] Arguing that decolonization was solely about sovereignty and not about human rights, he claimed that the UN was not built with the purpose of promoting human rights and that most anticolonialists were not consciously using the rights language in their struggle for freedom:

> As the agent of the greatest dissemination of sovereignty in world history, not of its qualification, anticolonialism's lesson for the history of human rights is not about the growing relevance of the concept across the postwar era. It is about the ideological conditions in which human rights in their contemporary connotations became a plausible doctrine after the mid 1970s: an era in which collective self-determination, so persuasive before, entered crisis.[26]

Other scholars disagreed with the reductionist and restrictive analysis of that historiography of the human rights concept. Steven Jensen and Roland Burke in their respective works, *The Making of International Human Rights: The 1960s Decolonization and the Reconstruction of Global values* and *Decolonization and the Evolution of International Human Rights*, disagreed with the stance taken by Reus-Smit and Moyn. Jensen proposed that human rights studies be done through the lens of what he called negotiating universality, which provides a comprehensive approach to international justice and human rights: "Human rights evolved through stages of diplomatic negotiations, political contestations, and larger historical processes, and throughout the whole period, the various actors were engaged in negotiating universality."[27] Burke shed light on how the question of human rights has been central to the decolonization process, to the independence movement across the globe, to the Non-Aligned Movement whose marker was the 1955 Bandung Conference, which set up the Afro-Asian block against colonialism and white supremacy. He added that the Bandung Conference was a driving force for human rights, like several other international assemblies for human rights such as the International Conference on Human Rights in Teheran in 1968.

The issue of human rights was a key item on the agenda of the Bandung Conference, which remained the cornerstone of the Non-Aligned Movement.

---

25 Samuel Moyn, *The Last Utopia: Human Rights in History* (Cambridge and London: The Belknap Press of Harvard University Press, 2010), 68.

26 Moyn, *The Last Utopia*, 86-7.

27 Jensen, *The Making of International Human Rights*, 13.

In many speeches delivered in the opening and the closing ceremonies, and in the final communique of the conference, there was a consistent mention of human rights:

> However, human rights were central to the political debate at Bandung, and provided much of the lexicon for the articulation of grievances and aspirations by the assembled nationalist leaders. ... Interest in human rights was a distinctive feature of the optimistic atmosphere that characterized the dawn of the postcolonial era. Rights were increasingly invoked in speeches to the conference, with only the related but more immediate preoccupations of racism and colonialism."[28]

The delegates of the Bandung conference, beyond their dissenting views on the concept of human rights, saw "self-determination as a fundamental precondition for all human rights. Anticolonialism involved rights, and respect for rights necessitated decolonization."[29]

In Africa, besides the fact that several leaders have claimed to be embracing the spirit of the human rights documents of the American Revolution, of the French Revolution, of the Communist Manifesto, and of the universal Declaration of Human Rights that Eleanor Roosevelt saw as the Magna Carta of mankind, some have consistently used the rhetoric of rights in their fight for the right to self-determination and self-government. Nnamdi Azikiwe, Lincoln University (PA) and Howard University graduate, Pan-Africanist, and founding father of Nigerian independence, has been one of the leaders in Africa who interlinked the anticolonialist struggle and the human rights movement. In his writings, speeches, and actions for freedom he has repeatedly used the rights language and claimed the spirit and the letter of various human rights declarations such as the Magna Carta, the British Petition of Rights, the American Declaration of Independence, Woodrow Wilson's 14 Points, the Atlantic Charter, and the Universal Declaration of Human Rights. In *Political Blueprint for Nigeria* (1943), he gave his vision of Nigeria which stood upon the cardinal principles of human rights.[30] He was responsible for the drafting of a *Freedom Charter* (1948) published by his political party, the National Council for Nigeria and the Cameroons (NCNC).[31] Roland Burke also underlined the

---

[28] Roland Burke, *Decolonization and the Evolution of International Human Rights* (Philadelphia: University of Pennsylvania Press, 2010), 18.

[29] Burke, *Decolonization and the Evolution of International Human Rights*, 35.

[30] Nnamdi Azikiwe, *Political Blueprint of Nigeria* (African Book Co.), 1943.

[31] Bonny Ibhawoh, "Testing the Atlantic Charter: linking anticolonialism, self-determination and universal human rights," *The International Journal of Human Rights*, Routledge

contribution of several key figures to the human rights struggle from various parts namely Kwame Nkrumah of Ghana. He emphasized the role played by Ghana under his leadership for the promotion of human rights during the Bandung Conference, during the Conference of Independent States of Africa (1958) and during the debates for the adoption of the International Convention on the Elimination of All Forms of Racial Discrimination (1965).[32]

The struggle against apartheid which culminated in the Free Nelson Mandela Movement was recorded in history as the greatest and the first major transnational and universal movement for human rights. During the Rivonia trial in 1964 at the end of which he was condemned, Nelson Mandela, claimed socialism while defining his ideological positionality and added that he reserved himself the right "to borrow the best from the West and the East" and expressed his admiration and that of many across the globe of human rights documents emanating from the British political experience which claimed glory and universality such as the Magna Carta, the Petition of Rights and the Bill of Rights. He devoted also lines to South African version of Magna Carta: the Freedom Charter.[33]

The Freedom Charter adopted in 1955 under the leadership of the African National Congress (ANC) made several references to the notion of human rights. The Freedom Charter highlighted the importance of a variety of rights that need to be guaranteed and achieved for every human being in South Africa: civil rights, political rights, economic rights, cultural rights, and human rights.[34] The icon of the struggle against Apartheid, the first Black president of South Africa Nelson Mandela, discussed the place in history of the Freedom Charter:

> Though the Congress of the People had been broken up, the charter itself became a great beacon for the liberation struggle. Like other enduring political documents, such as the American Declaration of Independence, the French Declaration of the Rights of Man and the Communist Manifesto, the Freedom Charter is a mixture of practical goals and poetic language. It extols the abolition of racial discrimination and the achievement of equal rights for all. It welcomes all who embrace freedom to participate in the making of a democratic non-racial South

Taylor and Francis Group, September 2014, http://dx.doi.org/10.1080/13642987.2014.951340.

[32] Roland Burke, 125-126.

[33] Nelson Mandela, "I am prepared to die" https://africanlegends.files.wordpress.com/2013/11/nelson-mandela-1964-speech_i-am-prepared-to-die.pdf.

[34] Nelson Mandela, *Long Walk to Freedom: The Autobiography of Nelson Mandela* (London: Abacus, 1995), 203-205.

Africa. It captured the hopes and dreams of the people and acted as a blueprint for the liberation struggle and the future of the nation.[35]

In the United States, the language of rights was also central to the golden age of the Civil Rights movement. It should be noted that the two world wars, especially the second, gave rise to a movement among black Americans called Double V (Double Victory) (Victory Abroad and Victory at Home). This movement was carried out by former black American soldiers who contributed to the victory of the allies on the battlefields in Europe and who found it legitimate to claim the end of racial segregation in the United States of America or victory over racism and lynching in the United States of America. In other words, they were encouraged to fight for their civil, political, and economic rights.[36] Dr. Martin Luther King seen as the greatest champion of human rights of his generation linked the civil rights movement, to the international peace movement (namely his opposition to the War in Vietnam and to nuclear race), to the global struggle for human rights, to the struggle against Apartheid and to the struggle for economic justice. Throughout his speeches and his struggle for justice, Dr. Martin Luther fought for a variety of rights, political, civil, human, economic. His very last campaign was called the Poor People's Campaign. In his Nobel Peace Prize acceptance speech he gave in Oslo on December 10, 1964, in Oslo, he identified the struggle for civil rights in the United States to the struggle against Apartheid in South Africa, and paid tribute to a number of freedom seekers such as Albert Luthuli, the ANC president who had received a Nobel Peace Prize in 1960.[37]

A few months before his assassination, Malcolm X who converted into a human rights advocate sought to take Blacks' human rights struggle before the United Nations in conjunction with Dr. Martin Luther King, Jr., who would later confess: "We have moved from the era of civil rights to the era of human rights."[38] Malcolm X was one of the first to shift the narrative about the Civil Rights Movement struggle in the United States when he sought to internationalize it and labeled it a black human rights struggle:

We have to make the world see that the problem that we're confronted with is a problem for humanity. It's not a Negro problem; it's not an

---

[35] Mandela, *Long Walk to Freedom*, 203.

[36] Plesch, *Human Rights after Hitler: The Lost History of Prosecuting the Axis War* (Washington: Georgetown University Press, 2017), 158.

[37] Martin Luther King, Jr, *The Autobiography of Martin Luther King, Jr.*, edited by Clayborne Carson (New York: Warner Books, Inc., 1998), 258.

[38] Dr. Martin Luther King, Jr. pronounced these words at the SCLC staff retreat in Frogmore, South Carolina, in May 1967.

American problem. You and I have to make it a world problem, make the world aware that there'll be no peace on this earth as long as our human rights are being violated in America...If we can't be recognized and respected as a human being, we have to create a situation where no human being will enjoy life, liberty, and the pursuit of happiness.[39]

The human rights lexicon rhythmed the march of the Civil Rights Movement. It was therefore logical to see Lyndon B. Johnson, who, while seeking to rally the American people through their representatives to act on the Voting Rights Act said that it was not about states' rights or national rights but about human rights.

In the context of the Cold War, the Afro-Asian block forged at the Bandung Conference played an incremental role in the progression and the expansion of human rights. The calls to the UN in the forms of letters and petitions to address human rights violations, which were ignored in the aftermath of the creation of the UN, started to receive acute attention thanks to countries of the Third World or of the Afro-Asian block in the 1960s. Human rights victims, particularly in the central and the southern parts of Africa and in oppressive regimes, were calling upon the UN to live up to its mission and adhere to the promises of the UDHR and to various conventions it has adopted. Roland Burke analyzed this paradigm shift:

> This was a stunning departure from the attitude of the Commission on Human Rights, which had expressly denied itself the power to study any petitions in 1947. For two decades, the Commission scrupulously avoided any serious consideration of the countless letters it had accumulated, and only began to reverse its position in the late 1960s, several years after the pioneering decisions of the various anti-Apartheid and decolonization committees.[40]

The issues of race and religion occupied a very important place in the conversations about human rights during the UN fora.[41] Two other major moments in the expansion of human rights deserve a particular attention: the International Conference on Human Rights which took place in Teheran in 1968 and the Helsinki Act of 1975.

The year 1968 was a very important moment in the world. It was a year when hopes, despair, grievances and griefs mixed. On the one hand, suffice it to mention the surge of the anti-Vietnam War movement, the multiple students'

---

[39] Malcolm X, *By Any Means Necessary* (New York: Pathfinder, 1970), 104.

[40] Burke, *Decolonization and the Evolution of International Human Rights*, 60.

[41] Jensen, *The Making of International Human Rights*, 146.

movements for more freedom, namely the May 68 protests in France which had shaken the foundation of French politics and the African-American students' movement which led to adoption of the African-American studies. On the other hand, 1968 registered the Soviet Union invasion of Czechoslovakia to crush the Prague Spring and the assassinations of Dr. Martin Luther King, Jr. and of Robert Kennedy, two symbols of the Civil Rights Movement struggle in the USA. The United Nations decided to declare that year the United Nations International Year for Human Rights. A commemorative conference took place in Teheran (Iran) that year. Social activists and human rights advocates from different parts of the world with competing agendas met and discussed a variety of human rights issues namely, colonialism, Apartheid, slavery, the question of occupied territories by Israel, the state of human rights in the Soviet Union and in the Soviet-controlled countries, and the evolution of civil rights in the United States of America. Even though the resolutions were not binding, the conference had the merit of internationalizing the human rights question.[42]

The Helsinki Act of 1975 was a declaration which sanctioned a meeting of 35 heads of state of all European countries, Canada, and the United States. It was the culmination of debates, discussions, negotiations, diplomatic ventures of committees, commissions, and delegations on a whole range of issues: security, trade, borders issues, détente, religious tolerance, and human rights. The greatest accomplishment of the Helsinki Act of 1975 was that it placed the question of human rights in the central stage of global politics.[43]

The Helsinki Act of 1975 occurred in the context of the mid 1970s wave of democratization followed by a period of transitional justice with its corollary of national prosecutions in Southern Europe. That movement of democratic transition coupled with transitional justice later touched Latin America in the mid 1980s. The journey of the notion of human rights thus evolved, expanded, and led to the establishment of national and regional courts which eventually culminated in the quest for a universal international tribunal, which took the name of the International Criminal Court. I discuss in the section that follows these processes which constitute the justice cascade that eventually led to the International Criminal Court.

The journey of the idea of an international criminal court

Parallel to the journey of the concept of human rights, there was undeniably another journey, that of the creation of an international arbitration institution that spawned the International Criminal Court. The latter [journey] gave birth

---

[42] Jensen, *The Making of International Human Rights*, 176.
[43] Jensen, *The Making of International Human Rights*, 236.

to a number of charters, conventions, and treaties which also ignited the awareness for international justice. Kathryn Sikkink, in her seminal work with the self-explanatory title *The Justice Cascade: How Human Rights Prosecutions are Changing World Politics*, discussed the various processes she identified as three separate streams that contributed to the growing consciousness about human rights, which she called the justice cascade, and which eventually culminated in the creation of the International Criminal Court.

The first stream began with the Nuremberg and Tokyo trials and ended with the creation of special regional tribunals, the International Criminal Tribunal for Rwanda (ICTR) and International Criminal Tribunal for Yugoslavia (ICTY). The second stream was the series of national prosecutions in Greece, Portugal, and Argentina. The third stream was a set of legislations, legal documents, charters, and judicial conventions, such as the Geneva Conventions of 1949 and the Torture Conventions of 1984, ratified after WWII and which served as the basis of discussion for the creation of the International Criminal Court.[44]

Before discussing the significance of the Nuremberg and the Tokyo tribunals, it is important to mention the early medieval practices of limiting military brutality which were noticeable in the national laws of Europe—in Naples in 1268 and in England in 1305. The Breisach trial of Governor Peter von Hagenbach in 1474 is considered a landmark in the history of international criminal arbitration, even though scholars disagree with its designation as an international trial. It is said to have laid the ground for the Nuremberg trials.[45]

In contemporary world history, the historical account that posits the question of the legality and the legitimacy of a trial begins in the nineteenth century with Gustave Moynier. He is known to be the first in Europe to mention, in 1872, the idea of an international justice court which should have two main functions, punitive and preventive. He proposed the creation of an international court after the Franco-Prussian War of 1870–1871. The idea of the creation of such a court did not come to fruition, because European states were concerned about the erosion of their sovereignty.[46] The 1899 meeting in Hague for peaceful settlements of conflicts also called the 1899 Hague Convention reiterated the idea for the

---

44 Kathryn Sikkink, *The Justice Cascade: How Human Rights Prosecutions are Changing World Politics* (New York: W.W. Norton & Co., 2011), 96-98.

45 Erik André Andersen, "The International Military Tribunals in Nuremberg and Tokyo: Epoch-Making and Standard-Setting, yet with Different Effectiveness," in *The Effectiveness of International Criminal Justice*, ed. Cedric Ryngaert (Antwerp: Intersentia, 2009), 4–5.

46 Paul G. Lauren, "From Impunity to Accountability: Forces of Transformation and the Changing International Human Rights," in *From Sovereign Impunity to International Accountability: The Search for Justice in a World of States*, eds. Ramesh Thakur and Peter Malcontent (New York: United Nations University Press, 2004), 21.

creation of an international court. The two World Wars led to subsequent attempts to create international justice courts: Leipzig, Nuremberg, and Tokyo. As a matter of emphasis, it is worth mentioning that the UNWCC served as "pretrial examining magistrate" as well as a model for the establishment of the Nuremberg and the Tokyo tribunals and subsequent tribunals.[47] Later, the idea resurfaced with the creation of the United Nations Special Courts and the International Criminal Court.

The outcome of World War I was a milestone in the history of international arbitration. The idea of the establishment of an international tribunal was not accepted by the United States and Japan. The former argued that the existence of such a tribunal would conflict with the American Constitution and advocated therefore that war crimes be judged within national jurisdictions. Provisions were thus made and inserted in the peace agreements, namely in the Treaty of Versailles signed on June 28, 1919.[48]

This treaty was perceived as a punitive agreement against Germany, blamed for being the violator of world peace. That treaty contained clauses related to the establishment of an international tribunal. Article 227 of the Treaty of Versailles stated that the German leader William II must be brought before a special tribunal for "supreme offence against international morality and the sanctity of treaties."[49] However, this trial never happened. The Netherlands, where the Kaiser had taken refuge, refused to extradite him. Instead, a special court, which oversaw the trial of Leipzig, was created to try the officials of defeated Germany. It was conducted in Germany, and the court was accused of protecting the defendants. Only a few were tried and got light sentence, which did not exceed six months.

The idea of the creation of an international criminal tribunal did not prosper during the interwar period, 1919–1939. Several associations under the leadership of the International Law Association, which drafted the constitution of such an institution, sought to help create the International Criminal Court; but the project fell short. Other groups supported the idea. The League of Nations adopted the convention for its creation in 1937, but the project could not be ratified by enough states.[50]

The end of WWII saw the resurgence of the idea of the existence of an international tribunal. On the eve of the adoption of the Universal Declaration

---

[47] Plesch, *Human Rights after Hitler: The Lost History of Prosecuting the Axis War*, 1.

[48] Andersen, "The International Military Tribunals," 7.

[49] The Versailles Treaty June 28, 1919: Part VII Penalties, Article 227, The Avalon Project, accessed February 27, 2022, https://avalon.law.yale.edu/imt/partvii.asp.

[50] Andersen, "The International Military Tribunals," 7.

of Human Rights, the United Nations adopted the Convention on the Prevention and Punishment of the Crime of Genocide and suggested the establishment of international tribunals to try war criminals and the creation of an international criminal court. After World War II, the four victors—the Soviet Union, the United States, France, and Great Britain—established the International Military Tribunals (IMT). The Nuremberg trial was the hallmark of the IMT in the aftermath of World War II. It set the stage for the existence of international tribunals. The notion of individualization of criminality and the principle of universal jurisdiction emerged in the field of international justice.

The four victors provided the prosecutors and the judges to try the defeated German leaders. In the case of Nuremberg, as Biddis pointed out, "it was more about punishment than justice."[51] Erik Andre Jackson reiterated this line of thought when he asserted the following: "That four great nations, flushed with victory and stung with injury, stay the hand of vengeance and voluntarily submit their captives, enemies to the judgement of law is one of the most significant tributes that Power has ever paid to Reason."[52] The allies wanted to avoid the pitfalls of the Leipzig experience but the Nuremberg trial epitomized the victors' justice or the "victors' law" according to Mark D. Kielsgard,[53] in the sense that the defeated were the only ones on trial. The disproportionate use of force by the United States against the civilian population of Japan—which suffered not one, but two, atomic bombs in Hiroshima and in Nagasaki on August 6 and August 9, 1945 respectively, causing the death of more than two hundred thousand civilians—was not questioned.

Many still question the ethical rationale of the use of nuclear bombs by the United States, which is the first nation (the only one so far) to have used atomic bombs in human history. The quest for world hegemony in the race against the Soviet Union pushed the United States, according to Oliver Stone and Peter Kuznick, to use nuclear bombs. In the last days of WWII, the allies were engaged in serious negotiations to carve up and take over regions and territories, as they were adamant to complete their victorious military expeditions against the fascist nations (Germany, Italy, and Japan). The possibility that the Red Army of the USSR might conquer Manchuria (Chinese territory which was under Japanese colonial rule since 1931) caused fear both in the United States and Japan. The United States in a show of force decided to drop the bombs. And

---

51 Michael D. Biddis, "From the Nuremberg Charter to the Rome Statute: A Historical Analysis of the Limits of International Accountability," in *From Sovereign Impunity to International Accountability*, ed. Thakur and Malcontent, 43.

52 Robert H. Jackson, Opening Address for the United States, November 21, 1945, quoted by Andersen "The International Military Tribunals," 3.

53 Mark D. Kielsgard, *Reluctant Engagement*, 8.

Japan, which suffered the bombs, continued to battle and only surrendered on US terms, as it preferred to surrender rather than to see its empire falling to the Russians.[54] These strategic interests of the United States were not discussed during the Tokyo and Nuremberg trials, nor the killing of hundreds of thousands of Japanese civilians.

After the Nuremberg and Tokyo trials, the question of international justice arbitration was put aside mainly because of the context of the Cold War, at the end of which the idea of a universal international arbitration resurfaced. However, the idea for the existence of an international court was kept alive and gained momentum thanks to a wave of national and regional prosecutions whose goal was to try political leaders, leaders of military juntas, or heads of states. These prosecutions were an offshoot or an outcome of the democratization process of Southern Europe in the 1970s. Three countries in southern Europe which were under authoritarian rule experienced democratic revolutions, from dictatorship to democracy, in the mid 1970s: Greece, Portugal, and Spain.

The wave of democratization in Southern Europe opened an era of transitional justice. Before elaborating on the question of transitional justice, for the sake of clarity and for the sake of the conversation, it is logical to give a brief overview of the political climate and the historical processes that culminated in the climax of a trend of a series of prosecutions whose objective was to hold accountable a number of political figures. I owe the bulk of the following account on the wave of democratization in Southern Europe which led to the growing awareness about international justice to Sikkink seminal work *Justice Cascade*.

In Portugal, on April 25, 1974, the Carnation Revolution, a bloodless military takeover ended the regime of Marcelo Caetano, born out of the Salazar dictatorship which was in power for 48 years. The revolution had two goals: to restore democracy and to grant independence to Portuguese colonies in Africa engaged in armed struggle for their freedom: Mozambique, Guinea Bissau, Angola, Cape Verde, and Sao Tome and Principe.

A few months after the Carnation Revolution, in Greece the military dictatorship, which overthrew the civilian government in 1967 and which was in power for seven years, was ousted from power, on July 23, 1974, thanks to a student revolt. The population was unhappy about the military regime which was on the verge of having a war it could not win against Turkey which had invaded Cyprus. This consolidated a wave of democratization in Europe which

---

[54] Oliver Stone and Peter Kuznick, "Chapter Four: The Bomb," in *The Untold History of the United States* (New York: Gallery Books, 2019, 131-80.

later touched Spain. In Spain, change began with the death of General Francisco Franco on November 20, 1975. He had ruled Spain for nearly 40 years, coming to power after winning a civil war (1936-1939).

Greece set the pace with the series of regional trials in 1975 followed by Portugal in 1979. Spain was the exception. The leaders of the Francisco Franco regime were not tried as they could agree on a negotiated transition different from the ruptured transitions experienced in Portugal and Greece.

The above-mentioned democratic transitions succeeded a period of détente during the Cold War. This was marked by the US president's visit to China, thus ending a three decade tension with that country, the withdrawal of the US troops from Vietnam in 1973. These revolutionary processes were also marked by another series of social movements, the students movements of the late sixties, namely in France and in the United States. These historical processes, along with the rise of a strong leftist movement in the world, the indignation caused by a US-backed military coup in Chile, led by Augusto Pinochet in 1973, which ended up with the assassination of the then sitting president Salvador Allende, and a growing peace movement led to a far-reaching momentum for a stronger consciousness of the struggle for human rights.[55]

Greece was the first to hold its state officials accountable for massive human rights violations. It held what are known as the Greek Junta Trials, a set of trials conducted during the transition. They included the trial of the instigators of the 1967 coup, the trial of soldiers involved in the repression of the Athens Polytechnic student revolt of 1973, and the trials of those who had committed torture against the civilian population throughout the rule of the military junta and particularly during the repression of the students' revolution. Konstantinos Karamanlis, a seasoned politician who self-exiled himself after the military takeover of 1967, was called upon to lead the transition and heeded the gradual demands of the people who called for trials to be held against the leaders of the Greek junta. The main defendants of the 1967 coup were sentenced to death, which Karamanlis commuted into life in prison. The trial of torturers was considered a human rights trial, unlike the trial of the instigators which was more like a political trial with expedited justice.

Portugal soon followed suit in relation to prosecuting military leaders, even though the Portuguese revolution occurred before the Greek revolution.[56] After the military takeover to end the Salazar regime, the Portuguese took to the streets and immediately expressed calls for trials to be held against the leaders of the eventually deposed regime. However, during the first five years of the

---

55 Sikkink, *The Justice Cascade*, 31-38.

56 Sikkink, *The Justice Cascade*, 43-50.

transition, Portugal was deeply divided along ideological lines, and the transitional government had one essential goal, to survive the coup attempts while building a new democratic society according to European norms. After a successful counter coup led by Captain Sousa e Castro, the new leader of the transition decided to organize the trials of hundreds of members of the political police, called *Polícia Internacional e de Defesa do Estado* (PIDE), for their defense of the Salazar regime. They had been in prison for over a year, without trial, since the revolution of 1974. The trials finally began in September 1976. They were quick and light sentences were pronounced. Several of the convicted did not serve their full sentences, to the displeasure of several human rights activists. Both types of trials in Greece and Portugal demonstrated the possibility to hold state officials accountable.[57]

This movement reached South America. Several countries in Latin America which also experienced democratic transitions and transitional justice held trials and convicted their leaders of juntas, namely in Argentina (1985), Bolivia (1986), Haiti (1986), Guatemala (1988), El Salvador (1990), Panama (1990), and Chile (1991).

Argentina ushered in a new era and set the pace for transitional justice in 1985 when it returned to democracy. The trial was one of the major decisions that democratic Argentina took in order to make leaders who committed various human rights violations accountable for their actions during the military rule which lasted from 1976 to 1982. Hundreds of officers appeared before the court. The main defendants were the nine commanders-in-chief of Argentina who served during that period and the president, Jorge Videla. Human rights groups created during the military rule, often led by members of Argentinian victims of human rights abuses (torture, killing, disappearance, and kidnapping), gradually played a major role with the support of their international backers and succeeded in making the call for trials a national cause. The trials initially planned to be conducted by a military court were finally brought before a civilian court.

After months of hearings held from April 22 to December 9, 1985, the leaders of the three military juntas were convicted for massive human rights violations. The court deliberated on 280 illustrative cases among the 709 cases presented by the prosecution. The prosecutor, Julio César Strassera, ended his indictment with this famous "¡Nuncas mas!" which means "Never again!" The assistant prosecutor of the trial was a certain Moreno Ocampo who became the first prosecutor of the International Criminal Court when that institution was established. The first two leaders of the first junta Jorge Rafael Videla and Emilio

---

[57] Sikkink, *The Justice Cascade*, 51-55.

Eduardo Massera were sentenced to life imprisonment. The trial of the juntas was a milestone and a landmark for criminal accountability and for the justice cascade in that country:

> The early trial of Juntas in Argentina contributed to an increase in judicialization there. Since 1985, there has been a significant increase in the number of cases submitted to the Supreme Court and to federal and state courts. The trial of the Juntas encouraged "the discovery of law", as ordinary citizens began to perceive the legal system as more viable and legitimate if it could be used to hold the most powerful former leaders of their country accountable. People observed that if the law could be applied even to the powerful, maybe they could use it to pursue their own goals.[58]

If there was a legal case that was the epitome of the justice cascade in the latter years of the twentieth century, it was that of Augusto Pinochet, the very man who came to power in Chile through the bloody coup d'etat which led to the assassination of Salvador Allende and who stayed in power from 1973 to 1990. The attempt to try him, on October 16, 1998, occurred three months after the adoption of the Rome Statute on July 17, 1998, which established the creation of the International Criminal Court.[59]

October 16, 1998 marked an important turning point in the history of international justice. Augusto Pinochet, who was in England for health treatment, was arrested there and ordered to stand trial and appear before a court in Spain. The Spanish court responded favorably to the request of activists and members of the Chilean civil society who brought Pinochet before Spanish justice for the crimes against humanity, genocide, and torture he had committed during his long reign of 17 years. Spain based its action on the principle of universal jurisdiction.

The principle of universal jurisdiction was adopted after the Second World War in the various founding acts of the creation of the United Nations, in particular through the precepts of the 1949 Geneva Conventions. But this principle was difficult to execute. Execution was limited to areas such as piracy and terrorism. The principle of universal jurisdiction has now been extended to various other areas such as the use of nuclear weapons. The ratification of these conventions in different countries of the world has led to their

---

[58] Kathryn Sikking, *The Justice Cascade*, 82.

[59] One should not confuse the Rome Statute which created the International Criminal Court and the Treaty of Rome or the Rome Treaty which created the European Economic Community in 1957. However, some of the ICC stakeholders call the founding document of the court the Treaty of Rome or the Rome Treaty.

incorporation in the respective criminal codes of these countries and to the adoption of the principle of universal jurisdiction in these countries.

In the name of that principle, any court in the world that abides by it can receive a complaint against world leaders who commit crimes with impunity and could not be prosecuted because of the immunity conferred on them by their official political function. A trend has emerged in international justice with a number of trials similar to that of Pinochet in Latin America. These trials helped to consolidate the rule of law and indicated that no one was above the law. They served as the basis for establishing a culture of reducing crimes against humanity, establishing the framework, the norms, and the habits whose nature reduced the propensity to commit crimes with impunity. The regional tribunals that were established for Sierra Leone, for Yugoslavia, for Rwanda, as well as the creation of the international criminal court of justice, have reinforced these standards which are now part of the expansive and incremental awareness for international justice Kathryn Sikkink called the justice cascade.

In light of what I have elaborated in this section, it is evident that the formation of the International Criminal Court is not a spontaneous generation but a predictable outcome of consistent attempts, constant efforts, and of recurrent and resilient campaigns for justice:

> Sometimes we might think that all of the action happened in Rome in 1998, when the delegates gathered to draft the Statute of the ICC. But Rome was an outgrowth of processes that started in Nuremberg and continued in Athens, Buenos Aires, Madrid, London, and Geneva- accelerating in the last thirty years. When the delegates met in Rome, there was an extensive back story that made the International Criminal Court possible but not inevitable.[60]

The idea of an international court was reintroduced in 1989 at the United Nations General Assembly by Trinidad and Tobago that wanted such a court in order to prosecute drug dealers.[61] The prosecution of crimes against humanity was not its objective. Then the crises in Yugoslavia and Rwanda broke out with their crimes against humanity. Under the auspices of the UN, some special courts were established to investigate human rights violations and crimes against humanity in these two countries and in some specific geographic regions, namely in Sierra Leone and in Cambodia.

---

[60] Sikkink, *The Justice Cascade*, 98.
[61] Sikkink, *The Justice Cascade*, 118.

The International Criminal Court, the most recent instrument in the field of international arbitration, seems to be the most refined tool. Contrary to the special tribunals, which were geographically located for some specific cases of human rights violations, the ICC is perceived by several stakeholders as more universal and global and can in theory investigate any crime on the face of earth in the field of international law.

In the beginning, several stakeholders in Africa welcomed the idea of an international court in a context that presaged the consolidation of democratic values on the continent. Nelson Mandela rose to power after the dismantling of apartheid, and Africa was turning its back on the one-party system in order to embrace multiparty systems. Several African nations and African civil society organizations initially welcomed the project of the existence of the court positively and greatly contributed to its creation and to the decision related to the creation of an independent Office of the Prosecutor. The Southern African Development Community (SADC) openly threw its support behind the idea of creating the ICC in 1997 and issued a declaration that later served as a building block for the adoption in February 8, 1998 in Dakar by twenty-five African governments. The declaration issued in Dakar was known as Declaration on the Establishment of the International Criminal Court.[62] At both meetings African countries seemed to have a consensual view about the incoming court. They wanted it to benefit from independent funding, with an independent prosecutor, free from the interference of world powers and the United Nations Security Council. Later the Africans'enthusiasm turned into mistrust and distrust toward the court.

During its 52nd General Assembly, the United Nations adopted a resolution to organize a conference for the creation of an international criminal court. That conference was held from June 15 to July 17, 1998, in Rome and drafted a treaty for the establishment of the International Criminal Court. Stéphanie Maupas gave an account of the debates, which registered a variety of dissenting positions about the mission and the funding of the court and the role of the prosecutor. She revealed that before the universal agreement on crimes against humanity, several countries wanted to add their respective individual concerns to the list of crimes to be prosecuted: Caribbean countries (drug crimes) and Arab countries (terrorism). The debate of the crime of aggression was deferred because it touched on sensitive issues such as the American embargo on Cuba, the Israeli colonization, and the crises in Chechnya and Tibet. The assembly instead agreed to forge an accord on crimes against humanity based on existing legal terms already articulated in the Geneva Convention.

---

[62] ICC, *How the International Criminal Court works* (The Hague: ICC, 2020), 15.

The delegates were divided into three major groups. The first group, which was in favor of a strong and independent court, was composed of Switzerland, Croatia, Argentina, Egypt, South Africa, many francophone African countries, and several European Union states, with the exception of France, which was in the second group, composed of the five permanent powers, which enjoyed the veto right in the United Nations Security Council. This second group wanted to have control over the court. The other members of the council are the United States, the Russian Federation, China, and the United Kingdom. The third group, which was the most conservative, was composed of India, Mexico, and several Arab countries and wanted a strong court but with limited powers.[63]

The debates intensified about the role of the prosecutor. African countries vehemently opposed the interference of the United Nations Security Council, the dominance of Europeans over the affairs of the court. They found themselves in circumstantial alliance with the group of conservatives who opposed the European-dominated international order in force since WWII. The permanent members of the UN Security Council did not want an all-powerful prosecutor. The question of the conflict between domestic laws and international law further divided the delegates, among whom some were worried about the sovereignty of their respective countries. The court decided to reconcile both conflicting positions with the notion of complementarity which requires the International Criminal Court to prosecute when states are unwilling or unable to do so regarding grave human rights violations such as war crimes and crimes against humanity.

Other topics in the central part of the heated discussions were related to the sentence to be administered to the criminals, abortions of forced pregnancies in case of rapes, and nuclear weapons. The idea of capital punishment, defended by the Caribbean and the Arab representatives was rejected, following the spirit of Nuremberg, and the maximal sentence was adopted. The fear of promoting abortion was the basis of the positions of the Vatican and the Islamists. The notion of rape was retained and was added to the list of crimes to be prosecuted. Nuclear powers vetoed the idea of adding nuclear weapons to the list of prohibited weapons. Chemical weapons were withdrawn from the list also.

The ICC aims at being a universal jurisdiction, but since its onset it had to acknowledge its own limitations in this regard. The most powerful nations did not want their citizens to be brought before the court, and France only accepted to sign the treaty if it could make some reservations that were granted. The

---

[63] Stéphanie Maupas, *Le Joker des Puissants: Le Grand Roman de la Cour Pénale Internationale* (Paris: Don Quichotte Editions, 2016), 54–55.

United States openly declared that it would do everything possible to fight against the principle of the universality of the court. Its representatives maneuvered, siding with countries bound to it through economic and military ties, to win them over, using at times blackmail and threats.[64] India disagreed with the ICC claim that it is universal and disapproved the role assigned to the United Nations Security Council. China rejected the claim that it is independent and neutral and denounced the lack of checks and balances, thus opposing the excessive powers given to the prosecutor as well.[65] Another critic of the consultations during the conference comes from Geoffrey Robertson who argued that the participants "deliberately fudged the lawfulness of landmines and nuclear weapons as weapons of international law."[66]

On July 17, 1998, the Rome Statute was adopted, with 120 countries voting in favor, seven against, and twenty-one abstentions. The United States, Israel, and the People's Republic of China led the list of countries that voted against the Rome Statute. The court went into effect on July 1, 2002, after the Rome Statute obtained sixty ratifications. David Davenport, a dissenting voice, decried the methodology and tactics used during the conference:

> [W]as bundling the key elements of the court into a package that became a take-it-leave-it proposal, not subject in the end to further compromise…"the package"…Additionally, the Rome Statute provided no possibility of a nation signing "with reservations" reflected in the Vienna Convention on the Law of Treaties as a standard part of international treaties…As with the element of time deadlines, such a nonnegotiable approach is most out of character with the thorough, consensus-based processes of international law.[67]

Even though the delegates sought and managed to gain the support of the United States during the constitutive conference for the successful creation of the court, the United States still voted against the Rome Statute and has fought the court, since its birth. Jesse Helms, chairman of the US Senate Foreign Relations Committee, broke down why the court is not good for America, as he made clear his opposition to the Rome Statute in July 1998:

---

[64] Maupas, *Le Joker des Puissants*, 55–65.

[65] David Hoile, *Justice Denied: The Reality of the International Criminal Court* (London: The Africa Research Centre, 2014), 23–24.

[66] Geoffrey Robertson, *Crimes Against Humanity: The Struggle for Global Justice*, 4th ed. (London: Penguin Books, 2012), 519.

[67] David Davenport, "The New Diplomacy," *Policy Review*, no. 116 (December 2002/January 2003), https://www.hoover.org/research/new-diplomacy.

The Rome Treaty is irreparably flawed...In short, this treaty, this treaty represents a very real threat to our soldiers, our citizens and our national security interests. I must...be clear: Rejecting this treaty is not enough. The United States must fight this treaty...we must aggressively be opposed to this court...The United States shall not permit a US soldier to participate in any NATO, UN, or other international peacekeeping mission, until the United States has reached agreement with all of our NATO allies, and the UN, that no US soldier will be subject to the jurisdiction of this court.[68]

However, the establishment of the ICC as a culminating tool for the long-held dream of international justice was welcomed with a chorus of satisfaction. Kofi Annan, former Secretary-General of the United Nations, viewed the court as "a gift of hope to future generations, and a giant leap forward in the march towards universal human rights and the rule of law."[69]

Benjamin B. Ferencz, the last surviving prosecutor of the Nuremberg trials, who had 22 Nazi officials indicted, stressed the imperative need for the creation of such a court: "As long as combatants in armed conflicts insist that they alone can judge the morality and legality of their deeds there is no way to end conflicts through the rule of law."[70] He does not shy away from his satisfaction: "Criminal law cannot stop all crimes but it certainly has a deterrent effect."[71] More than 40 African countries signed the Treaty of Rome, thus making them heavily represented in the ICC membership. (See the map on the next page about the membership of the ICC).[72]

---

[68] Jesse Helms, Subcommittee on International Operations of the Senate Committee on Foreign Relations of the United States Senate, July 23, 1998, 105th Congress, 2nd Session, S. Rep. No.105 in Hoile, *Justice Denied*, 69.

[69] Akbar Khan, "Ten Years of International Criminal Court Practice -Trials, Achievements and Tribulations: Is the ICC Today What Africa Expects or Wants?" in *The International Criminal Court and Africa: One Decade On*, ed. Evelyn A. Ankumah (Cambridge: Intersentia, 2016), 434.

[70] Benjamin B. Ferencz, "Foreword," in *The International Criminal Court and Africa*, ed. Ankumah, v.

[71] Ferencz, "Foreword," vi.

[72] Claire Felter, "The Role of the International Criminal Court," Council on Foreign Relations, February 23, 2021, https://www.cfr.org/backgrounder/role-international-criminal-court.

Members of the International Criminal Court

Note: Burundi and the Philippines joined the ICC but later withdrew.

Sources: International Criminal Court; United Nations.

COUNCIL *on*
FOREIGN
RELATIONS

Figure 1: Members of the International Criminal Court.
Source: Council on Foreign Relations, February 23, 2021

The International Criminal Court in brief

This section discusses the agencies, the prosecutorial rights, and the funding of the court. In accordance with Article 34 of its statute, the ICC is composed of four separate bodies: the Presidency, the Judicial Divisions, the Registry, and the Office of the Prosecutor.[73]

- The Office of the Presidency is held by the president aided by the first and second vice presidents. The members of that office are elected by an absolute majority by their peers for a three-year term renewable once. Article 38 discusses the functions of the Presidency. The Presidency oversees the well-being of the court, establishes chambers, and supervises the work of the Registry, except for the Office of the Prosecutor.[74] The Presidency may propose to increase the number of judges, and may discharge a

---

[73] United Nations, *Rome Statute of the International Criminal Court* (The Hague: International Criminal Court, 2011), 17.

[74] United Nations, *Rome Statute of the International Criminal Court,* 19.

judge (Article 41) and the prosecutor or a deputy prosecutor (Article 42-6) from the functions assigned to them. Moreover, the Presidency can conclude cooperation agreements with states.[75]

- The Judicial Divisions of the International Criminal Court are composed of three departments or three Judicial Divisions, which hear matters at different stages of the proceedings: Pre-Trial, Trial, and Appeals. They are a total of 18 judges elected by the Assembly of States Parties for a non-renewable nine year term (Article 39).[76]

- The Prosecutor's Office consists of the prosecutor and two assistant prosecutors who deal respectively with the investigation and the accusation. The prosecutor is elected by the Assembly of States Parties of the International Criminal Court for a nine-year term.[77] The first person to assume the position of the prosecutor was Luis Moreno Ocampo, deputy prosecutor during the trials of the Juntas in Argentina in 1985, a US-trained prosecutor who was elected in 2003. His election was an appeasement to the United States. Fatou Bensouda, who worked under him as his deputy, succeeded him and occupied the position of the ICC prosecutor from 2012 to 2021. She was in charge of the office during most of Laurent Gbagbo's trial.

- The Registry oversees the nonjudicial aspects of the administration and service of the court. It is headed by a clerk elected by an absolute majority of the judges for a five-year term and placed under the authority of the president of the court. It provides administrative support to the organs of the court and to the legal teams of the defendants (Article 43).[78]

- The Assembly of States Parties (ASP) is the oversight body of the managerial affairs of the International Criminal Court. It discusses the budget, elects the prosecutors and the judges, and adopts significant documents, such as "Rules of Procedures and Evidence." The Assembly of State Parties meets once a year either in New York or in The Hague. It is composed of a representative of each signatory state. The representatives of the Assembly of State Parties are urged to reach decisions through consensus. If they

---

[75] United Nations, *Rome Statute of the International Criminal Court*, 20.
[76] United Nations, *Rome Statute of the International Criminal Court*, 19.
[77] United Nations, *Rome Statute of the International Criminal Court*, 20.
[78] United Nations, *Rome Statute of the International Criminal Court*, 21.

cannot reach a consensus, they vote. Each member has one vote (Article 112).[79]

Regarding the prosecutorial dimension of the court, the ICC can prosecute under one of the four following conditions: (a) suspects who are citizens of countries that ratified the Treaty of Rome can be prosecuted; (b) suspects who reside on a territory of a state that ratified the Treaty can be prosecuted;[80] (c) the Office of the Prosecutor can take upon itself (*proprio motu* prosecution) to undertake an investigation or to prosecute suspects, Article 15(1);[81] (d) the Security Council of the United Nations can authorize an investigation and prosecution of suspects who can be citizens of a country that has not ratified the Treaty of Rome, Article 13 (b), article 16.[82] A state that has ratified the Rome Statute can request an investigation and prosecution, article 15 *bis* (State referral).[83]

Even though the Rome Statute in its Articles 13 (b) and 16 gives the prosecutorial right to the United Nations Security Council, three countries (the United States, China, and the Russian Federation) of the five permanent members of the Security Council refused to place themselves under the jurisdiction of the court. The other two (France and the United Kingdom) made some prohibited reservations about the Treaty of Rome. All members of the Security Council decide whom to investigate and whom to prosecute.[84]

Since the inception of the court, its prosecutorial rationale has been the center of acute scrutiny. The style of its first prosecutor has added to the worries of the institution. He carefully ignored the calls to prosecute the crimes of the United States in Iraq and pretended not to know about Laurent Gbagbo's request for the investigation of the crimes committed in 2002. He announced an investigation of the Congolese-born Thomas Lubanga for his alleged role in the commission of crimes against humanity in Congo. He welcomed the invitation by Yoweri Museveni, who wanted him to open an investigation into the activities of the Joseph Kony, a rebel leader, while he closed his eyes to the crimes committed by the Ugandan leader's forces in the fight against the rebel forces and in Eastern Congo.

---

79 United Nations, *Rome Statute of the International Criminal Court*, 53.

80 United Nations, *Rome Statute of the International Criminal Court*, 9.

81 United Nations, *Rome Statute of the International Criminal Court*, 9.

82 United Nations, *Rome Statute of the International Criminal Court*, 9, 10.

83 United Nations, *Rome Statute of the International Criminal Court*, 10

84 Kamari M. Clarke, *Affective Justice: The International Criminal Court and the Pan-Africanist Pushback* (Durham and London: Duke University Press, 2019), 2.

The style of the first ICC prosecutor was also a source of controversy. He was accused of being more preoccupied with his image, his spectacular media appearances, and his obsession to expand his network than with really advancing the cause of justice. He could count on the media and strategic support of Hollywood celebrities such as George Clooney (for the case of Darfur) and Angelina Jolie. When the state parties were about to vote for the successor of Luis Moreno Ocampo, the diplomats were driven by the same rationale as expressed in the following words: "The Argentinian [Ocampo] was chosen to seduce Americans. His successor was to reconquer Africa scoured by nine years of investigations which targeted mostly the continent. The court that saw itself as universal jurisdiction was perceived in 2011 as a European court which exclusively judges its former colonies."[85]

The source of ICC funding is also problematic. States' parties, private companies, and corporations contribute to the funding of the court, thus putting a question mark on its impartiality and neutrality. According to data provided by David Hoile, European countries provide more than 50% of the ICC budget. In 2012, the big six of the European Union—Germany, France, United Kingdom, Spain, Poland, and Italy—alone contributed 42% of the court budget, which was over one hundred million euros.[86] Several scholars were definitively convinced that the ICC was and is a European court.[87] Besides the controversial prosecutorial rationale, the ICC has been the reflection of issues and weaknesses inherent to international justice.

International justice and unresolved issues

An overview of the international justice journey sets the pace to critically analyze issues and patterns germane to international justice. The literature review reveals that these patterns are immanent to the conversation about the International Criminal Court: the selectivity of cases, the victor's justice, the question of national sovereignty, the conflict between national law and international law, lawfare, and the double-dealing and double standards of those who are in positions of power.

The question of sovereignty

The ICC does not prosecute states but individuals, thus the individualization of crimes, and only prosecutes when states are unwilling or unable to prosecute those who are accused of war crimes and crimes against humanity (the notion

---

[85] Maupas, *Le Joker des Puissants*, 84.

[86] Hoile, *Justice Denied*, 17.

[87] Hoile, *Justice Denied*, 35.

of complementarity). Both notions, the individualization of crimes and the notion of complementarity, are points of dissenting views inherent to the evolution of international justice. The former seems less controversial than the latter, which posits the fundamental question of the sovereign rights of nations. Several thinkers and scholars argue that the question of sovereignty is not relevant in a world that is becoming more and more globalized, but it increasingly occupies central stage in international justice circles' conversations because of the *modus operandi* of the ICC.

National sovereignty characterizes the legitimate quest for self-determination of states and nations. It cherishes the independence of individual nations or states from other states or from international bodies such as the United Nations or its Security Council or the International Criminal Court. There is the widespread idea that the notion of sovereignty is solely used by some African countries in order to avoid and escape any international arbitration or the jurisdiction of the ICC for the alleged crimes of which they are accused. All countries, great powers, lesser powers, and small ones—the West and the rest—do not want to cede their sovereign rights to a globalized structure or to an international jurisdiction that vows to be universal. The crux of the matter is that all nations, even if they do not have a uniform understanding of the concept, remain jealous of their sovereignty.[88] When Russia signed the treaty and later refused to ratify it, it claimed that it sought to preserve its sovereignty. When American president Donald Trump appeared before the United Nations General Assembly and attacked the ICC, he claimed that it was in the name of US national interests and sovereignty.

The West and the ICC

I intend to demonstrate and highlight that the noble principles of the ICC are differently implemented depending on who the court's targets are. In international affairs driven by the realist theory, nations are in perpetual competition, and the strongest end up using the institutions and tools at their disposal to advance their national security interests to the detriment of others. In light of the last five hundred years of history, European nations enjoy a position of power that they want to maintain.

On November 8, 2005, the ICC presented its "First Report" to the United Nations General Assembly. The European Union publicly endorsed the resolutions related to the court and since has forcefully mobilized all bodies of its institution to assure and secure international support of the International

---

[88] David A. Nill, "National Sovereignty: Must It Be Sacrificed to the International Criminal Court?" *Brigham Young University Journal of Public Law* 14, no. 1 (1999): 132.

Criminal Court: the community, the Common Foreign Security Policy and the police, and the Judicial Cooperation in Criminal Matters.[89] One of the institutions Europeans control that was activated to support the ICC was the Africa, Caribbean, and Pacific Agreement (ACP), also known as the Cotonou Agreement, which was signed in 2000, renegotiated in 2005, and renewed in 2021. It was eventually renamed the Samoa Agreement. It is composed today of 79 countries that include 48 African states. It is a set of trade agreements that bind countries from Europe, the Caribbean, the Pacific, and Africa. The members of the commercial agreement are all bound into a multidimensional accord, which initially started as a common commercial trade deal, later took on a political dimension, and now encompasses judicial and criminal matters, namely issues related to the International Criminal Court. Several observers have denounced the lion's share that the European Union countries hold. They use it as a diplomatic tool to advance their foreign policy interests, to coerce other member countries (namely, African) to take decisions not always in the interest of Africa. It has been instrumental in bringing several countries to sign the Treaty of Rome and in preventing any withdrawal from the court.

Article 11.6 of the Cotonou Agreement commits its members to "(a) share experience on the adoption of legal adjustments required to allow for the ratification and implementation of the Rome Statute of the International Criminal Court and (b)…The parties shall seek to take steps towards ratifying and implementing the Rome Statute and related instruments."[90] Through this article, Europeans sought to make membership of the ICC a condition to remain a good member of the Cotonou Agreement. European countries threatened to withhold disbursement of funds and economic assistance to any country that was unwilling to abide by the regulations of the Cotonou Agreement. Case in point, Sudan:

> Sudan has chosen not to ratify the revised Cotonou Agreement by the legal deadline of 30th June 2009. This is due to a clause in the Agreement—which Sudan signed some time ago—encouraging the ACP to take "steps towards ratifying and implementing the Rome Statute and related instruments." The Rome Statute is the treaty that established the ICC; so far the revised Cotonou Agreement is the only binding legal instrument including an ICC-related clause…Since Cotonou provides the legal framework for relations between the EC and the ACP states, non-ratification by Sudan prevents the EC from implementing bilateral development cooperation in Sudan under our main financial instrument for development to developing countries, the 10th European Development Fund (EDF). This means that the EC will not be

---

[89] Hoile, *Justice Denied*, 39.

[90] Hoile, *Justice Denied*, 39.

able to disburse the 300 million Euros pledged at the May 2008 Sudan consortium for the period 2008–2013.[91]

In the following, the European Union clearly adjusted its new foreign policy, which combines from then on economic development and cooperation and trade to the adherence of the ICC clauses:

> The EU systematically seeks the inclusion of a clause supporting the ICC in negotiating mandates and agreements with third countries. So far, the revised Cotonou Agreement of 2005 which applies to 75 African, Caribbean and Pacific countries is the only binding legal instrument including an ICC-related clause. However, an ICC clause has been agreed to in the Partnership and Cooperation Agreements (PCAs), Trade Cooperation and Development Agreements (TDCAs) and Association Agreements (AAs) with Indonesia, South Korea, South Africa, Ukraine and Iraq. ICC clauses are currently being negotiated in the PCAs and AAs with Singapore, Thailand, Malaysia, The Philippines, Brunei Darussalam, Vietnam, China, Libya, Russia and Central America. The TDCA with South Africa was signed in September 2009 and the PCA with Indonesia in November 2009. Article 11 of the Cotonou Agreement forms the "standard clause" to be followed when negotiating other agreements, although it is of course necessary to adopt a case-by-case approach.[92]

In light of the preceding, it is therefore a myth to believe that African countries have freely and willingly maintained their adherence to the Rome Statute. In a hypocritical move, while using its soft power as a means of coercion, the European Union has been critical of the United States. The latter took measures to weaken the ICC or to cut military and economic assistance to countries that refuse to sign binding bilateral immunity agreements it proposed to them. Some of these measures are the Nethercutts Amendment and the American Servicemembers' Protection Act (ASPA). Congress passed the Nethercutt Act, named after US Congressman George Nethercutt, who pushed for a bill— which was adopted in December 2004—as a part of the Foreign Operations Appropriations Bill. This law is even broader than ASPA and allows the withdrawal of Economic Support Fund assistance to all countries, including some key US allies who have ratified the ICC Treaty but who did not sign the Bilateral Agreement of Immunity with the United States.[93]

---

[91] Hoile, *Justice Denied*, 39.

[92] Council of the European Union, General Secretariat of the Council, *The European Union and the International Criminal Court: May 2010* (Council of the European Union, 2011), 5.

[93] Hoile, *Justice Denied*, 40.

The furious reaction of John Bolton, a US national security expert, to the news that the ICC contemplated the idea of investigating crimes against humanity committed by the American forces and its intelligence community in Afghanistan and those committed by Israel against the Palestinians sums up the wrath of the United States against the ICC. US president Donald Trump reiterated the same feelings in a speech he delivered on September 25, 2018 before the 73rd United Nations General Assembly. He opposed globalism and argued that the United States has the right to preserve and protect its sovereignty. This position revives the long-standing stance of the United States vis-à-vis the ICC. In retaliation to the intention of the ICC to prosecute the crimes committed by US servicemen, the US government revoked the American visa of the ICC prosecutor, Fatou Bensouda, thus denying her entry to American soil. In reaction to this retaliation, the court adjusted, and its judges issued a declaration stating that an investigation into Afghanistan does not serve the interests of justice.[94] This statement was welcomed by the then US president Donald Trump, who argued that it served the interests of the rule of law.

Even though it is known that the United States has never been on good terms with the court, it is imperative to note that its leaders have dealt with the court differently. Three successive American presidents before Donald Trump had three different styles in dealing with the ICC. Under Bill Clinton, the United States watered down the treaty and signed it but could not ratify it due to opposition from several American stakeholders. George W. Bush fought the court and undermined it. Barack Obama restored a form of partnership with the court at the UN Security Council, voted to authorize the prosecution of alleged crimes committed by the Kadhafi regime but refused to submit the Rome Satute to the Senate for ratification.[95] None of them sought to put the full support of the United States behind the ICC, because all of them, in the name of American exceptionalism, did not want to see an American soldier or citizen be brought before a court outside the United States' jurisdiction. Deborah Madsen situates the significance of the concept of American exceptionalism in American history and politics: "American exceptionalism permeates every period of American history and is the single most powerful agent in a series of

---

[94] Sara L. Ochs, "The United States, the International Criminal Court, and the Situation in Afghanistan," *Notre Dame Law Review Reflection* 95, no. 2 (December 2019): 94.

[95] Sara L. Ochs, "The United States, the International Criminal Court, and the Situation in Afghanistan," 92.

arguments that have been fought down the centuries concerning the identity of America and Americans."[96]

American exceptionalism infers American self perception, and self-identification imbued with the self-conviction about the uniqueness of the United States to be endowed with the divine gifts to promote freedom, to bring to the world changes and to lead the march of civilization.[97]That concept which invokes the promise and the mission of the American nation, the distinctiveness of the American union which was perfected throughout history by the contributions of subsequent generations takes another connotation when it is applied to international law, international justice, to international relations, or to foreign relations. It is a major pillar of American foreign policy. This legal understanding of the concept is clearly expressed by Michael Ignatieff, quoted by David Hoile:

> American Exceptionalism also influences the practice of American policy, nowhere more so than in US approaches to international law and justice. Law, after all, constrains power, and the United States, like any great power, is likely to support a law-bound international order only if it ties up the power of its competitors more than it constrains its own. Other great powers have subscribed to this realist calculus in advancing international law. America is exceptional in combining standard great-power realism with extravagant idealism about the country's redemptive role in creating international order.[98]

To circumvent the court, some countries that joined it have amended their respective criminal codes to ensure that none of their nationals be brought to The Hague, or they expressed some reservations to the Treaty of Rome. Among these countries were two important players in world affairs, members of the United Nations Security Council: the United Kingdom and France. These two signed the treaty but made some prohibited reservations, according to Amnesty International.[99] France attempted to redefine the notion of "war crimes" and vowed not to recognize the court jurisdiction for seven good years over war crimes when and if they were committed by its citizens or on its

---

[96] Deborah L. Madsen, *American Exceptionalism* (Edinburgh: Edingburh University Press, 1998), 1.

[97] Jon Meacham, *The Soul of America: The Battle for our Better Angels* (New York: Random House, 2019), 9-10.

[98] Michael Ignatieff quoted by Hoile, *Justice Denied*, 70.

[99] Amnesty International, "International Criminal Court: Declarations Amounting to Prohibited Reservations to the Rome Statute," November 2005, https://www.amnesty.org/en/wp-content/uploads/2021/08/ior400322005en.pdf.

territory.[100] The western powers which undermine the ICC jurisdiction and authority still manage to use it to advance their respective interests or to break leaders (several from Africa) whom they see as adversaries or enemies. The next section deals with the duplicity of the western powers in their interaction with non-western countries (namely from Africa) in relation with the International Criminal Court.

The ICC, the West, and Africa: double-dealing and double standards

In this section, I intend to underline how the international justice system is being manipulated by the very powers who have either refused to support it or expressed some reservations towards it. The creation of the ICC was initially welcomed on the continent of Africa with strong support and strong enthusiasm, mainly for two reasons. The first reason was due to the rise of a stronger African civil society in a political environment marked by the progressive disappearance of the one-party-system model and the consolidation of democracy on the continent of Africa. The second reason, which derives from the first, was related to the political will of a new race of African leaders who genuinely expressed their willingness to combat impunity.[101]

The selectivity of the ICC prosecution turned the initial African enthusiasm into mistrust. Several critics of the ICC affirm there is an "(anti)-African bias" because the bulk of the court investigations concern African nations, while the court has been unable to start any serious investigations on some crises known to have caused heinous crimes. As an illustration, suffice it to mention the following eight cases before the court: Democratic Republic of Congo (DRC), Uganda, Central African Republic (CAR), Darfur (Sudan), Kenya, Libya, Ivory Coast, and Mali. It is important to underline that there are four self-referrals (Uganda, DRC, CAR, Mali), two ordained by the United Nations Security Council (Darfur and Libya), and two by the Office of the Prosecutor *proprio motu* (Kenya and Ivory Coast).[102]

The claims of the prosecutor to investigate crimes committed by non-Africans have been so far a wishful thinking. In January 2015, prosecutor Fatou Bensouda opened an investigation into the crimes committed in 2008 during the brief Russian Federation-Georgia war. In December 2017, she asked the

---

[100] Hoile, *Justice Denied*, 21.

[101] Makau W. Mutua, "Africans and the ICC: Hypocrisy, Impunity, and Perversion," in *Africa and the ICC: Perceptions of Justice*, eds. Kamari M. Clarke, Abel S. Knottnerus, and Eefje de Volder (Cambridge: Cambridge University Press, 2018), 52–53.

[102] Chris Maina Peter, "Fighting Impunity: African States and the International Criminal Court," in *The International Criminal Court and Africa*, ed. Ankumah, 15–16.

judges for permission to open an investigation into crimes committed in Afghanistan, including those of the US forces and the CIA. The Office of the Prosecutor also reopened a preliminary examination of the alleged crimes of the British Army in Iraq and one on crimes committed in Palestine by the state of Israel, following the ratification by the Palestinian Authority of the Rome Statute in the beginning of 2015. The ICC turned a blind eye to the American invasion of Iraq, which occurred one year after its creation, and ignored the moral call to investigate the NATO military expedition in Libya. The prosecutor also claimed to investigate modern-day slavery of the African migrants in Libya. None of the intentions to investigate these cases turned into reality and into real prosecution.

The ICC became a tool at the mercy of the Western powers, driven by hegemonic goals, who use it in the context of lawfare, defined as "...the use of the law as a weapon of war, or more specifically, the abuse of the law and legal systems for strategic political and military ends."[103] The position of these powers remains that of a double-dealing one as they use, misuse, and therefore abuse the court to advance their national security interests and to subdue some of their foes, thus throwing a stain on the credibility of the institution. Several leaders and stakeholders from the West, including the US president Joe Biden have suggested that the Russian president Vladimir Putin should be tried for the crimes related to the Russian invasion of Ukraine which was launched on February 24, 2022. It is important to recall that the United States has not ratified the Rome Statute, claims American exceptionalism, and is viewed as a warfare state[104] which uses lawfare to advance its geopolitical and strategic interests.

Kofi Annan, former UN Secretary-General, who initially was full of praise for the ICC, joined another chorus—that of those who questioned its credibility: "The question of credibility will persist so long as the most powerful with the veto right refuse to join the court."[105] The credibility of the court has been questioned recurrently in various cases: namely Congo, Kenya, Darfur, Libya, and Ivory Coast. In practice, in the execution of its mission, the ICC has alienated an important part of its stakeholders, a growing number of Africans who see it as an African court because most of its prisoners are of African origin and the bulk of the cases of the court concern African nations. The next section gives an account of the reactions of several African stakeholders to the ICC work

---

[103] David B. Harris and Aaron Eitan Meyer, "Lawfare: A Supporting Arm in Modern Conflict," *The Lawfare Project*, April 4, 2011, https://www.thelawfareproject.org/articles/2011/4/4/ ilawfare-a-supporting-arm-in-modern-conflictibrthe-lawfare-project.

[104] James Boggs, *The American Revolution: Pages from a Negro Workers Notebook* (New York and London: Monthly Review Press, 1963), 42.

[105] Kofi Annan, *Interventions: A Life in War and Peace* (New York, Penguin, 2012), 153.

and the double-dealing and the double standards from both world powers and the ICC itself.

In the lines that follow, I shed light on the uproar, the showdown, and the standoff between the court and Africans (African political elite, African activists and scholars) regarding some specific cases: Hissèn Habré (former president of Chad), Omar al-Bashir (former president of Sudan), Uhuru Kenyatta and William Ruto (the then president and vice president of Kenya), and Laurent Gbagbo (former president of Ivory Coast). These cases have stirred a multiplicity of views from a variety of stakeholders (political leaders of the African countries, the African Union, and the civil society and several leaders of opinion) who do not have a monolithic view of the issue of international justice.[106]

The attempts to try former president of Chad, Hissèn Habré—who ruled from 1982–1990 and who was accused of crimes against humanity in Belgium—had already caused some discomfort within African diplomatic circles. For several critics, it reminded them of the deportation of African leaders during slavery and colonialism. The former Chadian president was eventually tried in Senegal after a 25-year campaign. He could not be brought before the ICC, which only hears crimes committed after July 1, 2002.

Three ICC investigations damaged the relationship between the court and a variety of African stakeholders, mainly the African political elite: in Sudan against Omar al-Bashir, in Libya against the late Libyan leader Muammar al-Kadhafi's regime, and in Kenya against its then sitting president, Uhuru Kenyatta.

The deterioration of the relations between the ICC and the African leaders started in 2004 over the situation in Darfur. The five permanent members of the council turned to the court in 2005 for the crimes of Darfur. The United States voted to refer the Sudanese case to the International Criminal Court, and it is believed that it financed the investigations and the procedure that led to the indictment of Sudanese President Omar al-Bashir. UN resolution 1564 of September 18, 2004 authorized the investigation of crimes against humanity in Darfur. The commission established the responsibility of the Sudanese government and its former president Omar al-Bashir and recommended he be brought before the International Criminal Court for his alleged direct role in the killing of civilians and for his desire to destroy three main ethnic groups, the

---

[106] Gerard Kemp, "Taking Stock of International Criminal Justice in Africa: Three Inventories Considered," in *International Criminal Justice in Africa: Challenges and Opportunities*, ed. Beitel Van der Merwe (Nairobi, Kenya: Friedrich Ebert Stiftung, 2014), 11.

Fur, the Masalit, and Zaghawa.[107] The first ICC prosecutor Luis Moreno Ocampo clearly stated that the double responsibility of Bashir was established, moral and penal, in the genocide of Darfur, because he was the head of the state and because he oversaw and directed a genocide to prevent an uprising of the people of Darfur. In light of President Bashir's relations with the West, several scholars considered that the ICC had been instrumentalized as a tool of pressure and repression against a president who was leaning toward China.[108] Leaders of the African and Arab worlds expressed their opposition against the indictment of the Sudanese president by the International Criminal Court. The first arrest warrant was issued against the Sudanese president on March 4, 2009.

This was the first episode of a strained relationship between the court and the African leaders represented by the African Union. The African Union summit held in Sirte in July 2009 asked its members not to cooperate with the ICC regarding the indictment of the Sudanese president whom the court was seeking to arrest in his official visits to Kenya, Malawi, or South Africa: "[The Assembly] decides that in view of the fact that the request by the African Union has never been acted upon, the AU member states shall not cooperate pursuant to the provisions of Article 98 of the Rome Statute of the ICC related to immunities, for the arrest and surrender of President Omar al-Bashir of the Sudan."[109]

Former president of Malawi, Bingu wa Mutharika, then president of the AU, was one of the very first to openly denounce Omar al-Bashir's arrest warrant during the 2010 AU summit when he declared: "To subject a sovereign head of state to a warrant of arrest is undermining African solidarity and African peace and security that we fought for so many years. ... There is a general concern in Africa that the issuance of a warrant of arrest for ... al-Bashir, a duly elected president, is a violation of the principles of sovereignty guaranteed under the United Nations and under the African Union Charter. Maybe there are other ways of addressing this problem."[110]

The successor of the late Malawian president, Joyce Banda, faced tremendous pressure from the international community, led by the US-based development partners, to arrest al-Bashir of Sudan and hand him over to the ICC, in case the

---

107 Peter, "Fighting Impunity," 17.

108 Pierre Dagbo Godé, *La Diplomatie Africaine: Théorie et Pratique* (Paris: L'Harmattan, 2014), 122.

109 African Union, "Decision on the Abuse of the Principle of Universal Jurisdiction," Assembly of the African Union Thirteenth Ordinary Session, July 3, 2009.

110 Max Du Plessis, *The ICC that Africa wants* (Pretoria: Institute for Security Studies, 2010), 18.

latter decided to attend an African Union meeting about to be held in that country. She was willing to comply in order to satisfy the demands of these development partners, whose funding she needed in order to deal with the dire economic conditions of her country. She eventually declined to host the meeting, which was relocated in Addis Ababa in Ethiopia.[111]

The denunciation of the ICC by the former president of Malawi set the pace for a series of open attacks by African leaders and eventually led to the threat of a collective withdrawal from the court of African countries. At the request of Kenya, the African Union decided to take a stance on the issue of the African collective withdrawal from the ICC and organized a summit that debated the burning question of the relationship between Africa and the ICC on October 11–12, 2013. After two days of meeting, African countries instead decided to send a strong message to denounce the harassment of the ICC against Africa, but they still committed to honor their responsibilities vis-à-vis the court. The African Union opposed the prosecution of any sitting African president and called for the suspension of the prosecution of Uhuru Kenyatta. At the meeting called by the AU to discuss the Kenya case before the ICC, Kenyan president Uhuru Kenyatta charged the ICC: "We would love nothing more than to have an international forum for justice and accountability, but what choice do we have when we get only bias and race-hunting at ICC? ... If so, what justice can be rendered by a court which disregards our views? ... Like other African countries, Kenya did not achieve its independence with ease. Blood was shed for it."[112]

African leaders refused to open an ICC office at the AU headquarters in Addis Ababa. The tension further escalated between the African Union and the court around the continental body's heads of states summit, June 14–15, 2015 in Johannesburg (South Africa). The host country was expected to honor its obligations as a state party of the court, since it had signed membership on November 27, 2000. The court expected the South African government to disinvite the Sudanese president—or to arrest him and hand him over. Instead, the host country managed to preserve the safety of al-Bashir and facilitate his return to his country.[113] South Africa, like members of the African Union and state parties of the ICC, was torn between two competing obligations: the respect of Article 98 of the Rome Statute, which suggests the obligation of ICC state parties to arrest any alleged criminal wanted by the court, and Article 23

---

[111] Clarke, *Affective Justice*, 22-24.

[112] Peter, "Fighting Impunity," 27.

[113] Max Du Plessis, "Exploring Efforts to Resolve the Tension between the AU and the ICC over the Bashir Saga," in *The International Criminal Court and Africa*, ed. Ankumah, 246.

of the African Union, which asks its members not to cooperate with the ICC.[114] Godfrey M. Musila lamented: "In four short years, the AU moved from a stance supportive of the ICC, to less than enthusiastic and obstructionist."[115]

The threat from Africa to withdraw from the International Criminal Court occurred in three episodes. Burundi was the first African country which actually withdrew from the court as a reaction to the court's plan to investigate human rights abuses committed by the then president Pierre Nkurunziza against his countrymen. The Burundians protested against a constitutional change he made to extend his tenure as the president of the country.

The Gambia threatened to leave the court in November 2016 as a way to protest about what the then leader of the country Yahya Jammeh, who allegedly committed various human rights abuses during his term in power, considered judicial harassment of the court against African leaders. A Gambian official vehemently charged: "Despite being called International Criminal Court, [it] is in fact an International Caucasian Court for the persecution and humiliation of people of colour, especially Africans."[116]

South Africa, which was a staunch supporter of the ICC, had a strained relationship with the court under Jacob Zuma. The former president of South Africa was also instructed and pressed to arrest Omar al-Bashir on South African soil, in order to hand him over to the court. South Africa ignored the court's request. In the face of international pressure, the country wrote a letter of withdrawal from the court to the UN on October 2016. Judge Phineas Mojapelo of the High Court in Pretoria blocked the withdrawal, arguing that the letter of withdrawal was unconstitutional, null, and void because it had not been preceded by an approval of the South African Parliament.[117]

The tension between African leaders and the court escalated over the Kenya case, which inflated the growing discontent against the international justice system. The Kenyan 2008 presidential election—which opposed the sitting president Mwai Kibaki with Raila Odinga, the leader of the opposition—led to an electoral stalemate. It resulted in the death of hundreds of people and led to

---

[114] Du Plessis, "Exploring Efforts," 255.

[115] Godfrey M. Musila, "The Role of the African Union in International Criminal Justice: For Good or Bad?" in *The International Criminal Court and Africa*, ed. Ankumah, 322.

[116] Al Jazeera, "Gambia withdraws from the International Criminal Court" Al Jazeera, October 25, 2016, https://www.aljazeera.com/news/2016/10/26/gambia-withdraws-from-international-criminal-court.

[117] Joseph Cotteril, "Court rules against South Africa decision to leave ICC" Financial Times February 22, 2017, https://www.ft.com/content/f7561a18-f8ee-11e6-9516-2d969e0d3b65.

prosecution by the ICC. The former ICC prosecutor, Luis Moreno Ocampo, had played along with the West by choosing his targets and designating two potential candidates for the 2013 presidential election, Uhuru Kenyatta and William Ruto (representing two different sides), while sparing their favorite, Raila Odinga.

The two leaders at odds with each other decided to join hands during the 2013 presidential election, thus creating a sacred union for peace and victory. Uhuru Kenyatta became president with William Ruto as his vice president.[118] The United States was accused of meddling in the electoral process and of attempting to sway the votes of the Kenyans. Johnnie Carson, then Assistant Secretary of State for African Affairs in the Obama administration, declared before the election that "choices have consequences" when pressed to answer questions about the candidacy of Kenyatta and Ruto in light of their prosecution before the ICC: "We live in an interconnected world and people should be thoughtful about the impact that their choices have on their nation, on the region, on the economy, on the society and on the world in which they live. Choices have consequences."[119]

The two opposing sides, represented by the two indicted by the ICC, created a new political formation called Jubilee Coalition. Uhuru Kenyatta and Ruto, with this sign "UhuRuto" on campaign insignia, managed to escape not only the court but they also sought to implement a form of restorative justice which is at odds with the model of punitive justice of the ICC. The presidential ticket UhuRuto was perceived as the symbol of national healing of Kenyans, national unification of Kenya sustained by a campaign slogan in Swahili "Tuko Pamoja" which means "We are together." But the hashtag #Kenyadecides was more of a political stance of defiance by the presidential candidates against external interference. Clarke depicts the feeling in the Kenyan press as follows: "The message that the ICC process is deeply political and reproduces older patterns of European colonialism in African affairs, while ignoring Europe's responsibility for its part in Kenya's contemporary violence, continues to resonate and circulate throughout the Kenyan press."[120]

---

[118] Stéphanie Maupas, "Victoire pour le Kenya à la Cour pénale internationale," *Le Monde*, December 9, 2014, http://www.lemonde.fr/idees/article/2014/12/09/victoire-pour-le-kenya-a-la-cour-penale-internationale_4537601_3232.html.

[119] Gabe Joselow, "US Official Says Kenya's Elections Have 'Consequences,'" VOA, February 7, 2013, https://www.voanews.com/a/us-official-says-kenya-elections-have-consequences/1599063.html.

[120] Clarke, *Affective Justice*, 143.

This caused tension and contention between Kenya and the ICC on one hand and the African Union and the ICC on the other hand. Kenya was divided along two conflicting positions: attachment to the popular sovereignty of the people expressed through the ballots, and pressure from the international arbitration of the ICC to prosecute the newly elected president. For many, the demands for international justice by the ICC against Uhuru Kenyatta underlined the preeminence of international laws over national laws, and thus were an attempt to undermine the sovereignty of the independent state of Kenya.

The prosecution of Uhuru Kenyatta had resonance and significance. He is the son of former president of Kenya, Jomo Kenyatta, who was a freedom fighter and who was imprisoned by the British colonial rulers for his alleged involvement in the Mau Mau resistance. He spent six years in prison and was freed, later to lead his nation to independence in 1963. In the minds of many in Kenya, the ICC prosecution of Uhuru Kenyatta was a resumption of the assault his father went through. The Rwandan president Paul Kagame denounced the will of the international community to derail the efforts of Kenyans to build peace after the two leaders previously prosecuted by the ICC came together to run on the same ticket and won the presidential election of 2013. Their election was also seen as cement for restoration and peace in Kenya.[121] Despite Uhuru Kenyatta's election, the ICC persisted in insisting that he be handed over. Hailemariam Desalegn, then Ethiopian prime minister and elected chairman of the African Union (AU) in 2013, openly accused the International Criminal Court of racism against African leaders: "African leaders have come to a consensus that the [ICC] process that has been conducted in Africa has a flaw...The intention was to avoid any kind of impunity...but now the process has degenerated to some kind of race hunting."[122]

The third case that exposed the court's collusion with some powerful nations was that of Libya. The five permanent members of the Security Council who turned to the court in 2005 for the crimes of Darfur resorted to it six years later for those crimes committed during the Libyan crisis. In the middle of the conflict, European officials threatened to resort to it, thus transforming it into a tool of pressure and a "sword of Damocles." They hoped to provoke defections in the ranks of the Kadhafi regime which was facing a rebellion in 2010-2011. An uprising started in the eastern part of the country in Benghazi, in the context of the Arab Spring which resulted in the overthrow of Hosni Mubarak of Egypt, Abidine Ben Ali of Tunisia, and eventually in the assassination of the former

---

[121] Maupas, "Victoire pour le Kenya."

[122] Godé, *La Diplomatie Africaine*, 133.

Libyan leader Muammar al-Kadhafi. The Libyan rebels benefitted from the military intervention and bombing by the NATO forces.[123]

The United Nations took two resolutions, the first of which (1970) imposed a no-fly zone on Libyan air space and the other (1973) whose goal was to allow NATO to intervene in order "to protect the civilians supposedly massacred" by the Kadhafi regime.[124] The West and its surrogates called the military uprising against the former Libyan regime, led by some militants linked to the terrorist group Al-Qaeda, a revolution that would bring democracy and freedom to Libya. They supported the insurgents and rebels, and eventually NATO intervened, resulting in the assassination of Kadhafi and the overthrow of his regime. A decade after the fall of Kadhafi, Libya is in shambles, divided into portions in the hands of competing groups in the context of insecurity and unlawfulness.

The ICC issued three arrest warrants against the former Libyan regime, in the middle of the crisis, against Muammar al-Kadhafi, his son Saif al-Islam designated heir to the throne, and the head of his military intelligence Abdullah al-Senoussi. During the crisis, several institutions and personalities, including the news organization *Al-Jazeera*, Hillary Clinton, Susan Rice, and the former ICC prosecutor Moreno Ocampo, repeated in chorus that Kadhafi had ordered Viagra for his soldiers so that they could rape women in the context of a careful conceived state strategy whose goal would be to humiliate the insurgents. This turned out to be fake news, as there was no evidence of such accusation, which was spread in international circles and media.[125]

In order to show support to the rebels, the former leaders of the United Kingdom and France, David Cameron and Nicolas Sarkozy, flew to the capital of the rebellion in Benghazi. There they mentioned the indictment by the ICC of the Libyan leader, who was eventually captured, sodomized, and beaten by the rebels, who exposed his body in a public market to be seen by the common man in Libya and by people across the globe thanks to social media and news organizations. Moreno Ocampo refused to open an investigation into the assassination of Kadhafi, which was not a war crime in his opinion. This selective prosecution was denounced by the Russian Federation on May 2012. The court ignored calls by Nigeria and South Africa to investigate the human rights abuses suffered by the African migrants accused of being the mercenaries of the regime and those endured by the descendants of black slaves called Tawerghas (expelled from their place of origin, Tawergha). Both

---

[123] Campbell, *Global NATO*, 18.

[124] Campbell, *Global NATO*, 67–73.

[125] Maupas, *Le Joker des Puissants*, 22–23.

groups had been victims of the insurgents' vendetta. But the court mobilized several networks in diplomatic circles for the transfer to The Hague of Addullah al-Senoussi and Saif al-Islam, who were eventually captured by the rebels after the fall of the Kadhafi regime.

The staggering numbers of the military expedition, which lasted seven months (March 31 to October 31) revealed that NATO flew more than 26,000 sorties, including more than 9,000 strike sorties, and launched more than 100 Tomahawks in various parts of Libya. Observers concluded that thousands of civilians were killed by the NATO air strikes, but the court did not welcome the idea of investigating its crimes. Moreno Ocampo argued that the Western military expedition did not have any criminal intention against civilians and based his decision not to investigate the NATO crimes on a UN report which concluded that only 60 civilians were killed and 55 people injured by the bombings.[126]

When Fatou Bensouda took over, she managed to prosecute the Kadhafists and found herself in an imbroglio with the United Nations and Western powers, who were unwilling to provide her with the necessary cooperation that her office needed. The new government of Libya committed to try Abdallah al-Senoussi and Saif al-Islam Kadhafi in Libya. Fatou Bensouda had proposed a diplomatic solution for the Tawergha issue at the United Nations. Her suggestion remained another wishful thinking.[127] The Libyan rebels have been exculpated. Since then, not a single Libyan insurgent has appeared before the ICC judges. Saif al-Islam—who was in prison in the stronghold of the rebels in the eastern part of the country which sparked the rebellion—was released in the spring of 2018. He attempted to run for president in Libya and his candidacy was rejected by the authorities of his country.

One case has captivated the imagination of a variety of stakeholders, even though it was not of interest for African presidents who barely discussed it during the African Union meetings, that of Laurent Gbagbo, which is discussed in the next section of this book.

France, the ICC, and Ivory Coast

The role of France in Africa also compromises the legitimacy of the ICC's actions. France can maneuver to ask for the prosecution against any leader who does not want to respect its dominance over its former colonies. French leaders alongside American officials hinted during the electoral stalemate that Gbagbo

---

[126] Campbell, *Global NATO*, 163–169.

[127] Maupas, *Le Joker des Puissants*, 50.

would be prosecuted by the ICC, even before an arrest warrant was issued against him.

Paul D. Schmitt discussed the credibility issue of the ICC in light of France's role in Africa and in international justice. Before elaborating on the credibility issue, Schmitt gave a brief overview of France's support for international justice. In its support of international justice and of the ICC, France modified its code of criminal procedure in August 2010 and aligned it with universal jurisdiction requirements regarding war crimes and genocide. It also amended Article 53 of its constitution as an illustration of its endorsement of the Rome Statute.

Besides the legal compliance with international law recommendations and universal criminal matters, France helped and contributed to the indictment of a number of prominent figures, including Mauritanian Army officer Ely Ould Dah, accused of ordering acts of torture against militants of a failed armed rebellion that occurred in 1990–1991. Kaled was condemned in absentia for his alleged role in cases of torture in Tunisia. A French judge built a case against nine close aides of President Kagame and urged that they be the recipients of international arrest warrants for their alleged role in the assassination of a French ally, Habyarimana, former president of Rwanda, who died in a plane crash, a tragic event that led to the Rwandan genocide. In 2006, French troops escorted Thomas Lubanga, the first to be tried by the ICC, to The Hague. In 2010, French police also facilitated the arrest in Paris of Calixte Mbarushimana, a former DRC rebel. France also helped build the case for the ICC in its indictment of President Bashir of Sudan in 2005. It was one of the powers to publicly suggest Kadafhi, the late former leader of Libya, be tried by the ICC.[128]

Regarding the specific issue of French involvement in international justice that observers have attributed to neo-colonialism, Paul D. Schmitt declared:

> France is particularly vulnerable to the "neocolonialist" critique given its historical and ongoing role in Africa. Once an imperial power, France maintained a significant presence in Africa, both before and after decolonization and has often intervened militarily to preserve favoured regimes, in the spirit of Françafrique. Further, it has long been one of the court's major supporters, as it was one of the first signatories of the Rome Statute and has taken an active role in encouraging the prosecution of crimes carried out during wars in Libya, Côte d'Ivoire, and Mali. France's unique standing as both former colonial power and present military intervener in Africa can serve to undermine France's

---

[128] Paul D. Schmitt, "France, Africa, and the ICC: The Neo-Colonialist Critique and the Crisis of Institutional Legitimacy," in *Africa and the ICC*, eds. Clarke, Knottnerus, and Volder, 131–132.

endorsement of the Court as a proper instrument of post-conflict justice.[129]

The Gbagbo case has exposed how the French officials manipulated the court. Even before the arrest of Gbagbo and his transfer to The Hague, the very first officials to allude to his eventual indictment by the ICC were Westerners. Nicolas Sarkozy declared during the electoral stalemate about Laurent Gbagbo: "It is up to him [Gbagbo] to choose what image he wants to leave to history. If he wants to leave the image of a man of peace, there is still time, but time is running out, and he has to go...Or, does he want to leave the image of someone who shot at completely innocent civilians? And in this case, there are international courts and the ICC. The ICC prosecutor himself has said that he has closely monitored the situation and those who have caused the shooting will be brought to justice."[130]

The then minister of foreign affairs of France, Alain Juppé, declared months later in April 2011: "As for Gbagbo's fate, it's neither for me nor for the French government to decide. There will be judicial proceedings: Ivorian, if that's what the Ivorian government decides, or international if the International Criminal Court continues the investigation unto Gbagbo."[131] Questioned by a journalist about a possible ICC prosecution against him for his alleged crimes in the Ivorian crisis, Guillaume Soro, former rebel leader, said bluntly: "I headed, as Prime Minister and Minister of Defense, the Republican Forces of Ivory Coast who have acted in concert with the international community, I say, the international community."[132] The chief prosecutor Moreno was therefore justified to welcome at The Hague Blaise Compaoré on November 9, 2011. He also met with Guillaume Soro, former rebel leader, in New York on December 15, 2011, and later he sent him a message of congratulations for his election as the Speaker of the House of Ivory Coast.[133]

Guillaume Soro, the rebel leader added his note to the chorus of threats about the ICC ordained and planned indictment of Gbagbo: "But if Laurent Gbagbo is going to keep killing civilians ... it will obviously be his duty to report to the

---

129 Schmitt, "France, Africa, and the ICC," 128.

130 Le Monde, "La Pression Internationale contre Laurent Gbagbo s'accentue," *Le Monde*, December 17, 2010, https://www.lemonde.fr/afrique/article/2010/12/17/sarkozy-enjoint-a-gbagbo-de-quitter-le-pouvoir-avant-la-fin-de-la-semaine_1454779_3212.html.

131 Alain Juppé, "France/UN/Côte d'Ivoire – Libya/French role/NATO role," interview given by Alain Juppé, Ministre d'Etat, Minister of Foreign and European Affairs, to "France Info," Paris, April 12, 2011.

132 Pigeaud, *France Côte d'Ivoire*, 332.

133 Pigeaud, *France Côte d'Ivoire*, 332.

International Criminal Court."[134] After the fall of the former president of Ivory Coast on April 11, 2011, France sped up its plan to definitively neutralize him by executing a covert operation with the complicity of the ICC. The Treaty of Rome was not ratified yet by Ivory Coast at the time of Gbagbo's arrest. The court had not yet started any investigation and had not yet issued an arrest warrant against him, but a plan was in progress to have him prosecuted by the ICC. The motives of the legal prosecution against Gbagbo were not judicial but political: "But in reality, a secret plan was afoot to make sure Gbagbo was definitively removed from any future involvement in Ivory Coast politics."[135] Fanny Pigeaud revealed the emails exchanged between a French official, Stéphane Gompertz, in charge of the African Affairs and the then chief prosecutor of the ICC, Luis Moreno Ocampo:

> In Paris, the head of the African affairs department of the French foreign ministry, Stéphane Gompertz, sent out an email that same day, April 11th, 2011, addressed to several officials and diplomats within both the ministry and also at the presidential office, the Elysée Palace. In his email, Gompertz said a French official who worked with Luis Moreno Ocampo, then chief prosecutor of the International Criminal Court (ICC) in The Hague, had "just called me." "The prosecutor would like 1/ that Ouattara does not release Gb," continued Gompertz, referring to Gbagbo, "and 2/ a state in the region send the case to the ICC as fast as possible," adding: "Ocampo will try to contact Ouattara or one of his close entourage.[136]

It is imperative to recall that Ivory Coast acknowledged the ICC jurisdiction in 2003. This acknowledgement was confirmed in 2010 and reconfirmed the following year, but it was not until 2013 that Ivory Coast ratified the Rome Statute. The prosecutor started a *proprio motu* investigation in October 2011. Gbagbo was finally transferred to The Hague on November 30, 2011. Again, the timing of his transfer was not coincidental. The new regime and its international supporters, including the ICC, wanted him out of the country, secluded in The Hague before the legislative elections, which were planned for December 11, 2011: "True, President Alassane Ouattara had been firm since he

---

[134] Tim Cocks and Andrew Quinn, "Exile or Sanctions: Ivory Coast's Gbagbo Told," *Reuters*, December 17, 2010, https://www.reuters.com/article/us-ivorycoast/exile-or-sanctions-ivory-coasts-gbagbo-told-idUSTRE6BG3ID20101217.

[135] Fanny Pigeaud, "The Devious Manoeuvres behind ex-Ivorian Leader Laurent Gbagbo's Trial at ICC," *Mediapart*, October 8, 2017, https://www.mediapart.fr/en/journal/international/081017/devious-manoeuvres-behind-ex-ivorian-leader-laurent-gbagbos-trial-icc?_locale=en&onglet=full.

[136] Pigeaud, "The Devious Manoeuvres."

took power in April that Mr. Gbagbo would face justice at The Hague, and those close to him worked hard to make sure the transfer happened before the 11 December legislative elections."[137] Gbagbo appeared before the court on December 5, 2011. For his appearance, he alluded to French neo-colonialism: "I was arrested under the French bombs. It was the French army that did the job."[138] The above-discussed diplomatic and political incidents contributed to enrich an array of views among African leaders of opinion.

The ICC: African bias and dissenting voices

A decade after its creation, the International Criminal Court's inability to undertake fair prosecution and to provide fair trials caused a mounting legitimate suspicion against the court of targeting Africans. One proponent of the court acknowledged, "While it cannot be seriously argued that the investigations already opened in Africa are unwarranted, the Prosecutor must be mindful that atrocities are also being committed across the globe, an over focus on Africa not only damages the court's credibility as an international institution but also its global mission to combat impunity."[139] Another advocate of the court, Desmond Tutu, gave a lukewarm assessment of the way the court tried to implement justice: "While it is indeed troubling that the International Criminal Court mostly seems to call to account dictators with brown skin, Tony Blair is not in the same moral category as Charles Taylor. The war in Iraq was not a systematic genocide or ethnic cleansing. All of this may well be tested in court one day."[140]

Philippe Sands, a pro-ICC scholar who had been in favor of an international arbitration and of the existence of the International Criminal Court, could not ignore an obvious weakness of the court:

> The more serious concern is the danger of lopsided international justice, a world of laws that are "spider webs through which the big flies pass and the little ones get caught," as Balzac put it. Look on the website of the ICC and see who is in the dock. Every one of the faces and names is African. Yet Africa plainly does not have a monopoly on international crime, and this unhappy and lopsided picture tends to give force to the critique that international justice is pro-Western and controlled by the

137 John James, "Gbagbo transfer to the Hague shocks supporters," BBC, November 30, 2011, https://www.bbc.com/news/world-africa-15962777.

138 Schmitt, "France, Africa, and the ICC," 137.

139 Khan, "Ten Years of International Criminal Court," 435.

140 Giles Fraser, "Desmond Tutu Should Not Have Snubbed Tony Blair," *The Guardian*, September 3, 2012, https://www.theguardian.com/commentisfree/2012/sep/03/desmond-tutu-snubbed-tony-blair.

victors. One wonders quite what it will take, for example, for a proper international investigation of the well-documented allegations of torture and other abuse at Bagram and elsewhere in Afghanistan, a country that has been a party statute since 2003.[141]

Fatou Bensouda, the ICC chief prosecutor rejected the anathema of the ICC "African bias." She summed up her perspective in the following words: "However, this is unfortunately not the story relayed in the media. Again and again, we hear criticisms about our so-called focus on Africa and about the court being an African court, having an African bias. Anti-ICC elements have been working very hard to discredit the court and to lobby for non-support and they are doing this, unfortunately, with complete disregard for legal arguments."[142]

There are genuine dissenting views on the question of international law between the African Union and the ICC. For the African Union, "International justice is seen as an impediment to peace and that the two are mutually exclusive." The ICC "stands for justice for victims irrespective of the situation."[143] Several other scholars, such as Olufemi Taiwo, do not agree with the AU perspective and denounce it as a morally bankrupt institution:

> The irony is lost on our rulers that they are demanding the world's respect while they disrespect their citizens. What respect do African leaders have for the more than 1,000 Kenyans who perished in the post-election violence? Or for the tens of thousands that have fallen victim to Omar al-Bashir's goons and killer squads in Darfur? Or the 3,000 or more Ivorian citizens that perished when Gbagbo elected to defy the expressed will of the plurality of Ivorian voters?[144]

The ICC chief prosecutor, Fatou Bensouda, weighed in on the debate and expressed two fundamental points of her stance and her worldview as she

---

[141] Philippe Sands, "International justice is needed—even if it takes 100 more years to perfect it," *The Guardian*, May 16, 2012, https://www.theguardian.com/law/2012/may/16/international-justice-needed-expert-view.

[142] David Smith, "New Chief Prosecutor Defends International Criminal Court," *The Guardian*, May 23, 2012, https://www.theguardian.com/law/2012/may/23/chief-prosecutor-international-criminal-court.

[143] Stephen Lamony, "African Court Not Ready for International Crimes," African Arguments, December 10, 2012. https://africanarguments.org/2012/12/10/african-court-not-ready-for-international-crimes-by-steven-lamony/.

[144] Olufemi Taiwo, "The African Union and the Moral Abdication," *Pambazuka News*, November 20, 2013, https://www.pambazuka.org/governance/african-union-and-moral-abdication.

claimed the support of some members of the African civil society whom she praised. The first point is expressed as follows: "The decade-old court has sought justice for millions of victims in the Democratic Republic of the Congo, Uganda, the Central African Republic, Darfur in Sudan, Kenya, Libya and Ivory Coast. ... We have done it with strong cooperation of African State Parties and we have benefitted from the commitment and support of our partners within African civil society."[145] The second point of Fatou Bensouda contrasts with the ICC prosecutorial rationale and strategy in several countries, namely in DRC, Kenya, and in Ivory Coast: "Real justice is not a pick and choose system. To be effective, to be just and to have a lasting impact, justice has to be guided solely by the law and the evidence. Our focus is on individual criminal behaviour against innocent victims. My focus is on Joseph Kony, on Bosco Ntaganda, on Ahmad Harun, on Omar al-Bashir."[146]

Makau W. Mutua, in his paper "Africans and the ICC: Hypocrisy, Impunity, and Perversion," as an advocate of the ICC attempted to give a dialectical analysis of the relations between the ICC and Africans. First, he sided with the above-mentioned thinkers who argued that the ICC will suffer from a legitimacy issue as long as it is incapable of prosecuting non-Africans: "In my view, the ICC will not be able to blunt the charges of a racist agenda if it cannot produce indictments of senior officials from continents other than Africa. It will not suffice to promise investigations outside Africa. ICC Chief Prosecutor Fatou Bensouda must aggressively pursue perpetrators without regard to station, race, identity, and national origin for the ICC to be seen to do justice without fear, favour, or prejudice."[147]

He elaborated on why Africans are generally suspicious of international law, as it was used to legitimize a series of systems of exploitation, expropriation, and dispossession, such as slavery, colonialism, and neo-colonialism and rejected the view of those who, among the African leaders, want to dismiss the credibility and the legitimacy of the court:

> Yet those who attack the ICC seem to suffer from historical amnesia and selective memory. Their arguments want to place all the blame for the trauma of Africa on the European West. This is an apology for the sins of their fathers and hypocritical Pan-Africanism by ruling elites and their ideologues. They deliberately pervert history to hoodwink ordinary Africans and play on white guilt. I reject this false historical narrative

---

145 Smith, "New Chief Prosecutor."

146 Smith, "New Chief Prosecutor."

147 Mutua, "Africans and the ICC," 47.

and its sinister attempt to hijack the stories of genuine Pan-Africanism
and the pain of victims to maintain bankrupt African elites in power.[148]

This is a valid statement but one which falls short, because Makau does not
expand on the detrimental role of European colonial powers who put into place
a global structure and used all means to undermine a spirit of national
sovereignty and economic independence of the non-West, namely Africans.
Chris Maina Peter sided with Makau; he echoed his stance and depicted a
picture of impunity in Africa and argued that African leaders reject Western
interference in their national affairs but yet denounce those who maintain
themselves in power through the rigging of elections and others who convert
their military uniforms into civilian coats.[149] Chris Maina Peter failed to take
into account the disastrous impact of external forces in Africa when he
declared: "Therefore, while the 1960s were years of hope, the 1970s turned into
a nightmare for the majority of Africans. It was during that period that dictators
like Idi Amin Dada of Uganda, Emperor Bokassa of the so-called Central African
Empire, and Macias Nguema of Equatorial Guinea ruled with iron fist."[150]

This above-mentioned narrative suggests that Africa is suffering only from
the stigmas of past systems of exploitations, as if the continent were completely
free and that the faulty African leaders were the exclusive victimizers of the
African people, using their free will to kill and impoverish their citizens. His
argument implies also that the international relations system is not driven by
the realist theory and ignores the weight of neo-colonialism in Africa. The ICC
may say that it is apolitical and that it does not only target Africans, the truth is
that when we observe the racial origin of those who are in the dock of the court,
the argument of the court cannot stand.

Kamari Clarke, in light of this situation, proposed an anthropological
understanding of justice she calls "Affective Justice." This stipulates that legal
triumphalism, which looks at criminal matters solely from the exclusive lenses
of victim/perpetrator paradigm, is limited and does not express multiple
understandings of justice. That prism, she argues does not encompass nor does
it redress historical wrongs and injustices. She suggests that taking into account
the historical landscapes, the geographical spaces, current geopolitical
contingencies, and emotional imaginaries charged with a long and unending
tradition of exploitation marked by subsequent systems of exploitation,
dispossession, and of dehumanization such as the Atlantic slave trade,
colonialism, apartheid, and neo-colonialism is necessary to acknowledge and

---

[148] Mutua, "Africans and the ICC," 48.
[149] Peter, "Fighting Impunity," 11–12.
[150] Peter, "Fighting Impunity," 11-12.

interpret the multiple stories, narratives, and meanings of justice. She contends that:

> [The theory of affective justice] departs from the atomized victim/ survivor/perpetrator models or state-centric theories of sovereignty. Instead it clarifies that international criminal justice as a site of contemporary contestations can only be understood as an assemblage of component parts that are activated through complex interrelationships.
>
> ...At the center of the rule of law movement are not only histories of proclamations, treaties, laws, categories like "victims" and "perpetrators", and so forth; there is also the sensorium-feelings, smells, sounds, historical narratives-that informs the work of international justice. They inspire feelings of righting past wrongs, which is at the heart of the international justice project.[151]

As she builds the case for affective justice, Clarke sheds light on the stance of a group of the ICC stakeholders who, claiming Pan-Africanism, have rejected the exclusive understanding of justice by the court and its prosecutors. In the course of her research for her book, *Affective Justice: The International Criminal Court and the Pan-Africanist Pushback*, during which Clarke and her team interviewed hundreds of the ICC stakeholders including staff of the African Union in Addis Ababa, she became more aware of a narrative on the continent of Africa embedded in the Pan-African discourse, often, in good faith, expressed by people and agencies of all walks of life:

> Time and time again, as we spoke with interlocutors on the African continent—politicians, academics, leaders, judges, investigators, diplomats, lawyers, children, survivors of violence, the homeless, and members of NGOs and of civil society, it was clear that international law—with its temporal and spatial particularities—was seen as both a beacon of possibility and the basis for the continued plunder and inequality in Africa. But with justice articulated through the support or rejection of the ICC or the support or rejection of an African court with criminal jurisdiction it was also clear that the validity of my colleagues' positions at the meeting that day, and many meetings before and after, were not rendered legitimate because of their experience or facts, but because of the profound affective performance and sentimentalism that accompanied their speech acts and the institutionalized forms that reinforced such narratives.[152]

---

151 Clarke, *Affective Justice*, 21.

152 Clarke, *Affective Justice*, xxiii.

The experts of international justice have resisted calls to take into account these voices which have been marginalized as they have been seen as belonging to the periphery. Clarke rightly and rightfully advocates an African-centered and driven understanding of international justice which opposes and deconstructs the western hegemonic understanding of justice:

> This reorientation of justice focuses on the way histories of plunder and unequal political economic formations in African countries are encapsulating alternate iconic affects—not just the anticolonial freedom fighter but figures like the displaced villager as well. These are now being packaged and disseminated through counter campaigning strategies and affective performances which insist that legal solutions must be firmly linked to a broader dismantling of neocolonial structures of oppression that Africans encounter at every level, from the rural villager to the cosmopolitan head of state. Thus, through the power of reattribution, an emergent African geography of justice is developing as a counterpoint to what is seen as hegemonic structures of Western approaches to international justice.[153]

In her seminal work dedicated to the Pan-Africanist pushback against the ICC, Clarke omitted another manifestation of the Pan-Africanist pushback: The rejection of the court by a number of its stakeholders, a community of Pan-Africanists not those who represent the African Union or the African leaders but those who are common citizens of Africa. They have stood up against western hegemonic implementation of justice. If there was a case which has mobilized Pan-African agents over a decade it was that of Laurent Gbagbo, the first African head of state to be prosecuted and indicted by the ICC. Clark barely addresses the Laurent Gbagbo's trial in her insightful and seminal work of more than 300 pages. The next chapter focuses on the singularity of Laurent Gbagbo's trial, which still shares several common features with other African cases and which remains a vivid illustration of the expression of both the realist theory and neo-colonialism.

---

[153] Clarke, *Affective Justice*, 30.

Chapter 3

The ICC and Ivory Coast: justice, peace, and neo-colonialism

As elucidated in the previous chapter, the Laurent Gbagbo's trial was not an object of concern for the AU leaders. There was a sententious consensus about the case of the former Ivorian president, as if it was not a case through which the rationale of the ICC could be questioned. Several stakeholders demonstrated a selective militantism and concern. They were vocal about the Kenyan case and silent regarding Laurent Gbagbo's trial. Their silence can be equated to an avowal of an endorsement of injustice. The self-righteous freedom fighters and justice advocates did not seek to find out if Ivory Coast had effectively abided by the democratic principles under Alassane Ouattara or if Laurent Gbagbo's detention in Korhogo respected the Geneva conventions regarding the conditions of prisoners.

This chapter begins by raising these issues. The bulk of it discusses the investigation, the prosecution, the trial per se, the conflicting approaches, of the prosecutor and of the legal defense teams. This chapter examines how weaknesses inherent to international justice were manifested and reflected in the Laurent Gbagbo's trial. It also spotlights how the prosecutorial approach and the handling of the case by the ICC have exposed distinctive flaws specific to the Gbagbo case. Regarding the incarceration of the former president of Ivory Coast in the northern part of the country, the Ivorian government wanted to present a rosy image of Gbagbo's detention conditions. The few visitors he met like the Council of Elders led by Kofi Anan, former Secretary General of the UN and Nobel Peace Prize Desmond Tutu, and the UN Chief mission Choi were given the impression that the former president was in a house arrest in a decent residence. The reality was that he was placed in a jail cell in a solitary confinement. The head of the correctional officers was the rebel Kouakou Fofié who was under the UN sanctions for crimes he perpetrated in 2002.[1] The former president of Ivory Coast could only have an idea of the weather only when the rain fell. He could barely see the sun. The correctional officers would occasionally take him to the decent residency, presented as his place of detention, to meet his rare visitors such as those mentioned above. He could

---

[1] Pigeaud, 310.

not meet his family members and could barely exchange with his lawyers. The UN Mission in Ivory Coast chief Choi after discovering the trickery brought it to the attention of Alassane Ouattara. After eight months in detention in the northern part of Ivory Coast, in the stronghold of the pro-Alassane Ouattara's forces, Laurent Gbagbo was transferred to The Hague on November 30, 2010. His first appearance before the court was December 5, 2011, six days before the legislative elections planned to take place in Ivory Coast on December 11, 2011. Before giving a brief historical account of Gbagbo's trial and analyzing the facts about the ICC's prosecution and investigation in Ivory Coast, it is important to unveil the conditions of his transfer, to discuss his first appearance before the court and the details about Blé Goudé's transfer and first appearance as well before the court.

Transfer of defendants to The Hague and joint trial

The new regime of Ivory Coast under President Alassane Ouattara facilitated the transfer of the former president from the prison of Korhogo to The Hague on November 30, 2011, thus executing an arrest warrant issued one week earlier, on November 23, 2011, by the Pre-Trial Chamber of the International Criminal Court.[2] Gbagbo's transfer from Korhogo to The Hague was worthy of a detective story or a Hollywood movie. The justice department of the city called for a trial. Judges travelled from Abidjan with a clear mission: to make sure he was handed over to the ICC without further delay. Later, they asked the UN to lift the travel ban that was put on him in the last moments of power. The Ivorian justice did not respect the procedural penal code in force regarding the holding of any trial; the defendant's lawyers were supposed to be informed five days in advance. They were invited but were not informed that an arrest warrant was issued against their client. An expedited and hasty hearing took place in the presence of the UN mission troops' representatives in Ivory Coast. After that parody of trial the former president was taken from Korhogo to Abidjan. He was thus in route to The Hague. Laurent Gbagbo uncovered the process that led him to the ICC during his first hearing in The Hague on December 5, 2011:

> They called me and later, they informed me, and they said: "Here is the arrest warrant." It was an improvised and hasty court hearing in the presence of the United Nations Mission in Ivory Coast soldiers and rebel leader Kouakou Fofié, all armed with kalachinkov…At the end of the hearing, I was in Kouakou Fofié's car, so he could take me back to the prison. And later I noticed he passed the prison. I told him "we passed

---

[2] Prosecutor v. Gbagbo, ICC-02/11-01/11-1, Decision on Warrant Arrest (November 23, 2011).

the prison." He replied "we are going to the airport. It is not lit, and the plane must take off at 18:30 GMT." And then I said: where am I going on a plane? He did not have the courage to tell me "You are going to The Hague." He said: "You are going to Abidjan."...Then I laughed because I understood it all.[3]

The former president of Ivory Coast did not hide the feeling of relief he had for being in The Hague. After only one week of presence in the The Hague prison, he could realize and he voiced it that the detention conditions in Korhogo and those in The Hague were not comparable. In the northern part of Ivory Coast where he was detained the conditions were less humane and he was getting sick, developing new illnesses. Later he added regarding the conditions of his detention in Korhogo, "I was in a small house, with a mosquito net, and a shower. I could not see the sun. Only on some rare occasions I saw the sun. I developed some other pathologies besides the ones I had...I was dying."[4]

Fatou Bensouda, Chief Prosecutor of the ICC declared that the hearings sole focus was about the criminal responsibility of the accused, about the trial per se and not about who won the 2010 presidential election. Later she presented her litany of grievances against the accused. She argued that there was enough evidence to establish the criminal responsibility of the former president of Ivory Coast Laurent Gbagbo for the following: crimes against humanity, murder, persecution, and rape. These crimes, she added, were committed during five specific incidents in Abidjan, which were the attacks during the protests related to the National Television (December 16–19, 2010), the Yopougon incidents which occurred between February 25 and February 28, 2011, the women's rally in Abobo (March 3, 2011), the gunfire in the Abobo market (March 17, 2011), and in Yopougon on April 12, 2011. The February incidents were dropped and it has been mostly about the four specific incriminating incidents even though the prosecutor has often harkened back to the initial forty-five incriminating incidents she had identified and which fluctuated throughout the trial. She did so in the subsequent documents she presented to the court, starting from the Document of Notification of Charges, submitted to the court on January 13, 2011. After hearing the charges against him, during his first appearance, former president Laurent did not plead guilty, contradicted the Chief Prosecutor Bensouda and raised the question at the center of the electoral stalemate of 2010–2011:

---

[3] Maupas, *Le Joker des Puissants*, 360.

[4] Maupas, *Le Joker des Puissants*, 363.

The Prosecutor said that we are not here to talk about who won the election and who did not win. But we cannot talk about the post-election crisis and not know how the election went. Who won the elections? Because it was the one who did not win them who caused the troubles. I think that's the logic. So, when I asked for the votes to be recounted, it was not a sentence in the air...we saw that in the city of Bouaké alone, 100,000 votes were added to the votes of my opponent. [Since 2002] I never believed that Ivory Coast was going to get out of the crisis through a war. I always thought we'd get out it through the discussion...so I traveled all over Africa. I evoked article 48 of the constitution and allowed Ouattara and Konan Bédié to be candidates...[5]

Laurent Gbagbo did not miss the opportunity to talk about the French troops that bombed his presidential palace along the UN blue helmets. He said that the French troops did the job meaning that there were the ones who arrested him and handed him over to the rebels. In his closing remarks, he sent a direct message to the Prosecutor Fatou Bensouda which demonstrated his commitment and readiness to take on that challenge, that other battle at the ICC against the ICC: *Madame, comme je suis ici, on va aller jusqu'au bout.* This means: "Mrs., as I am here, we will go all the way till the end."

The expression "*On va aller jusqu'au bout*" (We will go all the way till the end) became the leitmotiv or mantra of his supporters, convinced that they would eventually win and that the ICC would not be able to keep up the pace and the race. The expression became part of the public narrative in Ivory Coast. Online media mushroomed, such as OVAJAB Media with the acronym of the sentence "*On Va Aller Jusqu'Au Bout*" and LGTV which contains his initials (LG).

Stéphanie Maupas, a French journalist, correspondent at *Le Monde* in her book *Le Joker des Puissants: Le Grand Roman de la Cour Pénale Internationale* titled a chapter on the former Ivorian president's trial "*Jusqu'au bout*". Laurent Gbagbo's supporters—Ivorians, Africans, whites, and the ICC critics—have called the trial "the trial of shame."

The confirmation of charges hearing was supposed to be held on June 18, 2012. But on June 5, 2012, the defendant legal defense team led by the French lawyer Emmanuel Altit asked for its postponement. They raised a number issues and concerns. They initially questioned the competence of the court to try their client. They requested his release on bail. Later they claimed he was not fit to stand trial because of health issues. They also hoped to obtain the dismissal of the trial for these same health issues. Echoing what Laurent Gbagbo himself had said during his first appearance, the legal defense team

---

[5] Dossier de Presse V8-20190514 CPI. Le Procès de Laurent Gbagbo et de Charles Blé Goudé: Jalons et Enjeux, 5.

argued that their client endured inhumane and degrading treatment in Korhogo and developed some illnesses due to his detention's conditions.

The former president lawyers who were adamant to call off the trial added he endured also moral torture and that he was insulted repeatedly and received several threats from the prison guards. They concluded that he was suffering form post-traumatic disorders. The court asked an independent team of doctors to evaluate his health. A psychiatrist named Pierre Lamothe's assessment of Laurent Gbagbo's health convinced the court that he was fit to stand trial. Pierre Lamothe said that the former president of Ivory Coast may have short attention spans at times, a few brief memory losses but he was in enough good health to stand trial. He even added that Laurent Gbagbo was impatient to see his trial begin because he saw it as an opportunity to tell his side of the story for the restoration of his name and image.[6]

Another burning question was financial. It was related to the legal defense team's fees. The defendant had indicated that he was indigent, as his assets were frozen in Ivory Coast by the new Ivorian regime led by Alassane Ouattara, by the European Union, and by the United Nations Security Council. He therefore claimed that he could not take care of his legal defense fees. The ICC therefore had to pay for his legal team's fees. The ICC had to deliberate on the demands mentioned above, thus resulting in the trial's delay. Even though his lawyers did not succeed in calling off the trial, they could buy time and set up a workable game plan. The confirmation of charges pre-trial was finally held from February 19–28, 2013, 15 months after Laurent Gbagbo appearance before the court after his transfer from Korhogo. The goal of the hearing was to determine whether there was enough evidence to try him or not.

For the sake of clarity, it is important to reiterate that Fatou Bensouda accusation could be summed up in the following lines: Laurent Gbagbo conceived a Common Plan to remain in power as soon as he took power in 2000. In the execution of that Common Plan, his forces and some of his close collaborators reunited in a select group of inner circle attacked the supporters of Alassane Ouattara, defenseless civilians at the mercy of the incumbent president's forces and who were brutalised, injured, raped (women), and killed. After the Office of the Prosecutor presented the accusation, the Pre-Trial Chamber led by Sylvia Fernandez de Gurmendi was not convinced that the evidence presented met the criteria of crimes against humanity defined as acts of atrocities that defy the imagination and shock deeply human consciousness.

On June 3, 2013, the majority of the Pre-Trial, Christine Van den Wyngaert and Hans Peter Kaul Chamber took the decision to adjourn the confirmation of

---

[6] Maupas, 365.

charges because the incriminating evidence presented did not have a strong probative value and for lack of sufficient evidence against the former president of Ivory Coast.[7] The contrasting and dissenting view was expressed by the president of the Pre-Trial Chamber herself, Sylvia Fernandez de Gurmendi. One of the judges representing the majority was Judge Christine Van den Wyngaert who expressed a dissenting opinion when the court confirmed the charges against the accused. The other judge Hans Peter Kaul resigned a few weeks later and on July 21, 2013, he died in conditions none elucidated.

The majority refused to confirm the charges against the accused for two reasons which appeared to be two grievances: The first relates to the nature of the evidence presented. The second is related to the content of the evidence presented. The majority considered that the prosecutor Fatou Bensouda relied heavily on media articles, on human rights organizations reports, in sum on hearsay evidence devoid of probative value. She was asked to reduce the quantity of hearsay in her notifications of charges and bring more evidentiary information and reliable observations coming from the witnesses and from the victims.

Regarding the second reason, the majority argued that the evidence presented by the prosecutor has not reached the threshold of admissibility as its level was below the standard required at the confirmation of charges stage. She was requested to produce an amended version of the Document of Notification of Charges along six axes which were as follows:

1. The prosecutor was urged to describe the positions, movements and activities of all armed groups opposed to the "pro-Gbagbo" forces, namely the Invisible Commando and the *Forces Nouvelles*, particularly in and around Abidjan, between November 2010 and May 2011. Fatou Bensouda was asked to provide specific information on the confrontations between these armed groups and the pro-Gbagbo forces between 2010 and May 2011.

2. The Pre-Trial Chamber asked the Office of the Prosecutor to give a description of the organizational structure of the pro-Gbagbo forces, and to elaborate more on the interaction between the various sub-groups and how they fit into the overall structure. The Chamber wanted to know how Laurent Gbagbo's inner circle was coordinating and funding the activities of these sub-groups, reunited under the umbrella of the *Galaxie Patriotique*.

---

[7] Prosecutor v. Gbagbo, ICC-02/11-01/11-432, Decision adjourning the hearing on the confirmation of charges pursuant to article 61(7)(c)(i) of the Rome Statute (June 3, 2013).

3. The majority of the Pre-Trial Chamber judges requested the Prosecutor to be specific about the Common Plan. They wanted to know how and when the Common Plan was adopted and whom was behind it. They wanted to have more precisions on its *modus operandi*. It was expected from the Chief prosecutor to provide specific information on the meetings at which this policy or plan was adopted and about the internal communication of the organizational structure in charge of the implementation of the Common Plan.

4. The Prosecutor had mentioned 45 criminal incidents. The judges of the majority asked her to be more specific. She was urged to specify for each criminal attack against the pro-Ouattara population whether the authors acted according to the Common Plan. Moreover, she was asked to provide some details about the type of weapons the pro-Gbagbo groups used, the number of victims of the criminal acts, the type of suffering the pro-Ouattara victims endured, and finally she was asked to demonstrate the correlation between the events which happened outside Abidjan and in Abidjan.

5. The Prosecutor was asked to provide specific evidence about the December 16-19, 2010 incidents related to the national Radio and Television and about the April 12 violence. She was urged to support her allegations of sexual violence with forensic evidence.

6. The last axis was about the events that occurred in Abobo (March 3 and march 17, 2011). The majority asked the Chief Prosecutor of the ICC to provide any forensic or other evidence which could determine the origin of the firing, the authors of the firing and the type of ammunition used for the firing, and what and whom the targets were.[8]

The prosecutor was given more time to build a stronger case while Laurent Gbagbo who should supposedly benefit from the presumption of innocence was still kept in custody. The dissenting voice of the Pre-Trial Chamber, the president of that court, Judge Sylvia Fernandez de Gurmendi contended that the prosecutor had presented substantial probative elements which should have led the court to confirm the charges against the accused. She disagreed with the majority when they asked the prosecutor to further her investigation in order to bring to the court a more robust and substantive document of notifications of charges. Her argument was that the Pre-Trial Chamber was

---

[8] Prosecutor v. Gbagbo, ICC-02/11-01/11-432, Decision adjourning the hearing on the confirmation of charges pursuant to article 61(7)(c)(i) of the Rome Statute (June 3, 2013), ¶ 44.

going beyond the confines and boundaries of its responsibilities and was infringing on those of the Trial Chamber.[9]

On June 12, 2014, the confirmation of charges' hearing took place. The ICC stakeholders had the opportunity to hear the content of the amended version of the prosecutors' accusation. According to Bensouda, there were over more than a hundred incidents during which pro-Gbagbo forces including militiamen and mercenaries have committed a variety of crimes which led to the death of more than 1,000 civilians, from November 27 2010 to May 8, 2011. She added that the forces loyal to Gbagbo have arrested 520 people during that period, raped at least 40 women. The Document of Notifications of charges Amended claimed that the attacks were systematic and targeted pro-Alassane Ouattara forces along ethnic and religious lines. The document added that Laurent Gbagbo himself was the architect who mastermind a state policy geared towards the commission of violence and crimes against civilians along ideological and ethnic lines. She presented to the court 22,000 page documents, thousands of videos, and had mobilized 108 witnesses willing to testify against the defendant.[10] The court took the decision to confirm the charges against Gbagbo, alleging that the prosecutor provided further and relevant and probative evidence to support her claim pursuant to article 25 of the Rome Statute which deals with individual criminal responsibility of defendants.[11] Judge Christine Van den Wyngaert expressed her dissenting opinion and argued that the prosecutor case did not have a strong probative value. Article 25 relates to liability by instigation. Liability by instigation or indirect co-perpetration is the fact that the defendant encourages, solicits and orders the commission of a crime. Under Article 25, the defendant is not the perpetrator of the crime, but is the one by whose action the main perpetrator resolves to commit the crime. The material elements of the crime are: the planning of the crime; the fact of giving orders to commit the crimes and the act of inciting the commission of crimes. In sum the defendant is the co-author of criminal actions. The mode of criminal responsibility is called indirect co-action. But the prosecutor stated that the former president was also criminally responsible according to article 28 of the Rome Statute. She did so certainly to increase her chances of winning the trial. Article 28 is about the legal responsibility of the civilian and military superiors. After the confirmation of

---

[9] War Crimes Research Office, *The Confirmation of Charges Process at the International Criminal Court: A Critical Assessment and Recommendations for Change* (Washington, DC: American University Washington College of Law, 2015), 65-66.

[10] Maupas, 369.

[11] Prosecutor v. Gbagbo, ICC-02/11-01/11-656-Red, Decision on the confirmation of charges against Laurent Gbagbo (June 12, 2014).

charges the former president legal defense was denied the right to appeal the decision which meant that the trial was set to officially start.

As to Charles Blé Goudé, his January 17, 2013 arrest in Ghana, where he was in exile after the downfall of the former president of Ivory Coast, looked like a kidnapping. Brought to Ivory Coast, he was imprisoned and later was transferred to The Hague on March 22, 2014. His legal team initially led by the Dutch Knoops was later on exclusively composed of Ivorians, namely Claver Ndri and Zokou Seri. During his first appearance, Charles Blé Goudé declared on March 27, 2014 the following: "Tell me in which video I'm asking Christians to go kill Muslims, where I'm asking an ethnic group to kill another ethnic group! Who introduced political violence in Côte d'Ivoire?"[12] He continued to reject the idea of the Common Plan Laurent Gbagbo might have designed to remain in power at all costs and said that Alassane Ouattara was rather the one who had a Common Plan to oust the former president of Ivory Coast from power by means of force and violence. The leader of the Young Patriots addressed this direct message to the president of the Pre-Trial Chamber, Sylvia Gurmendi: "Madam President, millions of Africans are watching you and counting on you not to allow individuals to use this court to achieve ambitions that taint this court, because it is our court....I do not just seek to be free just as I do not seek to be right. There is only one thing that I want: the manifestation of truth. Only the truth will help the court to definitively situate my responsibility."[13]

The hearing confirming the charges against Charles Blé Goudé took place from September 29 to October 2, 2014, before the preliminary chamber I. The charges against him, identical to those brought against Laurent Gbagbo, were confirmed on December 11, 2015. The court decided to conduct a joint trial on March 11, 2015, which officially began on January 28, 2016.

The prosecutor reduced the number of her witnesses to 82. They were given codes names for security reason which all began with a capital P certainly for Prosecution followed by several digits. Most of them were flown to The Hague, hotel fees and air tickets paid for by the court so they could testify against the defendants. The body of the witnesses was composed of the main officers of the Ivorian army or the heads of the security forces units who served under President Laurent Gbagbo, a few low rank political leaders, ideologically close to the defendants, and Alassane Ouattara's sympathizers, and a number of alleged victims. After two years of hearings, the prosecutor was asked to submit

---

12 Dossier de Presse V8-20190514 CPI, 7.

13 Dossier de Presse V8-20190514 CPI, 7.

to the court a document called the Mid-Trial Brief in which she would summarize her argument or a case.

The year 2018 presented mixed signals for Ivory Coast with regard to justice and reconciliation, coupled with signs of détente and repression. In the early moments of that year, the justice system of the country sentenced Laurent Gbagbo to twenty years in prison for what was perceived by the government of Alassane Ouattara as a holdup of the national agency of the West African States Central Bank. In order to circumvent the economic sanctions against him in his last moments in power, Laurent Gbagbo had seized the country funds available in the local branch of the West African States Central Bank for state expenditures and the payment of the civil servants' salaries. That court sentence was seen as a signal that the state under Alassane Ouattara was not ready to see the former Ivorian president return to the country particularly before the 2020 election. The sentence was both a warning sign and a preventive act as there were growing rumours about the eventual acquittal from the ICC of Laurent Gbagbo. The Mid-Trial Brief was submitted to the Trial Chamber of the ICC in that context. Since the beginning of the trial, the ICC Chief Prosecutor drafted a number of documents in which she presented her argument. The Document of Notification of Charges submitted to the court on January 13, 2011 was the first major one in that series. Fatou Bensouda outlined her charges against the former president of Ivory Coast. When the confirmation of Charges was adjourned, she presented at the request of the Pre-Trial Chamber an amended Document of Notification of Charges. After two years of trial she was asked to submit to the court a Mid-Trial Brief. In this section of this work, in order to reduce redundancy, I opt to give a summary of the Mid-Trial Brief which is the culmination and the refined version of the prosecutor previous documents which all recurrently presented her line of attack. Moreover it was enriched with the testimonies, court hearings and cross-examinations which took place throughout the trial until the time of its drafting.

Mid-Trial Brief and Gbagbo's Common Plan to remain in power

The Mid-Trial Brief (MTB) is composed of ten parts. Part II is devoted to the Common Plan and the last two of the 10 parts spotlight the individual criminal responsibility of the accused. The prosecutor, Fatou Bensouda, stressed the four main incriminating incidents which were considered to be the representative crimes she decided to focus on. She argued that she has been concise as possible as she could and she justified the voluminous nature of the Mid-Trial Brief (the main document was 358 pages and there were five annexes) by the fact that she needed to insert into it all necessary information that would help the judges in the management of the trial. Laurent Gbagbo lead counsel,

Emmanuel Altit in a letter sent to the court on May 25, 2018 asked to receive without further delay the edited and improved version of the Mid-Trial Brief in French. He lamented that the first version of the document contained errors, inadequacies, and inaccuracies.

The main argument of the Mid-Trial Brief stood upon two major points. The first was that Laurent Gbagbo's refusal to leave power after the election that he allegedly lost led to the resumption of the civil war. The second, which is the main idea in the document, was that Laurent Gbagbo and his closest aides and allies, or inner circle, conceived a Common Plan as soon as he became president in October 2000 so he could remain in power at any cost and by any means necessary. Laurent Gbagbo was therefore criminally responsible pursuant to article 25 (3) of the Rome Statute.

The Mid-Trial Brief cast doubt on the legitimacy of Gbagbo's presidency. The prosecution argued that the 2000 presidential election in Ivory Coast was not fair because some candidates were excluded (Alassane Ouattara) in the name of *Ivoirité*[14] and rejected the idea that the trial be about who won the election in 2010, arguing that that question was not relevant for the trial. She argued that the defendant initially opposed the concept of *Ivoirité* and later used it to his advantage in order to eliminate Alassane Ouattara from the political and electoral arena in Ivory Coast. Regarding the debate about *Ivoirité*, the Mid-Trial Brief recalled Gbagbo's uncalled-for statement during the forum of reconciliation when he stated that Article 35 of the 2000 Constitution was conceived to resolve some questions, namely Alassane Ouattara's nationality issue, thus justifying the rejection of his candidacy.

The MTB also stated that Laurent Gbagbo managed to postpone the presidential election, which was supposed to be held in 2005, in order to prolong his power without any legitimacy. The former Ivorian president, according to the Mid-Trial Brief, activated his supporters so that they would disrupt and prevent the smooth process of the public hearings in 2006, which were necessary to complete the electoral listings.

With regard to the Common Plan, the Office of the Prosecutor argued that the former president of Ivory Coast masterminded and executed a strategy to keep power, be during the electoral stalemate of 2010–2011 or since his rise to power in 2000. The means he used, as reported by the Mid-Trial Brief, were the army commanded by officials he appointed based on ethnicity and loyalty, parallel or unofficial chains of command, mercenaries from Liberia who fought to

---

[14] Prosecutor v. Gbagbo, ICC-02/11-01/15, Office of the Prosecutor, The Mid-Trial Brief, ¶ 18 (March 29, 2018).

maintain him in power during the electoral crisis of 2011, militia groups, and the *Galaxie Patriotique*, led by Blé Goudé.

The *modus operandi* of the Common Plan, according to the Office of the Prosecutor, encompassed public statements by the defendants, Simone Gbagbo, and some other prominent members; the mobilization of the youth and self-defense groups; the incitation to violence; the use of violence; the conducting of meetings attended by members of the inner circle and high political and military officials; the blockade against the Golf Hotel where Alassane Ouattara and his military personnel and political aides found refuge; the crimes against opposition leaders; the control over the national radio and television (RTI); the demonization of the United Nations mission in Ivory Coast; and the failure by Laurent Gbagbo to punish crimes committed by his supporters.[15]

The words of the former leader of Ivory Coast were used as incriminating evidence. Suffice it to mention one of his addresses to the security forces and one of his campaign slogans. To the security forces whose loyalty he wanted to secure, he said: "*Si je tombe, vous tombez*," which means "If I fall, you fall."[16] His campaign slogan was "*On gagne ou on gagne*," which means, "We win or we win." The Mid-Trial Brief stressed the alleged roles of Blé Goudé and Simone Gbagbo besides those of some high-ranking officials of the army and those of Gbagbo party leaders.

The MTB argued that Blé Goudé, the former youth minister and the leader of the *Galaxie Patriotique*, received funding from Gbagbo's presidential office and urged young people to enroll in the army. His anticolonial and nationalist stance was perceived as a hate crime. He was accused of mobilizing and having the power to mobilize the youth with the intent of committing violent crimes and of using hateful language coupled with xenophobia against West African immigrants and France. The prosecutor added that Alassane Ouattara's supporters had been identified as public enemies who became natural targets by the former president's supporters. Through his words and works, Blé Goudé contributed to create an environment of hostility favorable for the commission of crimes and hate crimes.

The prosecution held the former Ivorian president accountable for his supporters' acts and words, as he never punished or sanctioned any of them. The Mid-Trial Brief argued that Laurent Gbagbo's refusal to punish the gendarmes, the alleged perpetrators of the crime, led to the charnel house of

---

[15] Prosecutor v. Gbagbo, The Mid-Trial Brief, ¶ 642.

[16] Prosecutor v. Gbagbo, ICC-02/11-01/15-T-138-Red2-FRA, Witness P-0010, Transcript of the Hearing, ¶ 13–24 (March 28, 2017).

around 50 people in October 2000, and set up a pattern of impunity that emboldened his followers to commit more crimes.[17] The prosecution added that the reign of impunity in 2000 became the foundational point of a pattern of impunity in subsequent human rights violations in 2003, 2004, 2006, and 2010–2011 by members of the Galaxie Patriotique and by the Defense and Security Forces. In 2003, the *Galaxie Patriotique* opposed the Marcoussis Agreement by organizing anticolonialist rallies on the basis that it was a peace agreement that undermined the sovereignty of Ivory Coast and eroded Laurent Gbagbo's legitimate power. In 2004, two major incidents occurred in the field of human rights violations, which were added as incriminating evidence against the defendants. A rally organized by the newly created coalition of opposition groups known as G7—which included the PDCI, the RDR, and the rebel groups—was repressed, and this resulted in the death of between 120 and 350 militants of Alassane Ouattara, according to the Mid-Trial Brief. For the prosecutor, the rebels (who had retreated to Bouaké) were not the targets of repression but the civilians who wanted to organize a peaceful demonstration.

Following the failed Operation Dignity, launched by Laurent Gbagbo to free the northern part of the country which was held by the rebels, the French, accused of attempting to overthrow the former president, became the targets of anti-French mass movements. The Mid-Trial Brief stated that while several supporters of the former Ivorian president constituted a human shield around his presidential palace and raised barricades, several others moved towards Biétry, and there, they committed acts of terror and crimes such as rape, beatings, and pillaging against the French citizens.

In 2006, Laurent Gbagbo's youth groups suspected non-Ivorian northerners and West African migrants of trying to "infiltrate" the electoral lists in order to inflate the voting population of the opposition and of the rebels. They clashed with Alassane Ouattara's supporters during public hearings at the end of which the deserving ones were to be granted their ID cards. The disturbance of the public hearings delayed the creation of the electoral listings, whose completion would have accelerated the electoral process, argued the prosecution. Moreover, Laurent Gbagbo was accused by the prosecution of having death squads for the purpose of physically eliminating militants and supporters of the rebellion and of Alassane Ouattara. The name of an artist, the late Camara H., was mentioned as an illustration in this regard. The Office of the Prosecutor stated also that military officers played a significant role in consolidating the Common Plan. They kept Laurent Gbagbo in power, campaigned for him, voted

---

[17] Prosecutor v. Gbagbo, The Mid-Trial Brief, ¶ 18.

for him, pledged allegiance to him, and showed him loyalty and held several strategic meetings with him during the 2010–2011 electoral stalemate.

The Mid-Trial Brief devoted paragraphs to the question of the requisition of the army, which, according to the Office of the Prosecutor, meant that the former president bore the moral, criminal, and penal responsibility of acts of violence during the implementation of that requisition. The former Ivorian president took decree number 2010-306 on November 14, 2010, which was followed two weeks later by a curfew on the eve of the runoff. The curfew was extended after the second round of the elections. The Office of the Prosecutor argued that the Common Plan evolved and escalated on November 27, 2010, to encompass "a state or organizational policy aimed at a widespread and systematic attack against Ouattara's supporters."[18] The features of the escalation encompassed the army requisition, the extension of the curfew, the implementation of a communication strategy that resulted in an intensified suppression of dissenting voices and opinions in national media on the control of state institutions, and the integration of militiamen and new recruits into the army.

Blé Goudé who, during the recurrent and regular mass mobilizations he led and organized, had called upon Ivorians willing to pay the ultimate sacrifice to defend the sovereignty of Ivory Coast, the regime of Laurent Gbagbo, the institutions of the Republic of Ivory Coast, and to expel the intruders, the invaders, France, and the United Nations mission out of the country to do so with bare hands.

The Mid-Trial Brief argued that he shared the spirit and the letter of the Common Plan and accused him of being an obstacle to peace processes and to political progress. The Office of the Prosecutor stated that besides his mobilizing abilities, the former Ivorian president's youth leader demonstrated great communications skills in the implementation of a communication strategy that combined verbal and nonverbal language. As an illustration of the nonverbal communication strategy, the prosecution concluded that Blé Goudé used a coded language that could only be decoded or deciphered by his close aides; when answering a question in an interview about the black cap he used to wear, he declared, "This was a language."[19] The state media namely the National Radio and Television was accused by the prosecution of spilling and spreading the venom of hatred against African immigrants, France, and the United Nations.

---

[18] Prosecutor v. Gbagbo, The Mid-Trial Brief, ¶ 6 (29 March 2018).

[19] Prosecutor v. Gbagbo, The Mid-Trial Brief, ¶ 340.

The prosecution mentioned the regular erection of roadblocks and barricades by supporters of Blé Goudé after some of his speeches, namely the one he delivered on February 25, 2011. The prosecution stated that he provided his support to the creation of paramilitary groups, such as *Groupement Patriotique pour la Paix* (GPP) led by Touré Moussa Zeguen, and his strategic support to the militia group, Front for the Liberation of the Great West, the *Front de Libération du Grand Ouest* (FLGO) based in the western part of the region and led by Maho Glofiéhi; that he helped new recruits enroll in the army; that he oversaw their training; and that he distributed weapons to youth during the electoral stalemate. He was nicknamed General of the Street (*Général de la Rue* in French); the new recruits he helped integrate the army in 2003 were called Blé Goudé soldiers. This was confirmed by General Mangou, former chief of the army, P-0009.[20] The former leader of the *Galaxie Patriotique* launched a series of frequent attacks against the UN mission in Ivory Coast, which was accused of being in collusion with the pro–Alassane Ouattara forces and which was no longer a peacekeeping mission but rather an army of occupation. He accused the mission and France for preparing a genocide in Ivory Coast.[21] When Laurent Gbagbo ordered the United Nations mission to leave the country on December 21, 2010, the Young Patriots chanted "*ONUCI dehors,*" which means "UNOCI out," and stopped a convoy of the mission in Yopougon. The chief of the army, General Mangou, who shared the idea of the United Nations mission collusion with the pro–Alassane Ouattara forces[22] had to intervene to escort the convoy.

The prosecution also claimed that it was in possession of receipts collected at the presidential palace which showed that the respective leaders of the *Galaxie Patriotique* and grassroots organizations—including the agoras and the *parlements*, the paramilitary groups like the GPP, and the militia group FLGO— were receiving bonuses, funding, and financing for their activities for their actions whose ultimate goal was to keep Laurent Gbagbo in power.[23] The former leader of *Galaxie Patriotique*, on several occasions, on media, during rallies, and at formal and informal meetings called also on the population to be vigilant and to search for intruders and weapons in their neighborhoods. Witness P-0440 claimed he expressed, in a report he wrote and sent to his superior, head of a police branch, his apprehension about Blé Goudé speeches' impact on the commission of crimes as he emphasized that "in the course of

---

[20] Prosecutor v. Gbagbo, The Mid-Trial Brief, ¶ 32.

[21] Prosecutor v. Gbagbo, The Mid-Trial Brief, ¶ 348.

[22] Prosecutor v. Gbagbo, The Mid-Trial Brief, ¶ 429.

[23] Prosecutor v. Gbagbo, The Mid-Trial Brief, ¶ 270–276.

their searches for arms and rebels, suspicious individuals were automatically lynched and burned."[24]

Regarding Simone Gbagbo, the Mid-Trial Brief underlined her alleged supporting role in the implementation and application of the Common Plan. The Office of the Prosecutor revealed that after the fall of Gbagbo it found a document incriminating Simone Gbagbo, which was her diary. In some of her narrations, she supposedly acknowledged the use of mercenaries and suggested a forceful involvement of militia groups in order to defend the regime. The prosecution also claimed to have discovered a document entitled "*Réunion de Concertation*" (Consultation Meeting) in one of the rooms that supposedly belonged to Simone Gbagbo. It was used as additional incriminating evidence as it supposedly contained reports of a highly sensitive meeting and revealed an operational strategy intended to consolidate the Common Plan. According to the document, six cells were created, which worked in a coordinated way for an effective implementation of the Common Plan strategy: political, diplomatic, defensive, communication based, humanitarian, and mobilization focused.[25] The crimes the defendants were accused of were committed against political and leaders and civilians, according to the prosecution, along multiple lines, political (opposition militants and leaders), religious (Muslims), ethnic (Dioulas), and regional (northerners and citizens of West African countries).[26]

Moreover, according to the prosecutor the crimes were committed against political supporters, militants, and civilians known as Dioulas, as well as northerners, or people from neighboring West Africa countries such as Burkina Faso, Mali, and Niger on political, national, ethnic, and religious grounds. Two types of forces were used for the commission of crimes: regular and parallel. The regular ones comprised the police, the republican guard, the gendarmerie, and mercenaries. The parallel ones were mostly composed of soldiers and officers from Laurent Gbagbo's own ethnic group, Bété. The prosecutor's witnesses after their testimonies which were recorded appeared in court to supposedly reinforce their statements. Officers of the Ivorian security forces such as General Mangou, head of the Ivorian army, medical experts, and several other Alassane Ouattara's sympathizers gave their respective testimonies. Multitud of paragraphs were devoted to their testimonies.

The prosecutor identified two major categories of crimes: the main criminal incidents and secondary crimes. The document listed 34 incidents that were

---

[24] Prosecutor v. Gbagbo, The Mid-Trial Brief, ¶ 567.

[25] Prosecutor v. Gbagbo, The Mid-Trial Brief, ¶ 131.

[26] Prosecutor v. Gbagbo, The Mid-Trial Brief, ¶ 632.

supposedly criminal acts Gbagbo perpetrated against civilians that showed common features and patterns, as consequences of the actual implementation of the Common Plan. The main charges were related to four main events out of the 34 that caused death, injury, or rape of 316 victims between December 16, 2010, and April 12, 2011: the march of Alassane Ouattara's supporters on the headquarters of the national television and radio from December 16–19, 2010; the women's march in the municipality of Abobo, March 3, 2011; the explosion of a shell at the Abobo market on March 17, 2011; and the attacks on civilians and alleged supporters of Alassane Ouattara in Yopougon on April 12, 2011, a day after the fall of Gbagbo. The secondary crimes were a set of 41 crimes whose number dropped to 34 by the time of the submission of the Mid-Trial Brief. The prosecutor considered that these incidents constituted crimes against humanity pursuant to Article 7-1 of the Rome Statute. The prosecutor had also argued that the judges could deduct in light of the reference to the grievances against Laurent Gbagbo that a common plan existed even though there was no written document about the Common Plan. Consequently, he deserved to be convicted. The Chief Prosecutor of the ICC made sure to clarify that the document she has just presented was just a Mid-Trial Brief not her final words or a Trial Closing Brief, implying that she anticipated and expected the trial to proceed.

The Mid-Trial Brief document presented serious flaws and weaknesses that undermine its credibility. The Mid-Trial Brief did not expand on the 2002 failed coup d'état whose goal was to overthrow Gbagbo; the *modus operandi* of the rebels and their human rights violations since 2002 and during the civil war that followed the failed coup d'état; the act of aggression of Burkina Faso against Ivory Coast; the neocolonial war of France against Gbagbo's regime; the crimes against humanity the rebels perpetrated during the electoral stalemate; and the activities of the Invisible Commando in Abobo. These were like footnotes in the document. As despicable as the dozens incidents that the prosecutor attributed solely to Gbagbo might be, they could not be compared to the massacre of Duékoué, which was committed exclusively by Alassane Ouattara's forces at the end of March 2011 before the fall of Gbagbo. She did not devote not even a signle line to the Massacre of Duékoué.

When the Mid-Trial Brief referred to public figures who were killed during the 2002 failed coup d'état, only the names of General Robert Guéi and Marcellin Yacé, a musician, were mentioned.[27] For the sake of honesty and historical truth, the prosecutor should have mentioned some other famous names among the high officials of the gendarmerie killed by the rebels in Bouaké and

---

[27] Prosecutor v. Gbagbo, The Mid-Trial Brief, ¶ 25.

in Abidjan, or Emile Boga Doudou, Laurent Gbagbo's minister of security and interior. The rebels had attacked his house that night of September 2002 and killed him.

In reaction to the Mid-Trial Brief of the Chief Prosecutor of the ICC Fatou Bensouda, both legal teams of the accused submitted rebuttals to the court. The defense demonstrated that the two premises or postulates on which the prosecutor built her case were false, the two linked by a relationship of reciprocity: the existence of a circle of insiders and the design and execution of a Common Plan for the maintenance in power of Laurent Gbagbo by the inner circle and other structures such as the military hierarchy, the existence of a parallel force, the groups of mercenaries and the *Galaxie Patriotique*.

The defense questioned the probative value of several incriminating documents, videos, death certificates, lists of victims. In the different versions of the Document of Notifications of Charges that she presented to the court as the trial progressed, the number of victims fluctuated. Regarding the numbers of incriminating incidents, it is important to recall that Fatou Bensouda initially said there were hundreds of them. Later she decided to focus on 45. The overall incriminating incidents dropped from 45 to 41 and then to 34. She then argued that they were five core incriminating incidents. Later the core incidents she labeled representative crimes were no longer five but four. The pattern of inconsistency and fluctuation in the numbers of crimes and in the numbers of the victims of these crimes was recurrent. In order to avoid to the reader redundant information and tedious reading about the fluctuation of numbers, I select the December 16-19 incidents as an illustrative example of the prosecutor's inconsistency about the numbers of victims.

In the Document of Notification of Charges (DNC), she mentioned 91 victims, deaths (41), wounded (35), women raped (15).

In the DNC of May 16, 2012, the number of victims climbed from 91 to 121: deaths (54), wounded (50), women raped (17).

In the DNC of January 13, 2014, the number of victims slightly dropped below 121. They were now 115: deaths (45), wounded (54), women raped (16).[28]

She tried to fix most of the inconsistencies in the Mid-Trial Brief but she could not fix them all. The recurrent inconsistencies and inadequacies were repeated in the Mid-Trial Brief with regard to the identity, numbers, and causes of deaths of victims. The defense rightly argued that the exact number of dead, injured and raped presented by the Prosecutor is unknown. The number

---

[28] Prosecutor v. Gbagbo, Defense Motion on No Case to Answer, ICC-02/11-01/15-1199-Anx4-Corr-Red 28-09-2018 1/57 RH T Annex 4, ¶ 1-15 (September 28, 2018).

mentioned in the annex concerning the April 12, 2011 incriminating incident in Yopougon did not match with the one indicated in the MTB about the same incident. The prosecutor failed to provide the list of women allegedly raped for the February 25, 2011 incriminating incident.

The defense team rejected certain lists of victims, arguing that they lacked a probative value. Associations affiliated with Alassane Ouattara's political party drew up these lists, argued the defense. The *Comité de Suivi* (Monitoring Committee) and the *Association des Parents et Femmes Martyres d'Abobo* (APAFEMA) were two of these active organizations. The Monitoring Committee created in the aftermath of the December 19 incident drew up the list of alleged victims of the December 16-19 incriminating incident (CIV-OTP-0032-0054-0001-R03) and that of the March 3 incriminating incident.

As far as the list CIV-OTP-0058-0320-R02 was concerned, it was a compilation of nine lists put together by anonymous hearsay[29]by another organization, the *Comité des Victimes du Quartier Doukouré-Yopougon* (CVODY) after the February 25 incident. The defense argued that the list was fabricated, drawn up by individuals who were not neutral in the conflict; and who were even with Alassane Ouattara in the Golf Hotel.[30]

Similarly, the defense team rebutted the validity of two incriminating documents, CIV-OTP-0037-0151-R02 and CIV-OTP-0084-2629-R01, presented as two different lists of victims of the March 17 incriminating incident. These two different documents contained identical names. The prosecutor own witness P-0594, Professor Hélène Yapo Etté, first female medical doctor in forensic in Ivory Coast supposedly the author of these lists contended that she had never seen them before they were presented to her by the investigators.[31]

Emmanuel Altit team also rejected the validity of the 32 minutes 52 seconds long video, a supposedly incriminating recording of the March 3, 2011 event. Credible sources said that the Office of Legal Affairs of the United Nations on June 21, 2013 gave it to the Office of the Prosecutor. For Laurent Gbagbo's counsel, the video was edited and manipulated as it contained several shots, which appeared to have been inserted in it. Moreover, the prosecutor used it to demonstrate and establish the circumstances of the death of six out of the seven women supposedly killed during the so-called all-women march of

---

[29] Prosecutor v. Gbagbo, Defense Motion on No Case to Answer, ICC-02/11-01/15-1199-Anx4-Corr-Red 28-09-2018 1/57 RH T Annex 4, ¶ 139 (September 28, 2018).

[30] Prosecutor v. Gbagbo, Defense Motion on No Case to Answer, ICC-02/11-01/15-1199-Anx4-Corr-Red 28-09-2018 1/57 RH T Annex 4, ¶ 111-112 (September 28, 2018).

[31] Prosecutor v. Gbagbo, Defense Motion on No Case to Answer, ICC-02/11-01/15-1199-Anx4-Corr-Red 28-09-2018 1/57 RH T Annex 4, ¶ 160 (September 28, 2018).

March 3, 2011. This appeared suspicious to the defense insofar as the video should have been used to demonstrate the deaths of all seven women not six.[32]

The defense disputed the probative value of the forensic documents of the prosecution. The Office of the Prosecutor used these documents to prove the reality of the death or the injuries suffered by individuals presented as victims of the incidents. These documents provided some information on the autopsy conducted or on the external examination carried out after the exhumation of bodies or on bodies kept in morgues, or obtained from morgues. Laurent Gbagbo defense team contended that the Prosecution has not presented any civil status or medical information for the following:

- The 24 of the 28 dead, 49 of the 54 injured and 9 of the 11 raped (December 16, 2010 incident);

- The nine dead and for the 13 injured (February 25, 2011 incident);

- The three of the seven dead and for six injured (March 3 women's rally)

- The 19 of the 31 dead and for 35 of the 36 injured (March 17, 2011 incident);

- The 70 of the 73 dead, the two injured and for the six supposedly raped (April 12, 2011 incident).[33]

Regarding the issue of the identity of some of the victims of the post-electoral crisis, the defense cast doubt on the authenticity of the birth certificates of the alleged victims added to the incriminating evidence. In an attempt to prove the identity of the victims, their date of death and circumstances of their death, the Prosecutor referred to medical death certificates and certificates of non-contagion.

Many of the medico-legal documents presented by the Office of Prosecutor emanated from the office of Professor Hélène Yapo Etté, P-0564, first female medical doctor in forensic in Ivory Coast. She was the expert who issued these forensic documents concerning the allegedly victims of the two incidents of December 16, 2010 and March 17, 2011. She declared that her task was not about establishing whether the deaths were linked to the crisis, nor of establishing the circumstances and the date of death. She did not herself

---

[32] Prosecutor v. Gbagbo, Defense Motion on No Case to Answer, ICC-02/11-01/15-1199-Anx4-Corr-Red 28-09-2018 1/57 RH T Annex 4, ¶ 166 (September 28, 2018).

[33] Prosecutor v. Gbagbo, Defense Motion on No Case to Answer, ICC-02/11-01/15-1199-Anx4-Corr-Red 28-09-2018 1/57 RH T Annex 4, ¶ 16 (September 28, 2018).

identify the bodies and she did not have any information about how they were kept. She claimed to have carried out 147 external examinations in a single day.

During the cross-examinations, P-0564 confessed that part of the information she put in the report about the exhumed bodies emanated from people close to the morgues. One of the report at the disposal of the prosecutor was not signed. P-0564 added because it was not complete. P-0564 turned to be an exculpating witness. For the Prosecutor's office, the absence of conclusive DNA tests was not a problem arguing that justice had functioned for a very long time without them, thus ignoring the progress of science and technology, which made the standard of proof evolve.

Emmanuel Altit detected flaws in the allegations of P-0564 during the cross-examinations when she said that she analyzed 65 exhumed bodies on July 5, 2011 and attended 147 external examinations and moreover carried out a number of them. For the defense that was not humanly possible assuming that the examination of each exhumed body might have taken a minimum of 10 minutes. It meant that she had a full day of 24h 30 minutes. This implied that she did not sleep; she did not take any break not even to feed herself or to drink. With such a demonstration, the defense concluded that P-0564 was not the only one to do the examinations she claimed she did.[34]

The defense deconstructed the idea according to which the army under Laurent Gbagbo was an ethnic-based agency, as the prosecutor presented it. Besides Mangou, other high officers of the army were not from Laurent Gbagbo's ethnic group, but the prosecutor would name only those who shared the same ethnic group with Laurent Gbagbo such as Dogbo Blé, the head of the Republican Guard in order to sustain the view that the army was built around the Ivorian former president ethnic group. The head of the Ivorian army military operations during the war was Konan Boniface, from the Baoulé ethnic group.

P-0009, General Mangou, who was the chief of the army was presented by the prosecution as one pillar of the inner circle who helped in the implementation of the Common Plan. General Mangou himself declared that he only had professional relations with President Gbagbo and that at times he was only doing a coordination work, having been, at times, sidelined from the decision-making center and the operations center for the defense of the country. For the legal defense team, it was essential for the prosecutor to claim that he was part of the so-called inner circle. Because otherwise everything would collapse and there would not be a common plan. General Mangou was not part of the inner

---

[34] Prosecutor v. Gbagbo, Defense Motion on No Case to Answer, ICC-02/11-01/15-1199-Anx4-Corr-Red 28-09-2018 1/57 RH T Annex 4, ¶ 33-35 (September 28, 2018).

circle.[35] The position of the prosecutor was that President Laurent Gbagbo had set up the common plan as soon as he took power. This is a fallacious argument insofar as the *Galaxie Patriotique* emerged on the political scene in 2002 after the rebels' attack.

Moreover, for the defense, the prosecutor expressed lack of respect for the soldiers, pillars of the republic who sacrificed themselves to honor the republican legality in a time of war. High officers of the army threw blame at each other. General Mangou claimed that he did not have the troops he needed to fight against the rebels and argued that General Kassaraté mobilized only 500 gendarmes while General Brindou put at his disposal 1,250 police officers.[36]

The defense addressed several other issues raised by the prosecution such as the requisition of the army. Fatou Bensouda had accused the former Ivorian president of having had criminal intent or having given illegal orders with criminal intent. For the accusation, the fact that he had not declared Abobo a war zone, or the fact that he ordered 120 mm mortar shells on a densely populated area was an illustration of his criminal intent. Regarding the requisition and the issue of criminal orders supposedly given by the former president, P-0009, General Mangou declared that the requisition of the army was a normal procedure and the president did not need to give any further instruction.[37]

General Mangou and the other security forces witnesses explained that the political hierarchy did not interfere with the conduct and execution of the military operations exclusively led by the high military command. They also lamented the terrible destitution of the Ivorian security forces outgunned by a heavily armed rebellion. For the defense, the Office of the Prosecutor has presented itself as a defender of Alassane Ouattara, exculpating him despite the facts which cried out about his involvement in the rebellion and about his endorsement of the insurrectional rallies namely those of 2004 and 2011.[38]

Laurent Gbagbo defense team disagreed with the prosecution who attempted to present the Ivorian National Radio and television as a medium of hate and of propaganda against the UN and France. For them, the prosecution was not

---

[35] Prosecutor v. Gbagbo, Defense Motion on No Case to Answer, ICC-02/11-01/15-1199-Anx4-Corr-Red 28-09-2018 1/57 RH T Annex 5, ¶ 45-46 (September 28, 2018).

[36] Prosecutor v. Gbagbo, Defense Motion on No Case to Answer, ICC-02/11-01/15-1199-Anx4-Corr-Red 28-09-2018 1/57 RH T Annex 5, ¶ 327 (September 28, 2018).

[37] Prosecutor v. Gbagbo, Defense Motion on No Case to Answer, ICC-02/11-01/15-1199-Anx4-Corr-Red 28-09-2018 1/57 RH T Annex 5, ¶ 415 (September 28, 2018).

[38] Prosecutor v. Gbagbo, Defense Motion on No Case to Answer, ICC-02/11-01/15-1199-Anx4-Corr-Red 28-09-2018 1/57 RH T Annex 5, ¶ 531 (September 28, 2018).

interested in what could be valid in the news, in the speeches of leaders who were in power. A reference to the illegal funding of Nicolas Sarkozy campaign by Muammar Kaddafi was according to the office of the prosecution an anti-French sentiment even though this news was in public domain.[39]

For the two defense teams, the prosecutor could not answer with evidence to support questions about when, where, and by whom the Common Plan was designed. The lawyers considered that the impossibility by the prosecutor to show to the court and to the face of the world a written document which would attest to the existence of Common Plan was the perfect proof that Laurent Gbagbo never conceived a strategy to stay in power and in whose name he would kill civilians, supporters of Alassane Ouattara. The prosecutor contended to this that it was the very absence of a written document on the common plan which was the demonstration of the existence of a secret plan. The defense pointed out that the prosecutor downplayed the disastrous role of the rebels who have repeatedly and recurrently attacked the country, in 1999, 2002, 2004, and 2010-2011. The army loyal to Laurent Gbagbo was a republican force that was defending the country under attack and assault. The lawyers added that the prosecutor failed to take into account the activities of the Invisible Commando whose members camouflaged themselves in the population, took over police precincts, and conducted deadly military attacks against contingents of the army, causing casualties among civilians. They charged that the prosecutor tried to see and show in the normal and regular defense operations and protection deliberate criminal attacks against the civilian population. The prosecutor sought to criminalize the actions of the soldiers and officers, who in the name of the republican duty defended the Ivorian nation against rebels supported by Burkina Faso. The legal defense team turned their defense into an accusation of the prosecutor whose narrative and actions were likely to further divide the country when she presented a false image of the country where two blocks were against each other, ready to butcher each other in the name of ethnicity and religion. The lawyers contended that in doing so she was thus working against the mission of the ICC which is to help build reconciliation in countries. Also they brought to the attention of the court that the ICC Chief Prosecutor did not solicit the expertise of any Ivorian historian who would give an independent assessment of the socio-political environment of the country in which occurred the crises that led to the trial of Laurent Gbagbo, but instead she relied on an official of Alassane Ouattara's party. The legal defense team accused the Office of the Prosecutor

---

[39] Prosecutor v. Gbagbo, Defense Motion on No Case to Answer, ICC-02/11-01/15-1199-Anx4-Corr-Red 28-09-2018 1/57 RH T Annex 5, ¶ 568-569 (September 28, 2018).

to have conducted a bias field investigation, in 2011 during which, the defense added, the Office of the Prosecutor benefitted from the support of the Ivorian government led by Alassane Ouattara and consequently it did not search for bodies, did not resort to a ballistics expert, and did not undertake an independent verification.

The defense argued that the arguments of the prosecutor about the incriminating core incidents were based on falsehood and deceit. The December 16-19, 2011 was not a peaceful demonstration it was an insurrectional rally. The video of the supposedly evidence of the violence perpetrated by Laurent Gbagbo forces during the March 3, 2011 women's rally was problematic. The metadata associated with the video revealed that it was put together before the date of the actual event. The defense concluded that it was a photoshop. With regard to the March 17, 2011 incident, the defense contended that the video shown or presented was edited, did not show any date about the day the incident was recorded. Moreover, the only eyewitness testimony contrasted with those of other witnesses. Regarding the last incriminating incident of April 12, the defense simply said that it could not be imputed to the former president who had lost power the day before.

Charles Blé Goudé's legal team reinforced the defense line expressed by Laurent Gbagbo's lawyers but added that the Prosecution's last minute withdrawal of two incriminating incidents (March 3 and March 17) from the list of incriminating incidents initially held against their client was an indicator that the trial could be ended at any time because the evidentiary elements were not convincing. They rejected the prosecutor's accusation when she declared it was Blé Goudé's speech of February 25 that had led to the establishment of roadblocks around which violence was committed. They contended that no one asked those who set them up to do so. The roadblocks mushroomed spontaneously and their creators did establish them as an outcome of the instinct of survival in the face of the invasion, the intrusion, and the infiltration of Alassane Ouattara's warlords in Abidjan. Blé Goudé's lawyers challenged the prosecutor to objectively analyze the content of his speeches and identify phrases calling for violence instead of making abusive deductions, inferences and extrapolations. In light of the above both legal defense teams pressed the judges of the Trial Chamber to pronounce the No case to Answer that would set free the two accused who have been deprived from their rights to freedom and to the presumption of innocence.

According to the defense, the prosecutor had not been able to demonstrate that Laurent Gbagbo incited violence through his words and actions and that he ordered the commission of crimes. Drawing upon the arguments of the legal defense team of the former president of Ivory Coast, it is imperative for the sake of clarity to underline the differential nuances that exist between Article 25 and Articles 28 of the Rome Statute.

The prosecutor established that the former Ivorian president should be convicted pursuant to Articles 25(3) and 28(a) (b) of the Rome Statute. Article 25(3) deals with the indirect co-perpetration mode of liability whereas article 28 discusses the indirect criminal responsibility of two categories of hierarchical superiors. Regarding article 25, the implication of that criminal responsibility rests upon two tenets: The defendant can be convicted for acts that he or she did not directly commit and for acts of which he or she would not even have knowledge. The knowledge and intention of one of the other co-perpetrators is sufficient to allow the acts in question to be imputed to him or to her.

The two categories of hierarchical superiors whose indirect criminal responsibility article 28 discusses are military leaders and civilian authorities. Article 28 (a) is about military leaders whereas article 28 (b) is about civilian authorities. The difference lies in the degree of guilt related to the information about the crimes committed. The military command should have known and been aware of the crimes committed under his or her authority. It is held against the civil authority the fact that he or she deliberately refuses to take into account the information on the commission of the crimes. According to Laurent Gbagbo's lawyers, the prosecutor has not effectively demonstrated, beyond any reasonable doubt, with the utmost rigor, that their client has indeed conceived the so-called Common Plan. They contended that the prosecutor has not been able to prove that all criteria for the conviction have been fulfilled. In light of the above, they felt therefore justified to submit the motion for the No Case to Answer.

In the second half of the year 2018, the tide was turning against the prosecutor Fatou Bensouda and against the Ivorian president Alassane Ouattara. Simone Gbagbo, who was imprisoned in Odienné after the fall from power and from grace of the presidential couple, was later transferred at the Gendarmerie School in Abidjan. Brought before the court, she was sentenced to 20 years in prison on March 10, 2015 for charges related to the post-electoral stalemate such as attacking state authority, participating in an insurrection, and for disturbing public order. She was acquitted of the charge of crimes against humanity on March 28, 2017.

On August 6, 2018, on the eve of Ivory Coast Independence Day, the Ivorian president Alassane Ouattara granted her an amnesty as well as to hundreds who were still detained since the 2010-2011 electoral stalemate. She was therefore released. But the International Criminal Court, which had issued an arrest warrant against her on February 29, 2012, repeatedly demanded her transfer to The Hague, even after she was released from prison by presidential amnesty.

In 2017 several mutinies shook the country. Alassane Ouattara's soldiers took to the streets and paralyzed the country for days to demand they be paid thousands of dollars to each one of them. They were more 17,000. As they wanted to appear justified in their actions and convincing, they declared on national and international media that they had taken weapons to launch a rebellion and to fight for Alssane Ouattara since 2002 and particularly during the electoral stalemate of 2010-2011. They have repeatedly said that it was the war they conducted that took him to power and therefore they deserved to be paid consequently. They claimed that they have not received adequate compensation and were now using the means and power at their disposal to reach their goal. In other words they took publicly responsibility for the crimes they were accused of but that the ICC downplayed and ignored.

The court also pretended not to be aware that a collective of lawyers associated with grassroots organizations for the defense of human rights filed more than 4,000 cases for victims to it. Most of the files were linked to the Duékoué massacre. The Rome Statute does not provide for the submission of complaints emanating directly from individuals. The court which pretended not to know that such a file had been submitted to it did not react.

When the first mutiny erupted in Ivory Coast in the beginning of the year 2017 it had coincided with the launching of the Anti-CFA Franc Campaign which signaled another decisive moment for the revival of Pan-Africanism. Starting from mid 2018, it was becoming clear that Laurent Gbagbo's trial was turning into a difficult case to defend for the prosecution. One camp was prosecuted and another was spared. Debates heightened about the (un)fairness of Laurent Gbagbo's trial. There was a growing awareness about it and about the inconsistencies and incongruities of the case.

I will discuss in the section that follows the pitfalls of the trial. Some of them are by-products of the Rome Statute. Others are related to the prosecutorial rationale with regard to Laurent Gbagbo's trial. Some other ones are the consequences of ill-inspired decisions taken by the court which failed to take into account the historical context during which the trial was taking place: the growing momentum of Pan-Africanism in the age of social media. I call these pitfalls or failings incongruities of a trial.

Incongruities of a Trial

This section sheds light on the singular controversial aspects as well as the incongruities in Gbagbo's trial, which contributed to the growing discredit of the court. Each of these points demonstrates that the court cannot pretend to have conducted a fair prosecution, highlights its partiality, and taints its credibility. They include: collusion of interests between France, the UN, the international community, and the ICC; legal grounds for investigation and prosecution; suspicious sequential prosecution; Gbagbo's transfer and adjournment of confirmation of charges; Rome Statute and discretionary powers of the prosecutor; one-sided prosecution and violation of Article 54 of the Rome Statute; crimes wrongly attributed to Gbagbo's camp (December 16, 2010); selective activation of the *proprio motu* powers by the prosecutor; ICC prosecution: justice vs. peace, collectivization of crimes; and standoff concerning the request for bail.

Collusion of interests involving the ICC

There was undeniably a collusion of interests between Ouattara's camp, the international players, and the court. Moreno Ocampo affirmed in paragraph 18 of his request to the Pre-Trial Chamber III that a group of French lawyers representing Alassane Ouattara had provided him with evidence to prosecute Gbagbo: "On 15 March 2011, the Prosecutor received a memorandum from lawyers representing President Ouattara which compiled information on crimes committed in the context of the post-election violence in Côte d'Ivoire since 28 November 2010. The memorandum contains information on alleged facts, their legal characterization under the Rome Statute as well as considerations related to jurisdiction and admissibility."[40]

In the same document, the prosecutor stated that he had received a document containing alleged crimes against humanity committed by Alassane Ouattara's camp from Gbagbo's cabinet. The Office of the Prosecutor ignored the requests of Gbagbo's camp and went along with the petition of Ouattara's camp. This is a glaring lack of impartiality from the prosecutors and a clear expression of collusion between the Office of the Prosecutor of the ICC and Ouattara's camp, thus validating the narrative of the former president sympathizers.

There was also noticeable traffic of influence on the ICC by high officials from the West to indict Gbagbo. William Fitzgerald, Deputy Assistant Secretary for African Affairs of the United States; French president Nicolas Sarkozy; French Minister of Defense Gérard Longuet; and Young-jin Choi Special Representative of the United Nations Secretary-General for Ivory Coast; just to mention a few, all announced that Gbagbo would end up in the ICC. As an illustration, suffice it to mention the following: On April 7, 2011, Alain Juppé and Gérard Longuet, Minister of Foreign Affairs and Minister of Defense of France respectively,

---

[40] Prosecutor v. Gbagbo, Request for an Investigation, ¶ 18.

testified before the French senate about the Ivorian crisis. The former vowed that France would do everything possible to install Alassane Ouattara in the presidential palace. The latter affirmed that it (France) would transmit to the ICC evidence of human rights violations that occurred in Ivory Coast, suggesting that France would gather evidence for the ICC so that the court could prosecute Gbagbo.[41]

When Ivory Coast was about to organize the election held on December 11, 2011, Ocampo meddled in the internal affairs of the country and precipitated the transfer of Gbagbo to The Hague, not on judicial grounds but on political grounds. Ocampo gave the impression to the public that Gbagbo had to be taken to The Hague because his presence on the Ivorian soil, even though he was in prison in Ouattara's stronghold would undermine the organization of the legislative elections. In other words, the hasty transfer of the former president to The Hague was intended to be a boost (both political and judicial) to Ouattara so that he could have a free ride and a free reign and rule without any major challenge, thus the existence of a clear collusion between the Office of the Prosecutor and Ouattara's camp.

In addition, the public appearances and displays of the prosecutors with Ouattara and Soro add to the tainted image of the ICC. Moreno Ocampo's letter of congratulations on March 27, 2012 to Guillaume Soro, who was just elected president of the parliament, heightened suspicion about the ICC and reinforced the sentiment of that collusion.[42] The indictment of the former Ivorian president led to conflicting interpretations about whether the ICC was qualified to prosecute him or not.

Legal grounds for prosecution

The following question guides the discussion in this section: Did the court have competence to try Gbagbo? The International Criminal Court declared that it had competence to try the former president of Ivory Coast.[43] The debate about legal grounds for the prosecution in Ivory Coast revolves around the process by which Ivory Coast recognizes the jurisdiction of the court. Ivory Coast ratified the Treaty of Rome in February 2013 after Gbagbo was transferred to the Hague

---

[41] Alain Barluet, "Côte d'Ivoire: Paris planche sur l'après-crise," *Le Figaro*, April 7, 2011. http://www.lefigaro.fr/international/2011/04/07/01003-20110407ARTFIG00697-ci-paris-planche-sur-l-apres-crise.php.

[42] The letter was made public by Guillaume Soro himself, who posted it on his Facebook page on April 4, 2012.

[43] The Confirmation of Charges Document gives an account of the debate between the court and Gbagbo's lawyers about the legal competency of the ICC to try Gbagbo.

on November 30, 2011. This was just the culminating point of a process that started with the respective official requests of Ivorian presidents Laurent Gbagbo and Alassane Ouattara inviting the court to begin the investigation into crimes committed in Ivory Coast.

This process can be divided into three moments, or steps: the signing of the Rome Statute in November 1998 under President Henri Konan Bédié; the acceptance of the International Criminal Court's jurisdiction in April 2003, characterized by the formal request by Gbagbo on April 18, 2003; and the ratification of the Rome Statute in February 2013. Between the recognition of the court's jurisdiction in 2003 under Gbagbo and the ratification of the Treaty in 2013 under Alassane Ouattara, two letters were sent by the latter on December 14, 2010 and May 4, 2011 respectively, to the ICC to request the beginning of the investigation of human rights abuses in Ivory Coast.[44] The Office of the Prosecutor mentioned those letters and stipulated that they too served as legal grounds for the prosecution against Gbagbo. In the December 2010 letter, Alassane Ouattara asked the court to undertake an investigation on the 2004 crimes. In his second formal request, he asked the court to limit its investigations to the 2010 post-election violence. As previously mentioned, Moreno Ocampo did not investigate crimes committed by the rebellion in 2002 as they occurred before 2011.

The fact that the prosecutor (Moreno Ocampo) based his arguments on Ouattara's letters demonstrates one of the main collusions between the Office of the Prosecutor, the international community, and Alassane Ouattara. He aligned the court with the dominant discourse about the outcome of the controversial election. The electoral stalemate was still in force and was not resolved yet, with both candidates declared victorious by two separate bodies. The court echoed the position of France, the United States, and the UN, who all recognized Ouattara as the real winner of the election. They, in chorus, rejected the authority of the Constitutional Council that declared Gbagbo the winner of the election, only to put pressure on the president of the same judicial chamber to give an oath to Ouattara, who was finally sworn in by the very institution they had vilified, the Constitutional Council, on May 21, 2011. Sarkozy made sure he did not miss the swearing ceremony. Even though Laurent Gagbo was the target of the court some stakeholders had hoped that the ICC would conduct a fair prosecution of both camps. The choice of a selective prosecution was questionable as much as the rationale of the option of a sequential prosecution.

---

[44] Prosecutor v. Gbagbo, ICC-02/11, Request for an Authorization of an Investigation Pursuant to Article 15, ¶ 17 & 22 (June 23, 2011).

Suspicious sequential prosecution rationale

A decade after the crisis, the court has yet to investigate let alone prosecute a single person in Alassane Ouattara's camp. This throws legitimate and logical suspicion on the credibility of the ICC and reinforces the position of its critics, who doubt its claim of impartiality. Less than two weeks after Gbagbo's first appearance before the court, Moreno Ocampo gave a hint about the nature of the prosecution in Ivory Coast. He referred to the option of sequential prosecution during a press conference on December 15, 2011, during which he discussed plans about his handover to his deputy, prosecutor Fatou Bensouda. He added that sequential prosecution implied that more suspects from Gbagbo's camp would be prosecuted subsequently. He added that only when all suspects of Gbagbo's camp were arrested would the court prosecute suspects in Alassane Ouattara's camp. During the same press conference, he announced that Guillaume Soro, the former rebel leader who had just attended a meeting of the Assembly of States Parties to the Rome Statutes, had promised to fully cooperate with the court for the indictment of the former Ivorian president.[45] This was surprising because the leader of the rebellion, who should supposedly be criminally responsible, was the very person that Ocampo mentioned in that press conference. The truth of the matter was that after the incarceration of Laurent Gbagbo and Blé Goudé in The Hague, the Office of the Prosecutor had pressed hard to have Simone Gbagbo transferred to The Hague.

In the course of my battle for justice against the ICC handling of the Ivorian case, I met a high official at the Office of the Prosecutor who explained to me the rationale of sequential prosecution during a meeting on May 28, 2014 at the ICC headquarters. He claimed that it was intended to avoid the mistake they had made with the Kenyan case, where the ICC was conducting a simultaneous prosecution that was hampered by the sacred union of the two antagonists, the very suspects on both sides, Kenyatta and Ruto, which took the name of Rainbow Coalition or known as the presidential ticket UhuRuto. Eventually the ICC had to back down and stop the prosecution in Kenya. In the case of Gbagbo, one would think that the investigation of the crimes he was accused of would lead to a smooth confirmation of charges against him. Que nenni!

Gbagbo's transfer and adjournment of confirmation of charges

From Gbagbo's fall on April 11, 2011 to his transfer to The Hague on November 30, 2011, the prosecutor had not been able to gather sufficient and enough evidence to demonstrate criminal responsibility of the former Ivorian

---

[45] United Nations, "Press Conference by Prosecutor of International Criminal Court," December 15, 2011, https://www.un.org/press/en/2011/111215_ICC.doc.htm.

president to the point that the pre-trial judges adjourned the confirmation of charges. From February 19–28, 2013, the International Criminal Court held the pre-trial of Laurent Gbagbo in order to determine if there was enough evidence to try him. This demonstrates that Gbagbo's transfer was done in a hasty way. The Office of the Prosecutor presented a document of charges against the defendant to the Pre-Trial Chamber (the "chamber"), convinced that it contained quantitative and qualitative incriminating evidence for the indictment of the former Ivorian president.

The decision of the court on whether or not there was enough evidence to try Gbagbo was awaited and was finally announced on June 3, 2013. The Pre-Trial Chamber decided to adjourn the hearing on the confirmation of charges due to insufficient evidence. The chamber stressed that the Office of the Prosecutor based its charges on human rights organizations and press reports and that tangible evidence was lacking in the documents it provided. The prosecutor even used video evidence for another country to show an example of a crime against humanity committed by Gbagbo, which was a total blunder.[46] The chamber decided to give more time to the prosecutor to provide the requested evidence, till November 15, 2013.

The crimes were not called into question, but the evidence was deemed insufficient.[47] Six actions were indicated, which also included the activities of the pro-Ouattara forces from November 2010 to May 2011 in and around Abidjan.[48] The hasty transfer of Gbagbo to The Hague, which preceded the gathering of evidence against him that later happened not to be sufficient enough—to the point that the confirmation of charges was adjourned—reinforces the position of those who question the credibility of the court. In the document of charges, the prosecutor failed to mention other armed groups that also caused human rights violations, such as the Invisible Commando, the French troops, the UN troops, and the Forces Républicaines de Côte d'Ivoire (FRCI), the new name Alassane Ouattara gave to his former rebels on March 17, 2011. This failing draws also on the discretionary power of the prosecutor.

---

[46] Félix Tano, "L'Ajournement d'Audience pour Insuffisance de Preuves de la Cour Pénale Internationale: Un Acharnement Judiciaire," in *Cour pénale internationale: L'introuvable preuve contre le président Laurent Gbagbo*, Raymond Koudou Kessié, Hubert Oulaye, and Félix Tano, eds. (Paris: L'Harmattan, 2013), 80.

[47] Tano, "L'Ajournement d'Audience, 73.

[48] Prosecutor v. Gbagbo, Decision adjourning the hearing.

Rome Statute and discretionary powers of the prosecutor

Tradition has shown that "prosecutors can exercise and have exercised considerable discretion in selecting cases."[49] The Rome Statute, so acclaimed, contains some substantial weaknesses that impact the efficiency of the court and may raise some questions about the impartiality of the court. Two articles related to the initiation of an investigation (Article 53) and the confirmation of charges (Article 61) address the discretionary powers of the prosecutor of the court. The former stresses that it lies solely with the prosecutor to initiate an investigation if he or she considers that there are enough grounds for prosecution or an investigation. This discretionary power about the selection of charges is exclusively in the hands of the prosecutor.[50] The Pre-Trial Chamber does not have the power to interfere in the execution of the discretionary power of the prosecutor about which crimes to investigate. This may lead to a selective prosecution and to a selective investigation, and logically to a selective indictment, and consequently to selective justice, and ultimately to a lack of true justice. The prosecutor using his or her discretionary power decided that there was enough evidence against Gbagbo and not enough against Ouattara's camp.

Article 61 of the Rome Statute suggests that the prosecutor is the one who gathers and presents the charges and evidence. He or she alone is also the one who communicates the evidence on which he or she bases his or her case for the confirmation of charges. He or she alone can modify or withdraw the charges or present additional evidence. In the case of Gbagbo, Fatou Bensouda undertook a further investigation and presented additional evidence to build her case at the request of the Pre-Trial Chamber. Fatou Bensouda deliberately ignored the instructions of article 54 of the Rome Statute.

One-sided prosecution and violation of Article 54 of the Rome Statute

The one-sided prosecution and the obsessive motivation of the prosecutor to charge Gbagbo were in breach of Article 54 (1) (a) of the Rome Statute. That article entitled "duties and powers" of the Prosecutor states: "In order to establish the truth, extend the investigation to cover all facts and evidence relevant to an assessment of whether there is criminal responsibility under this Statute, and, in doing so, investigate incriminating and exonerating

---

[49] Cedric Ryngaert, "The Principle of Complementarity: A Means of Ensuring Effective International Criminal Justice," in *The Effectiveness of International Criminal Justice*, 168.
[50] United Nations, *Rome Statute of the International Criminal Court* (The Hague: International Criminal Court, 2011), 24, 28-29.

circumstances equally."[51] The prosecutor has the obligation to incriminate and exonerate. In the case of Laurent Gbagbo's trial, Moreno Ocampo first and Fatou Bensouda second conducted a hasty investigation whose purpose was to incriminate and not exonerate Gbagbo's camp and to refuse to investigate Ouattara's camp with the intent to exonerate it and exculpate its crimes.

The action of the prosecutor Moreno Ocampo during the electoral stalemate foreshadowed the selective prosecution against Gbagbo's camp. He gave an interview to *France 24*, in January 2011, during which he singled out Gbagbo and his camp, Blé Goudé and the generals of Ivory Coast troops then loyal to Gbagbo, and threatened them with the idea of possible prosecution. It was in the middle of the electoral stalemate, when the domestic antagonists were committing various human rights violations.[52] The court, which vows to prosecute and judge in fairness, did not issue any arrest warrant for the pro-Ouattara warlords, but did issue arrest warrants for Gbagbo, his wife, and the youth leader Blé Goudé. The international justice in this case is tainted with the stain of victor's justice.

The selective and partial investigation by the prosecutor set the pace for unfairness. The Office of the Prosecutor failed to conclude that the crimes committed by the pro-Ouattara forces from 2002 up to 2011 (even after the Pre-Trial Chamber asked for the extension and expansion of investigations) were crimes against humanity that deserved to be prosecuted. In the document "Request for Authorization of an Investigation Pursuant to Article 15," which he wrote to the Pre-Trial Chamber, Ocampo affirmed that there was enough evidence to prosecute Gbagbo's camp for crimes against humanity (paragraph 74) and that there was not enough evidence to prosecute Ouattara's camp for crimes against humanity (paragraph 75).[53]

There was no mention of the single largest massacre committed by Alassane Ouattara's forces since the upsurge of the post-election violence: the massacre of Duékoué. Several journalists wondered whether Alassane Ouattara would be prosecuted for being the commander in chief of the *Forces Républicaines de Côte d'Ivoire* (FRCI) and the *Dozos*, who committed the massacre of Duékoué and other human rights violations. During an interview with *France 24*, on the second day of the French and the UN bombing of Ivory Coast, Moreno Ocampo

---

[51] United Nations, *Rome Statute of the International Criminal Court* (The Hague: International Criminal Court, 2011), 24.

[52] *France 24*, "Le Procureur de la CPI met le Camp Gbagbo en garde," YouTube video, accessed December 4, 2014, https://www.youtube.com/watch?v=p6cA-KBHNOE.

[53] Prosecutor v. Gbagbo, ICC-02/11-01/15, Request for Authorization of an Investigation Pursuant to Article 15, ¶ 74, 75 (June 23, 2011).

was asked the following question: "Could Ouattara also be judged? The UN said that part of the massacre in Duékoué was carried by Ouattara's men." In answering this question, the prosecutor argued that there was still not enough evidence and clarity about the genocide of Duékoué: "We are concerned about the killing in the western part of the country. The information is still not clear. We are working on it...It is not clear yet...on the numbers and the timing."[54]Alassane Ouattara and his warlords that he has promoted in high positions seemed to be absolved of their crimes. The prosecutors have simply refused to acknowledge the crimes of the pro-Ouattaras form 2002 to 2011, even after the Pre-Trial Chamber asked the Office of the Prosecutor to expand the investigation.

Selective activation of the *proprio motu* powers by the prosecutor

The Office of the Prosecutor of the ICC did not use its *proprio motu* powers to investigate the crimes committed by the rebellion in Ivory Coast. The 2003 formal request of Gbagbo, which served as one of the legal grounds for the prosecution against him, did not convince the Office of the Prosecutor to investigate the rebels' crimes, which were well documented. Or, as already expressed, the prosecutor selectively decided to investigate only the crimes attributed to Gbagbo when she (Fatou Bensouda) used the *proprio motu* powers; she ignored those of Alassane Ouattara. Moreover the trial of the former Ivorian president deconstructs the notion of individual culpability, thus highlighting the inadequacies of the ICC prosecutorial rationale which furthered the division in the country.

Collectivization of crimes and alienation of ICC stakeholders

The nature of the crime also has a deterministic relationship with the process of reconciliation, which is not certainly the objective of the international court. The notion of collectivization of crimes speaks to the fact that prosecution against an individual in a context of war is prosecution against a collective or a community, also part of the international court's stakeholders. The crimes investigated and brought before an international jurisdiction suggest that they are international crimes. The crimes occurred during subsequent armed conflicts. This means that "there is always per definition a group fighting against another."[55] The notion of individual culpability adopted in Nuremberg

---

[54] *France 24*, "Ivory Coast: ICC Chief Prosecutor Luis Moreno Ocampo," YouTube video, April 5, 2011, https://www.youtube.com/watch?v=tm83P-pBSzA.

[55] George P. Fletcher, "The Law of War and Its Pathologies," *Columbia Human Rights Law Review* 38, no. 3 (Spring 2007): 521.

resurfaced during the establishment of special tribunals and became a cardinal element in the ICC.[56]

In the name of the individualization of crimes and culpability, the ICC prosecutes individuals who have supposedly committed crimes on behalf of groups and constituencies. The individuals who are prosecuted represent at least one armed group involved in the war. Or, in armed conflicts, armed groups fight each other. The individuals opposed to each other in an armed conflict represent conflicting collective forces: "In international criminal law, the accused person therefore often represents one collective and the victims another in the eyes of both themselves and the public, even though the trials are supposed to individualize the guilt."[57]

In Ivory Coast, prosecuting Laurent Gbagbo, in light of the preceding, shows that the ICC was prosecuting a collective group that Gbagbo represented. In this case, that collective group is multidimensional. It can be Gbagbo's ethnic group, the ethnic groups that he represents, his political party, all those who sympathize with him in Ivory Coast and outside Ivory Coast. The ICC seems to have overlooked "the collective dimension of the criminality."[58] The suspect Gbagbo and the community he represents are also stakeholders of the international criminal court. Many of them have vested interests in the success of the ICC. They too deserve fairness and justice.

The option of sequential prosecution and the one-sided prosecution against Gbagbo, who represents a community, demonstrate that the court has alienated an important community of its stakeholders. The collective dimension of the crimes also negatively impacted the process of reconciliation in Ivory Coast. The community that supports President Gbagbo had also the sentiment of being victim of human rights abuses committed by Ouattara's camp. The choice of punitive justice and of victor's justice reinforced the sentiment of a people who see themselves as persecuted and prosecuted and who do not have any interest in a wishful reconciliation process. These pro-Gbagbo victims felt harassed when Laurent Gbagbo was harassed and could not understand for instance why the bail-out was denied to him multiple times. The ICC Chief Prosecutor Fatou Bensouda who conducted further investigation wrongly attributed some crimes to the former Ivorian president.

---

[56] Clarke, *Affective Justice*, 146.

[57] Mikaela Heikkilä, "The Balanced Scorecard of International Criminal Tribunals," in *The Effectiveness of International Criminal Justice*, ed. Ryngaert, 35.

[58] Heikkilä, "The Balanced Scorecard," 35.

Crimes wrongly attributed to Gbagbo's camp

One of the charges against Gbagbo is about December 16, 2010, a supposedly peaceful demonstration that he crushed. The rally was not carried out by exclusively peaceful protesters and was not peaceful. It was a guerrilla warfare that some pro-Ouattara armed forces undertook. And the crimes that resulted from the combat were exclusively and wrongly attributed to Gbagbo's camp. The transcript of the video of the December 16, 2010 events stresses that the events were not peaceful and that the human rights violations were committed during an armed confrontation between Gbagbo's armed forces and Ouattara's troops. On December 14, 2010, Guillaume Soro declared to his troops at the Golf Hotel: "Soldiers, soldiers, I will go to the Ivorian Radio and Television to install the new managing director of the national television because the President of the Republic [Alassane Ouattara] asked me to do so. You must stand ready. You should be fired up…I count on you." Issiaka Ouattara, known as Wattao, another warlord, added: "As both of our bosses [Alassane Ouattara and Guillaume Soro] have already spoken, we have nothing more to say…We have to be ready for Thursday…They are now the rebels. They did not crush our rebellion. We, we are going to crush them." Ouattara decided to galvanize his men with these words: "Rally, Thursday at 8:00 GMT at the pool with all your military combat equipment. Recess is over.[59]

Despite such evidence, the chamber argued, in paragraph 39 of the Confirmation of Charges Document that it did not believe that the crimes committed occurred in the context of an armed confrontation between Alassane Ouattara's forces and Gbagbo's troops, as Gbagbo's defense claimed, and therefore rejected that argument. But the chamber did not make any mention of or any reference to the above-mentioned statements by Soro and his warlords that clearly indicate that they, indeed, undertook a military assault the day they claimed to be organizing a peaceful demonstration.[60]

The crimes committed that day could not be exclusively imputed to Gbagbo's camp. Several stakeholders questioned the Office of the Prosecutor rationale. It claimed to have used its *proprio motu* powers to begin the investigation and the prosecution against Laurent Gbagbo but did not do so against Alassane Ouattara and his forces who undertook a coup against Laurent Gbagbo in 2002 and who have attempted to launch insurrection recurrently since that year until the 2010-2011 military assault they launched to dislodge the former Ivorian president. The rationale of the ICC punitive justice and selective

---

[59] RTI, YouTube video, accessed March 30, 2011, http://www.youtube.com/watch?v=EF-ScWulSaM.

[60] Prosecutor v. Gbagbo, Decision on the Confirmation of Charges, ¶ 39.

prosecution contrasted with the ideal of national reconciliation in Ivory Coast and with the concept of restorative justice.

ICC prosecution: justice vs. peace and reconciliation in Ivory Coast

Africa has been the theater of competing and conflicting understandings of justice. Laurent Gbagbo's trial has been the reflection of these divergent judicial approaches: punitive justice vs. restorative justice. The judicial approach of the ICC (punitive) contrasts with the ontological traditional justice known to African communities (restorative). The concept of restorative justice gained credence with the rise to pre-eminence in the mid-1990 of the Ubuntu philosophy, whose fundamental values are humanness, caring, sharing, respect, compassion,[61] which served to build a multiracial democratic South Africa under Nelson Mandela. Seen as an African value system for the moral regeneration of post-apartheid South Africa, the Ubuntu philosophy whose essence is humanness or humaneness became gradually an ideological and theoretical compass for Africa's emancipation, unity, integrated sustainable development, and communal justice. The Ubuntu philosophy served as a framework for the Reconciliation and Truth Commission and various South African public policies. Desmond Tutu, leader of the Truth and Reconciliation Commission in South Africa, is credited to have articulated the Ubuntu theology. He drew on Ubuntu as a philosophy of conflict resolution for the healing of the South African nation wrecked by decades of apartheid. The idea of Ubuntu communal justice posits that individual rights are intertwined and interwoven with communal rights. The pillars of that traditional justice system are restoration and healing.

The success of the Truth and Reconciliation Commission in South Africa and the Gacaca tribunals in post genocide Rwanda inspired several thinkers and policy makers to advocate an alternative to punitive justice for the sake of peace and nation building in the aftermath of a conflict with horrific consequences. However, several others opposed the idea of transitional justice. Even though they agreed that it may help heal and help rebuild the community, they thought that it is not a deterrent to crimes against humanity and mass atrocities.[62] The question that looms large is the following: Is it possible to see the ICC in

---

[61] Johann Brodryk, *Ubuntu Life Lessons from Africa* (Pretoria: Ubuntu School of Philosophy, 2002), 32.

[62] Centre for Conflict Resolution, "Peace versus Justice: Truth and Reconciliation Commission and War Crimes Tribunals in Africa," Policy Advisory Group Seminar, Cape Town, May 17–18, 2007.

accordance with a project of transitional and restorative justice? To this question Leo C. Nwoya gave an insightful answer:

> First, while prosecution can serve a wide variety of purposes, especially following mass atrocities, it may always be a sensible choice for a country. Second, demanding prosecution in every situation whether by ICTR, ICC, or domestically, whilst top down, is also a very limited approach in that it overlooks the intricacies and difficulties of each conflict, thereby preventing the consideration of novel or underutilized alternative mechanisms of justice.[63]

In building his case, Leo C. Nwoya echoed the position of those who accuse the ICC of partiality for issuing five arrest warrants for the LRA members while it refused to prosecute members of the Ugandan government. To this criticism, Moreno Ocampo, the former chief prosecutor of the ICC, argued:

> Some people say that the only way to retain our impartiality is to prosecute both the LRA and the UPDF (government forces). However, I think that impartiality means that we apply the same criteria equally to all sides. A major criterion is gravity. There is no comparison of gravity between the crimes committed by the Ugandan army and by the LRA. The crimes committed by the LRA are much more grave than those committed by the Ugandan army.[64]

Moreno's response was grave in itself. When applied to the Ivorian crisis, it shows the double standard and the bad faith of the ICC. The notion of "gravity of crimes" in the Ivory Coast case should have pushed the ICC to prosecute Alassane Ouattara's crimes and those of his warlords, namely Guillaume Soro, or to investigate the Massacre of Duékoué. Asked why the ICC had not so far decided to investigate this most atrocious crime of the electoral stalemate, Fatou Bensouda dismissed the veracity of the criminal incident as lacking judicial substance. She added that the court was not going to rely on media reports.[65] In light of this, the non-prosecution of Gbagbo would have been in the interests of justice and true reconciliation: "Not prosecuting may under certain circumstances contribute more effectively to a durable peace and

---

[63] Leo C. Nwoya, "Transitional Justice and the ICC: Lessons from Rwanda," in *The International Criminal Court and Africa*, ed. Ankumah, 576.

[64] Nwoya, "Transitional Justice and the ICC," 576.

[65] Fatou Bensouda made that statement during the inaugural ceremony of an international conference held in Accra (Ghana) on "Africa and the ICC: Legitimacy, Selectivity, Impartiality and Responsibility." The conference took place on March 17–18, 2016 at GIMPA in Accra. She was responding to my denunciation of her handing of the Ivory Coast case and of the Laurent Gbagbo's trial.

political reconciliation."[66] The court in need of internal substantial structural changes should seek to find the proper balance between prosecutorial rationale and the imperative of transitional justice.[67]

The Forum of Former African Heads of States led by Joaquim Chissano who led Mozambique from 1986 to 2005 wrote a letter to Fatou Bensouda urging her to drop the charges against Gbagbo for the sake of peace, justice, and reconciliation. The forum warned that the way the trial was conducted and the way the charges were built against the former Ivorian president could lead to the resumption of the civil war in Ivory Coast. It suggested that his release would greatly contribute to peace and reconciliation in the country.[68] The situation of tension and conflict was rightfully expressed in the title of an article written by Reuters, "Gbagbo's Trial exposes old wounds."[69]

Let it be recalled that the court has been unable to undertake a simultaneous and comprehensive prosecution of all the potential suspects who presumably had a criminal responsibility in the Ivorian crisis. The approach of punitive justice undertaken domestically in Ivory Coast and by the ICC breaks the tradition of conflict resolution in Ivory Coast. During the one-party-system era, the first president of the country, Félix Houphouët-Boigny, regularly used the platform of "National Councils" as a catharsis and a means of healing the nation. In the democratic era, Laurent Gbagbo organized a forum of reconciliation. Even though it was imperfect, it gave the opportunity to a variety of stakeholders to share their pains and their views on the conflict. Alassane Ouattara, who decided to punish Gbagbo's camp and crush dissenting voices, broke with the culture and the tradition of peace and reconciliation in Ivory Coast. In that context of an expedited justice in Ivory Coast, the fact that the ICC refused to grant a bail to the former Ivorian president in the early moments of the trial was perceived as a judicial harassment.

Standoff concerning bail request

Laurent Gbagbo's lawyers used a variety of reasons to request his release on bail after his incarceration in The Hague, including at times his health issue. The

---

[66] Ryngaert, "The Principle of Complementarity," 147.

[67] Dersso, "The ICC's Africa Problem," 74.

[68] Africa Forum, "An Urgent African Appeal to the Prosecutor of the International Criminal Court: Côte d'Ivoire and Africa Need Former President Laurent Koudou Gbagbo in order to achieve Peace and Justice!" September 9, 2015.

[69] Ange Aboa and Joe Bavier, "Gbagbo's Trial Exposes Old Wounds," Reuters, January 28, 2016, accessed June 28, 2019, https://br.reuters.com/article/us-warcrimes-ivorycoast-gbagbo-idUSKCN0V621B.

court repeatedly denied him bail, thirteen times. The court stood its decision on the fact that the defendant would benefit from the existence of a network of supporters who could help him escape justice and that there was a risk that that network could hamper or compromise the proceedings through pressure or coercive actions on witnesses. The court also added that there was clear indication that Gbagbo could escape his eventual condemnation, considering the gravity of the charges against him.

The former Ivorian president was kept in captivity, and time and time again, the prosecutor was given chance after chance to further her investigation so she could build a stronger case against him. This is a double flagrant violation of Article 66 (1) of the Rome Statute, which is about the presumption of innocence: "Everyone shall be presumed innocent until proved guilty before the Court in accordance with the applicable law."[70] Even when the court decided to hold a trial, the possibility of granting a release on bail to Gbagbo was still relevant and sensible, as the court has not yet given a final verdict about whether he was guilty. After 7 years in captivity with no bail, the presumption of innocence of the defendant should have been honored and respected.

On Friday, December 14, 2018 the Prosecutor's Office and the defense lawyers waited until the end of the day to be informed that a "written decision" would be sent "by the end of the year," about a bail release to be granted to Laurent Gbagbo and Blé Goudé. The three judges who had convened this session decided to "urgently" assess the "risks" of a possible provisional release of Laurent Gbagbo and Blé Goudé. The principle of their release on bail was adopted after two judges out of three agreed to it, but the choice of a host country that would comply with the rules, rights, and obligations of the defendants delayed the announcement of their decision. After a couple of days of suspense, the court finally issued another communique informing its stakeholders that the decision about whether it should grant the release on bail to Gbagbo and Blé Goudé would be made public in mid-January 2019. Moreover, it was rumored that Belgium could be the host country and that Gbagbo should wear a GPS monitoring device or an ankle bracelet during his provisional freedom period. This caused an outcry by Gbagbo's supporters, who saw this as a way by the court to continue humiliating him.

The ICC staunch supporters failed to understand that it was difficult to dissociate the neo-colonial war against Ivory Coast from the incongruities of Laurent Gbagbo trial which exposed the ICC. The actions of the court and its

---

[70] United Nations, *Rome Statute of the International Criminal Court* (The Hague: International Criminal Court, 2011), 32.

handling of the Ivory Coast crisis have been perceived as a continuation of the same neo-colonial war. The section below underlines that aspect of the discussion.

Global superstructure, the ICC, and imperialism

I have designed the schematic of the structure of the global governance or superstructure which I have called the Wheel of Imperialism. The Wheel of Imperialism is the most complete form of a supra organizational structure that Westerners set up since slavery. It was refined during colonization and was perfected after independence was won and became the bedrock of neo-colonialism and collective colonialism.[71] Colonialism as it was established presented common features, a common *modus operandi*, mechanism, and system summarized in the following elements: colonial administration led by colonial powers; Afro-European armies for the preservation of colonial peace, law, and colonial order; forced labor; forced taxation; concessionary companies; colonies used as purveyors and providers of raw materials and cash crops for the western world; colonies used as captive markets where European goods were dumped; limited education of an African elite trained to work in the colonial administration. The goal of colonialism was the preservation of the colonial order and tthe expropriation of lands, resources, and of the people of Africa and of the world.

The creation of institutions in the aftermath of WWII in the name of peace, progress, and prosperity became the consolidation of a global structure in the hands of Western powers. They control or they are the creators of a variety of institutions in every sphere of human activity. In the face of the rise of nationalism in a number of situations, they are activated in a coordinated way to undermine the spirit of self-determination and sovereignty of dissenting voices around the world namely those of the African people. The architecture of the globalized system set up in the aftermath of WWII mirrors the features of the colonial order described above.

Kwame Nkrumah declared rightfully decades ago: "The forces arrayed against us are, and I use the word most carefully, formidable…They operate in world-wide combinations at all levels: political, economic, military, cultural,

---

[71] The expression "collective colonialism" was used by Kwame Nkrumah when he warned Africans about the threat that the European Economic Community represented for them. See William Zartman, *Politics of Trade Negotiations between Africa and the European Economic Community: The Weak Confront the Strong* (Princeton: Princeton University, 1971), 21.

educational, social, and trade…and not all, through intelligence, cultural, and information services. They operate from European and African centers using agents who, I am ashamed to say, are often unpatriotic sons of Africa…"[72] There was a vacuum in the field of international justice, and the ICC filled it. Below is the schematic of the structure of the global governance or superstructure that I have designed and that I call the Wheel of Imperialism, as described by Kwame Nkrumah.

Figure 2: Wheel of Imperialism. Source: Author

The wheel of imperialism is a supra organizational structure which exists to defend, to advance the interests of westerners or to enforce imperial order or to maintain imperial peace. It works in several ways and in stages that reflect the different levels of its functioning according to its objectives in a given situation. It provides security and projects power. With the attraction it offers it inspires admiration. All those who want to live decently and who have the skills to do so can hope one day to work in the institutions that make up the various agencies of global governance. Many people dream of working there. It does not always destroys immediately. When faced with a form of opposition, the

---

[72] CPP Ghana Online, "Nkrumah Speech Forces against Africa," YouTube video, October 7, 2012, https://www.youtube.com/watch?v=OeozQd5cemg.

imperial wheel first tries to charm, to seduce, to corrupt, then it tries to intimidate, to threaten, to frighten, and finally it sets itself in motion to crush, to break and to destroy. The steamroller of the imperial wheel, imbued with its will to power, crushes everything in its path. Then it becomes the leviathan.

When the decision is taken by the leaders of the imperial countries, the steamroller starts. All the institutions are activated or self-activate themselves, in a concomitant way, each playing its part in this concert of destruction for the triumph of the imperial order in very specific battles. The institutions of the steamroller, in harmony, in a form of synchronicity and symbiosis, play their role within the framework of their activities and in their respective spheres.

The military option to enforce the imperial order is usually the last resort. This explains the reason why powers have set up military bases across the globe in regions other than their respective countries. Long before the activation of the military dimension or before actual weapons are used most of the other institutions in all the spheres of activity are weaponized. The process of financial isolation is put into motion through measures of financial suffocation, namely economic embargo. The local branches of the international financial system in the country to break, like the western multinationals, obey the orders emanating from the source of the imperial power and they have to make sure financial and economic pain be inflicted to the nation.

Trade with the enemy country is suspended, thus causing commercial strangulation. Warfare claims its rights. Resolutions are voted in the United Nations as a means of retaliation or as a legal cover for military missions. They are disguised under the cover of a civilizing mission or a humanitarian intervention to save the peoples supposedly oppressed by their own leaders. Western media no longer give real information. They become channels of propaganda. Information is transformed into war communications. Censorship is justified. It must serve the imperial order. The so-called human rights organizations under the orders of the Western powers from which they receive funding or whose funding comes from certain legal and physical persons who work to advance the imperial agenda align themselves with THE roadmap and echo the propaganda. Intellectuals, draped in the mantle of the white man's burden, whose perspective has been shaped by racial prejudice, churn out articles and books infested with the tenets of social Darwinism and white supremacy.

Be with Laurent Gbagbo, Muammar Kadhafi, or any other leader who defies this order like Fidel Castro, Kwame Nkrumah or Mao Zedong or Vladimir Putin, the methods are the same. In that context, the actions of the ICC which singled out Laurent Gbagbo and exculpated Alassane Ouattara cannot be isolated from the *modus operandi* of the Wheel of Imperialism. They fall in line and they fit into the actions of the steamroller. They become part of the war effort. They became an expression of warfare. The attempts by the ICC to dissociate its actions from those of the neo-colonial forces that opted to break Laurent Gbagbo were null and void. After all, the ICC is controlled by the imperial powers and is a part of the surpra organizationl structure of global governance. Its existence has helped perfect the Wheel of Imperialism.

Despite its might, the Wheel of Imperialism remains a human creation subject to human laws and to divine laws. In its midst there are human beings who have not lost their soul and who are guided by a sense of humanity and who become the voices of reason and who fight to reduce its destructive power. Outside the Wheel of Imperialism or the leviathan there are generations of justice lovers, freedom seekers, truth advocates of all walks of life who, either in clusters or collectively fight for the betterment of mankind, to stop its destructive might and who usually benefit from favorable historical factors. The Wheel of Imperialism is a part of the world historical memory. As such its existence, its implementation, the memory of its past and current operations are challenged by the memory of pains inflicted to others who are willing to pay the ultimate price to conquer their dignity. The trial of Laurent Gbagbo contributed to remind to everyone the *modus operandi* of the Wheel of Imperialism. It also contributed to bring to the memory of Africans the tragic fate of all those who dared to say "No" to the imperial power and order.

Laurent Gbagbo's trial and the African collective memory

In this conversation about the ICC and Africa, it is imperative to make a distinction between certain leaders who do not have the moral authority to denounce the court, because of their unethical leadership or because of their involvement in several human rights abuses, and some in the African community who are genuine about true justice and who can rightfully denounce the ICC as a neocolonial institution. The history of international law regarding Africa is that of a series of subsequent laws and decrees that have been dipped in the ink of racism and that have sustained slavery, colonialism, and apartheid. The African collective memory is filled with recollections of the slave codes, the black codes, Jim Crow, the code of the indigenous, the hottentot code and the apartheid laws. There is a feeling of a legitimate suspicion toward any institution that is part of the global system and governance, particularly the ICC, that seems to be prosecuting Africans exclusively. These observations fuel and feed the mistrust of Africans vis-à-vis the International Criminal Court.

Laurent Gbagbo's trial was unique, as it has been the one that exposed to the world the true essence of the ICC as a tool in the hands of the most powerful. Defeated militarily, defenseless, believed to have lost the election, perceived as unpredictable by the West, seen as an adversary who deserved to be punished for his nationalist stance and defiance, the former Ivorian president was sent to a court based in The Hague. His tragic fate revived in the memory of millions of the members of the global African community how African/black leaders who opposed European colonial penetration and domination were persecuted, prosecuted, haunted and hunted down. It reminded them about nationalists who were sent away and who died far from their respective places of birth:

> The illegal capture and incarceration of President Gbagbo in a white jail has historical precedence. Toussaint Louverture of Haiti died in a white jail. Samory Touré died in a white jail. King Behanzin of Dahomey died in a white jail. Their crimes? They opposed the rape of Africa by the ravenous Occident. Their captures were also facilitated and applauded by some Africans. Each time and African fighter is arrested by the white world and Africans applaud, each time the African continent is plundered of its natural and human resources and Africans applaud, Africans give a standing ovation to the Gobineauian and Levy-Brhulian Aryanist theses of black inferiority and cerebral ugliness, a cerebral ugliness that can be made responsible for all the ugliness of the world, even that which is openly perpetrated by white malice.[73]

Laurent Gbagbo's fate is also a reminder of the assassination of Thomas Sankara, the humiliation and the killing of Patrice Lumumba, the repetitive assaults against the Quilombo communities of Zumba and Zumbi, the murder of Sylvanus Olympio, the tragedies and assassinations of Dr. Martin Luther King, Jr. and Malcolm X, the imprisonment of Nelson Mandela, and the overthrow of Kwame Nkrumah. Irrespective of what could have been the outcome of the election and the discourse that the Western propaganda attempted to construct about the crisis in Ivory Coast, Ivorian nationalists, Pan-Africanists, and internationalists felt a great indignation. They organized to express their opposition to the treatment inflicted to the former Ivorian president.

In Europe, particularly in France and in The Hague, in the wintry weather or in the rain, snow or sleet, or sunny moments, African social activists led by Ivorians, often draped in the orange-white-green colors of their country, gathered and organized rallies at each session of this trial for over eight years, by hundreds and thousands, to denounce French neo-colonialism and the ICC. Their resilience and their determination were reported regularly by major French media. Every session of the trial since the imprisonment of the former Ivorian head of state in The Hague has been an opportunity for Africans to denounce the victor's justice, the ICC, and French neo-colonialism. Taking

---

[73] Frindéthié, 176.

advantage of new information technologies and the social media, social activists and cyber activists have seized the opportunity to spread their side of the story and rally like-minded people across the continent and the globe. They have not missed a chance to ridicule the court, mocking it by organizing parodies of the trial.

Two young Africans based in Switzerland, the female from Ivory Coast and the young man from Cameroon, made a video in which they performed a parody of a trial hearing of Laurent Gbagbo and Blé Goudé. Sequences of the video were recurrently interrupted by their own contagious laughter. The young man played the part of the Deputy Prosecutor Eric MacDonald and the lady was one of the prosecution witnesses. In the beginning they could not agree on the identity of the witness as they wanted to mock the naming of the prosecutors' witnesses who were given codes that begin with a capital P followed by several digits..

"Are you...P-120? or aren't you P-121?"

"No, I am P-130 but if you want you can call me P-100,000. I am here to be a witness."

The prosecutor asked the witness to talk about the conversation she had with Blé Goudé when he told her to go and kill people. And the witness asked the prosecutor, in a unique Ivorian way of speaking, "You, you were there when Blé Goudé asked me to go and kill people?" The prosecutor replied, saying: "We met and spoke in Ivory Coast and you told me it was fine; and that you could come to court and tell the audience that Blé Goudé sent you to kill civilians." In her response, the witness revealed that she used the opportunity of the trial to migrate to Europe without having to swim across the Mediterranean: "Bengué [Europe] that you see, it is not easy to come here. You know yourself how these Eritreans swim across [laughter] the Mediterranean to come here." Then the prosecutor reminded her that her air ticket was paid and that she must respect her part of the contract. To this P-100,000 replied: "You paid my ticket to come here. Should I give a damn?"

As if the two young persons wanted to depict the surreal world being displayed in the courtroom, the exchange shifted, and they switched roles for a brief moment. A witness whose role in a courtroom is to answer questions was now asking the prosecutor what his name was. He replied "MacDonald." To this the witness, alluding to the American fast food brand MacDonald responded: "Isn't that the name of the new bread people eat at a store?" And the witness continued: "I thought you were the maker of that bread. You have not created that store, and you pretend to know that Blé Goudé sent us to go and kill people…"[74] The video ended with uncontrollable laughter. Several other cyber activists have made similar videos to mock the infamous trial of shame.

One of the moments of the trial which became a source of inspiration for ingenuous activism occurred on December 13, 2018. That day, the judges of the International Criminal Court discussed the possibility of the provisional release of Laurent Gbagbo. The deputy prosecutor (Eric MacDonald) declared that he would be in favour of such decision but on one condition: The accused Laurent Gbagbo should wear an electronic bracelet on his ankle. For African nationalists, the image of Laurent Gbagbo, former president of Ivory Coast, unjustly imprisoned in a white man cell was unbearable. Immediately, Ivorian internet users decided to make a mockery of that recommendation. They launched a "GPS Challenge," taking and publishing photos of themselves on social networks wearing on their ankles "electronic bracelets" such as drones, women's underwear, toilet paper, watches, big old cell phones, and fans.[75]

French major news organizations such as *Le Monde, Libération, le Nouvel Obsersateur, le Figaro, France 24*, and *Mediapart* dedicated countless reports to the trial. Their coverage shed a new light on the role of France in the Ivorian crisis and in Gbagbo's trial. Political analysts debated on major talk shows. Books were published by French writers and journalists on *Francafrique*, on the trial, and on the ICC, as they retold the Ivorian crisis and the fate of Gbagbo, who was vilified. The discourse on the controversial role of the ICC could not be ignored anymore. It moved from the periphery to the core of French political circles. There were some key moments in the reports made by French media that shifted French public opinion. Suffice it to mention the investigative piece by *Mediapart* "*Procès Gbagbo: Les Preuves d'un Montage*," which created an unimaginable buzz across the globe. The content of the article was made available in various languages, as it was published in coordination with major news organizations in Europe. Several other news organizations echoed the revelations published by *Mediapart*. The political involvement of the French political elite, their collusion with Alassane Ouattara's regime and the ICC for the indictment of Laurent Gbagbo, were denounced.

Pan-African news organizations were at the forefront of the struggle. One news organization based in Cameroon, a TV channel, Afrique Media, often the

---

[74] Nakouty Luyet, "Procès de Laurent Gbagbo et de Charles Blé Goudé: il faut sauver le temoin P 100000 Degamage," YouTube video, February 2, 2016, https://www.youtube.com/watch?v=WSu1dzsQQ28.

[75] *France 24*, "Video-Les internautes Ivoiriens lancent 'le bracelet electronique challenge,'" December 14, 2018, https://observers.france24.com/fr/20181214-cote-ivoire-internautes-bracelet-electronique-challenge-gbagbo.

target of French authorities who sought unsuccessfully to destroy it claimed glory thanks to its militantism, its anti-French neocolonialist stance, its commitment to a Pan-African narrative. It carried the burden for the freedom of Laurent Gbagbo in the field of media. Recurrently, regularly, constantly, and consistently, Afrique Media (through its shows which look like the under the baobab tree lengthy but enjoyable conversations) helped set the score straight with regard to Laurent Gbagbo's trial. That news organization, through its shows and reports, in line with the Pan-African mandate contextualized the significance of the trial in relation to the Africa historical memory. The image of Laurent Gbagbo captured by the French troops and on trial in the Hague became counterproductive for the West, as it awakened many in Africa. Besides groups of social activists who organized in various parts of the world, on the African continent, Cameroon became the hub of the resistance against French neo-colonialism and the court and for a good reason. The Ivory Coast crisis was reminiscent of the war of independence fought and lost by the Cameroonian nationalists of *Union des Populations du Cameroun* (UPC). Hundreds of thousands of Cameroonians and their leaders Um Nyobè and Félix Moumié lost their lives.[76]His incarceration in a western prison was seen and presented as a deportation. His capture was presented as a reminder of that of Lumumba. Through the trial they re-lived the tragedies of the African masses and people. As they watched the trial and the cross-examinations, they became more emboldened as the tide was turning against the prosecutor and her principals.

---

[76] Pigeaud, *France Côte d'Ivoire*, 348.

Laurent Gbagbo's trial, testimonies, acquittal, and the decision

This chapter, while it spotlights the atmosphere in the courtroom, highlights some of the prosecution witnesses' testimonies, sheds light on some cross-examinations, debates the oral pronouncement of the defendants' acquittal, and the written decision of the acquittal. The prosecutor's approach could not stand against factual truth which arose from the counter-examinations in the courtroom. Prosecution witnesses turned into Defense witnesses, recanted their initial testimonies. If the prosecutor succeeded in avoiding the debate about who was the winner of the elections since the beginning of the trial, she could not avoid other debates, in particular that of the armed confrontations which took place between the parties since 2002 and especially during the post-electoral crisis. The army officers she brought to testify against the defendants were army officers who lost brethren during the ten-year long confrontation. In the course of the blame game they engaged in, they highlighted some of the military confrontations which occurred during the post-electoral crisis between the army loyal to Laurent Gbagbo and the pro-Alassane Ouattara forces which took the official name of FRCI before the massacre of Duékoué.

Incriminating testimonies and incidents

The prosecutor argued that Laurent Gbagbo has designed and devised a common plan to remain in power and that in the course of the implementation of that plan he systematically sought to brutalise, neutralize, and kill dissenters mostly from Alassane Ouattara's camp. The burden of proof was therefore on the Office of the Prosecutor. Fatou Bensouda's responsibility was to prove beyond reasonable doubt that the commission of crimes were in line with the common plan. The court tried to obtain from testimonies the individual criminal responsibilities of Laurent Gbagbo and Charles Blé Goudé.

Fatou Bensouda compiled thousands of incriminating pages against the defendants. Several types of prosecution witnesses gave their testimonies: crime base witnesses, eyewitnesses, experts, military officials of Laurent Gbagbo's security forces, and the pro-Ouattara victims presented as the victims of the crisis. The incriminating documents put together to build the case encompass forensic evidence, medical reports, videos of speeches and of incidents, and Simone Gbagbo's diary. The witnesses' identities were protected.

Fatou Bensouda appeared only once since the beginning of the trial, the day of its opening. After that it was a team of her substitutes led by Eric MacDonald who led the discussions at the hearings.

The initial number of the prosecution witnesses (138) scheduled to appear in court was dropped to 82 as the testimonies were more exculpating than incriminating. This represented a defection of more than 40% of the witnesses. Some recanted their testimonies or testified in favor of Laurent Gbagbo and his youth minister Blé Goudé. Among the prosecution witnesses there was no senior UN official, no European official, no French soldier who were at the fore front during the post-election crisis. By the time of the decision of the chamber, which resulted in the defendants' acquittal, the defense did not have to present their witnesses. The time of cross-examination was significant because it allowed the court to learn some truth about the charges. The testimonies at the hearing, under oath and in adversarial proceedings, have a much higher probative value than the original reported and written statements.

Before discussing the crux of the matter of this chapter, the testimonies per se, I present the discussions that transpired during the hearing about the Common Plan, the blame game of the army officials, the accusation against Laurent Gbagbo regime about the blockade of the Golf Hotel, and the issue of the requisition of the former Ivorian leader's army.

Regarding the Common Plan that Laurent Gbagbo is accused of having conceived since 2000 to stay in power permanently, the Office of the Prosecutor acknowledged that the plan was not explicit and that its existence could be deduced from indirect evidence. Eric MacDonald argued if Laurent Gbagbo had relinquished power, the course of events would have changed drastically, and crimes would not have been committed. Out of the 82 prosecution witnesses, only one (Witness P-0048), an activist of the Alassane Ouattara's party, addressed the period of the time Gbagbo stayed in power (2000–2010). As noted by the defense, if a Common Plan has been implemented over a period of 10 years, it was incompressible that no one could find any direct evidence (testimony or document) of its implementation, noting that members of the opposition and the rebellion participated in the various governments since 2003.

It is important to note that the most awaited testimonies were those of the former hierarchy of the army once loyal to Gbagbo: Brindou M'Bia, former general director of the police; Georges Guiai Bi Poin, commander of the security operations coordination center, a joint elite unit composed of elements from the army, police, and the Ivorian gendarmerie called CECOS (now dissolved); Édouard Kassaraté, head of the gendarmerie; and the head of all the security forces, General Philippe Mangou. These high officials of the

Ivorian army played the blame game and accused each other of betrayal or claimed to have been loyal to their former commander in chief till the end.

General Mangou, registered as Witness P-0009, had had a strained relationship with the former Ivorian president in the last days in power of the former Ivorian president. His house was attacked with explosives. Some officers close to the deposed leader accused him of betrayal. They were believed to have been the perpetrators of the attack. General Mangou accused Mrs. Simone Gbagbo's aide de camp Seka Seka, accompanied by mercenaries, to be the perpetrator of his assassination attempt. He found refuge at the residency of the South African ambassador, with his wife and their five children, at the end of March 2011.[1]

He was later replaced by General Dogbo Blé, the head of the republican guard and of the presidential palace, who had been in prison since the electoral crisis of 2011. General Philippe Mangou told the court that he played the role of coordinator of the military operations, despite the position he assumed, arguing that a lot sensitive information was not reported to him. He later said bluntly that General Dogbo Blé became the effective chief of the army and the centerpiece of the former head of state's military strategy: "Dogbo Blé was at the same time commander of the Republican Guard and commander of the presidential palace. He reported only to President Laurent Gbagbo. Every time he was called for a meeting, he used to say that he was with the president. Between God and the angel, it is obvious that we turn to God. Moreover, in seven years of command, Dogbo Blé attended only twice a meeting of the staff of high command of the army."[2]

On October 5, 2017, when asked by the presiding judge Cuno Tarfusser if the Republican Guard and CECOS were granted secret parallel missions other than the duties of regular security defense forces during the electoral stalemate, General Mangou said these institutions were just carrying their normal responsibilities, which were to defend the institutions of the republic.[3]

The former head of the Ivorian army rebutted the accusations of betrayal and said that his army fought in difficult conditions without weapons and

---

[1] Abraham Kouassi, "Mangou Asked Gbagbo to Resign," International Justice Monitor, September 26, 2017, https://www.ijmonitor.org/2017/09/philippe-mangou-asked-gbagbo -to-resign/.

[2] *Baobab News*, "P1: Procès de Laurent Gbagbo et Blé Goudé du 25 septembre 2017," YouTube video, accessed June 18, 2019, https://www.youtube.com/watch?v=jwvcYh 5aWkA.

[3] Prosecutor v. Gbagbo, ICC-02/11-01/15-T-200-Red2-FRA P-0009, Transcript of the Hearing, October 5, 2019, p. 54, line 9–12 and pp. 58–59, line 13–18.

ammunitions. He rather accused of betrayal the head of the gendarmerie, General Kassaraté, and the chief of the police, General Brindou, because they had not put at his disposal an adequate number of soldiers from their respective units so he could better organize the war to fight Alassane Ouattara's warlords.[4] Perceived by Gbagbo's circle as disloyal, untrustworthy, and pro-Ouattara, Edouard Kassaraté rejected the accusations of betrayal against him while pointing fingers at some of his colleagues (the head of the police) as he claimed to have attempted to tell Laurent Gbagbo to relinquish power: "I saw that many generals were not in office and I took it upon myself to go and see Laurent Gbagbo to advise him to hand over power to Alassane Ouattara. I was surrounded (accosted) and threatened by the Republican guard soldiers with handguns, but the president was not aware of that incident. They called me a traitor. The president learned this and told me not to pay any mind to that. That's all, I returned to my office and we did not have the exchange."[5]

General Mangou Philippe revealed too that it was when he asked the former president to leave power that he almost lost his life. Mangou divulged that the former head of state "accidentally" financed the Invisible Commando when he thought that Zakaria Koné, a pro-Ouattara warlord, could be given one million dollars so that his men could infiltrate and destabilize the pro-Alassane Ouattara militiamen, the Invisible Commando. Mangou Philippe said he initially opposed such an operation and pleaded with the president to put this money at the disposal of the army so that his troops could better fight.[6]

General Kassaraté made a stunning revelation, which consolidated the narrative about the French neocolonialist involvement in Ivory Coast. He told the court that there was a French intelligence listening bureau located within the Ivory Coast presidential palace.[7] He informed the court that he had watched the report of the incriminating December 16 rally on TV and claimed that his signature at the end of what is believed to be his deposition was forged.

---

[4] *Baobab News,* "P2: Procès de Laurent Gbagbo et Blé Goudé du 25 septembre 2017 avec le Général Mangou Philippe," YouTube video, September 26, 2017, https://www.youtube.com/watch?v=jwvcYh5aWkA.

[5] APA News, "Le General Kassaraté révele avoir tenté de demander à Gbagbo de rendre le pouvoir a Ouattara," March 14, 2017, https://news.abidjan.net/articles/611397/le-general-kassarate-revele-avoir-tente-de-demander-a-gbagbo-de-rendre-le-pouvoir-a-ouattara.

[6] Abraham Kouassi, "Philippe Mangou: 'Gbagbo Accidentally Financed the Invisible Commando,'" International Justice Monitor, October 2, 2017, https://www.ijmonitor.org/2017/10/philippe-mangou-gbagbo-accidentally-financed-the-invisible-commando/.

[7] *Citoyen Media,* "CPI Francafrique Ecoute," YouTube video, March 14, 2017, https://www.youtube.com/watch?v=mZQAbCkMt0A.

Asked if he remembered some specific details about the meetings he had with other army officers and president Gbagbo, he said he could not recall and that he had a bad memory. In reaction to such a claim, Judge Cuno Tarfusser could not hide his irritation.[8]

The testimony of the head of CECOS threw another stain on the reputation of the ICC. General Guiai Bi Poin revealed the conditions under which he had been forced to testify against the defendant. He accused Alassane Ouattara and Guillaume Soro, as well as the ICC, and denounced the blackmail and the pressure put on him, and spoke about his detention, whose goal was to force him to provide incriminating evidence against the former president:

> One day during the month of August 2011, I was called by an adviser to the then Minister of Defense, Guillaume Soro, who told me that there were representatives of the International Criminal Court (ICC) who wished to talk to me. Shortly after, he put me in touch with a certain Mr. Bah who claimed to be working for the ICC. I did not object and I agreed to meet with him.

> He asked me questions about the post-electoral crisis. I gave him answers that seemed not to have satisfied him. Later, according to the feedback I received from someone else, the Ivorian authorities had been informed by the ICC and both have found my answers not satisfactory, considering my level of responsibilities that I had occupied. Until August 10, 2011, I was not in detention. I was put in prison from August 20 to December 27, 2011. Oddly enough, I was in detention and I met members of the ICC against my own will. I was taken from the prison to the investigating judge and then suddenly to the investigators of the ICC. I did not like it at all. I reproach them for taking me from prison, for making me believe that it was the investigating judge that I was going to meet; and suddenly I was told that it was the ICC investigators that I would have to meet.[9]

Regarding the discussions in court, it is worth noting that several witnesses recanted their testimonies, which were in total contradiction with their original written deposition. There were instances of courtroom theatrics and entertainment during the trial. During the cross-examination, there was a

---

[8] Stephano de Crete, "Partie 3 Procès Gbagbo/Blé 10 mars 2017 Kassaraté ex cdt sup gendarmerie ntle Côte d'Ivoire," YouTube video, March 10, 2017, https://www.youtube.com/watch?v=Bl1jzR4690M.

[9] Michele Laffont, "Le General Guiai Bi Poin révele "Comment j'ai été obligé de témoigner contre Laurent Gbagbo à la CPI," *Ivoire Business,* April 2, 2017, https://www.ivoirebusiness.net/articles/cpi-le-g%C3%A9n%C3%A9ral-guiai-bi-poin-r%C3%A9v%C3%A8le-%C2%AB-comment-j%E2%80%99ai-%C3%A9t%C3%A9-oblig%C3%A9-de-t%C3%A9moigner-contre-laurent.

witness who could not visibly tell the name of his own village, as it is demonstrated in the brief exchange that follows:

"What is the name of your village?"

"The name of my village? Let me see and check. My village…my village" he said while he was opening different sheets of paper to find out the right one on which the name of his own village was written.[10]

The next section is devoted to the supposedly incriminating incidents, including the debate about the blockade, to the decision-making process, and to the discussion about who was the originator of the orders given to the army of the deposed president during the conflict. On two very important issues, the blockade and the requisition of the army, the former head of the army, General Philippe Mangou, P-0009, denied that his troops sought to starve to death the hosts of the Golf Hotel, Alassane Ouattara, his close aides, and at least three hundred warlords. He informed the court that there was only one policeman on duty before the elections, whose responsibility was to monitor the traffic at the crossroads near the hotel. He added that this changed after the elections, because of an increase in the movement of people going in and out of the hotel, mainly the rebels.

The military officials decided therefore to have nearby a vehicle from which the movements of the pro-Ouattara soldiers could be monitored. General Philippe Mangou reported an exchange he had had on that issue with President Laurent Gbagbo, who, he said, did not ask him to put a blockade against the hotel. He added that the former Ivorian leader asked him to make sure that the soldiers already in the Golf Hotel did not leave the facility. He interpreted the instruction as a military order. As a result, he decided that the observation post that was there was to be readjusted and transformed into a checkpoint. He insisted that no order was given to deprive the people who were at the Golf Hotel of food.[11]

General Mangou continued his testimony and added that the rebels attacked that vehicle and confiscated the machine gun, which they took with them to the hotel. The security checkpoint needed to be reinforced and adjusted with the goal of keeping an eye on the rebel soldiers so that the authorities could be informed in a timely manner about any potentially suspicious movements toward the city and to prevent possible friction between them and the population whose safety needed to be ensured. He added that that

---

[10] AfroPlanete, "Justice: un Témoin qui ne Connait pas son Village," YouTube_video, January 22, 2019, https://www.youtube.com/watch?v=L-U_HPUrAWI.

[11] Prosecutor v. Gbagbo, ICC-02/11-01/15, Annex 3, ¶ 4 and 5 (September 28, 2018).

readjustment was done under the technical supervision and advice of the representatives of the United Nations mission.[12]

In the eyes of Laurent Gbagbo's lawyers, there was no blockade of the Golf Hotel for several reasons: many civilians and journalists, foreigners, foreign dignitaries and mediators, rebels and journalists were going in and out of the hotel. This was confirmed by Witness P-0088, a British journalist, who explained that he met dignitaries and interviewed a TV host there on March 23, 2011. The defense supported their argument by referring to the December 23, 2010 UNOCI report which clearly stated that civilians could enter the Golf Hotel. The legal team argued that the joint ECOWAS-AU mission of January 3, 2011 took place in that hotel. The United Nations Mission could freely enter the hotel, as it had the mandate to protect its occupants and to regularly provide them with supplies. Witness P-0625 explained that, for example, "our helicopters [those of President Gbagbo] were banned from flying but the UN and the French helicopters transported Alassane Ouattara and his relatives and they could fly wherever they wanted."[13] Alassane Ouattara's aides based at the Golf Hotel could go, even during the battle of Abidjan, to areas that were favorable to them. On March 6, 2011, a delegation of pro-Ouattara officials from the Golf Hotel went to Abobo to pay a visit to some people who were believed to be the relatives of the victims of the women's rally of March 3, 2011.

The debate about the requisition of the army was another significant conversation as the court was seeking to establish direct criminal responsibility of the former president in his capacity of commander in chief. General Mangou said: "As for the question of whether the army had any authorizations before acting, I say that we already had the authorization, since we were acting under requisition. Once the army is under requisition, it has to come out with all its means and fire power."[14] The fire power of the army was in question in the incriminating incidents.

Regarding the December 16 incident, the prosecution's line of attack stood on two points: Laurent Gbagbo and his close aides, including General Mangou and Blé Goudé, incited violence in speeches, and the former president actually ordered the repression of a peaceful demonstration. Speeches pronounced by the chief of the army and Blé Goudé days before the rally, in which they were supposedly inciting violence, were used as incriminating evidence. In these speeches, the former vowed to defend the constitution and the Ivorian republic, and nowhere had he mentioned the December 16 rally. The defense

---

[12] Prosecutor v. Gbagbo, Annex 3, ¶ 5.

[13] Prosecutor v. Gbagbo, Annex 3, ¶ 6.

[14] Prosecutor v. Gbagbo, Annex 3.

therefore concluded that there could not be a link between his speeches and the decision to repress the rally. The defense lawyers drew the same conclusion in relation to Blé Goudé, who in the speech considered incriminating asked his audience to organize to fight back with bare hands.

Regarding the actual event, P-0045, a former military officer who claimed to have listened to the police network during the battle of Abidjan, argued that he heard communications of officers who were planning to repress the December 16 rally, namely a movement of protesters around the zoo. The army officers dismissed his claim as they informed the court that they were not using the security forces radio network to communicate during the battle of Abidjan, as they knew they had been infiltrated and that the network was bugged. They said that they were using their personal cellular phones instead to coordinate activities.

The prosecutor could have asked the Ivorian authorities or the French government for the recordings as the French had at least one intelligence listening unit operating during the conflict. For the defense, such recordings would have revealed that there was indeed an armed conflict on December 16 between Alassane Ouattara's rebels and Laurent Gbagbo's security forces, who were performing legitimate defensive actions. According to the defense, the rally was well structured with clear intentions: to place plainclothes fighters among unarmed protesters and use protesters as human shields to approach and attack the security forces loyal to the defendant:

> It must therefore be noted that once again the Prosecutor cannot present to the Chamber a direct testimony of the alleged incident. It must be content with a hearsay, a confused and contradictory word, a hearsay ultimately without interest, since the words reported do not give any indication of what actually happened. Any useful indication to determine the form of the incident and to understand the circumstances: nothing is said about the violent nature or not of the demonstrators present at this place, on their behavior, on the attitude of the FDS, on any shots, on their provenance, etc.[15]

Several witnesses contradicted the prosecutor. Their testimonies corroborated the thesis that the December 16 so-called peaceful rally was indeed a violent one that involved armed groups. The director of the national police, P-0046, stressed the violent nature of the December 16 incident: "This is not a normal occurrence. You saw that, in the balance sheet, there were police officers who were killed. If police officers were killed, that means that it was by firearm. This is not a normal event and that's why the dispersion was ordered by the Minister

---

[15] Prosecutor v. Gbagbo, Annex 3, ¶ 113.

of the Interior."[16] Witness P-0010 added: "Our men who were killed that day, we were deeply moved, because many of them were killed with weapons of war, and especially not with any weapon of war: with anti-tank RPG-7 rockets which have totally burned down troop carriers. There, we were truly moved by these events."[17] According to the report of December 16, 2010, so often referred to by the Office of the Prosecutor, 19 people were killed, including four policemen and five soldiers, and 18 armed forces elements wounded. The defense argued that there were more than ten security forces killed, in Cocody, Abobo, and Yopougon. Regarding the December 16 rally, the chief of the army, General Mangou, P-0009, made a stunning and shocking revelation that substantiated the idea of French neocolonial active involvement in the conflict. He said that he felt obliged to report to the then Ivorian president an exchange he had with General Palasset, the commander of the French troops, after the Ivorian army overcame an attack by the rebels who had come from the Golf Hotel. The head of the French troops forbade him and his soldiers to pursue the attackers in the following words: "If you ever touch the Golf Hotel, consider that you are going to war with France. When I reported back to the president, he said, 'Do not move. Stay on the spot.'" The defendant lawyers consequently said that the former president's instruction was for peace and not for war.[18]

Another testimony, that of P-0578, weakened further the line of attack of the prosecution regarding the December 16 rally. P-0578 claimed to be an eyewitness who recorded six videos of the incident, which later were posted online. Later, the court found out that he was Alassane Ouattara's supporter who contradicted himself during the cross-examination. It appeared that he did not know how the videos were posted online. The idea that he was not the real author of the videos was accepted. The defense team played a video and asked Witness P-106—who claimed to have been an eyewitness or a crime-based witness of the December 16, 2010, rally—to confirm if the images that appeared in the video were those of the incident. He replied "yes," only to be reminded by a lawyer that the footage was shot in Kenya. Embarrassed and confused, the deputy prosecutor confessed in session that it was a consequence of the prosecutor's negligence.

The next incriminating incidents were those of the month of March in Abobo. For the prosecutor, Gbagbo's forces were responsible for the killing of civilians at the two main incidents that took place in Abobo in March 2011: the demonstration of March 3, 2011 and the supposed bombing of March 17, 2011.

---

[16] Prosecutor v. Gbagbo, Annex 3, ¶ 186.

[17] Prosecutor v. Gbagbo, Annex 3, ¶ 187.

[18] Prosecutor v. Gbagbo, Annex 3, ¶ 175.

During their testimonies, Ivorian military officials confessed to have learned of their occurrence only at the end of the day, informed by General Palasset, the commander of the French military contingents in position in Abidjan.

The main argument and the initial narrative of the prosecutor was as follows: Abobo was mostly inhabited by northerners, supporters of Alassane Ouattara, defenseless Muslims who repeatedly suffered assaults and attacks by the security forces of Laurent Gbagbo. These attacks were carried out with the sole purpose of terrorizing that population in order to allow the former Ivorian president to remain in power. The Office of the Prosecutor's task regarding the March 3, 2011 incident was daunting. First it had to prove that the victims were killed; it had to demonstrate their identity. Secondly, it had to demonstrate the condition surrounding their assassination; and thirdly, finally, it had to demonstrate that the order for their assassination came from both defendants. In the Mid-Trial Brief, the prosecutor who initially rebutted the presence and activities of armed rebel groups, mainly the Invisible Commando, acknowledged the involvement of pro–Alassane Ouattara armed groups but dissociated such context from the two incriminating incidents of the month of March.[19]

For the defense, the thesis of the prosecutor who stated that the security forces of the incumbent president targeted defenseless civilians was not credible for the following reasons:

1- The denial by the prosecutor of the presence of pro-Ouattara armed groups in Abidjan and, specifically, in Abobo;

2- The refusal of the prosecutor to accept that there were weapons caches belonging to the rebels in Abidjan before the 2010 election;

3- The fact that the military officials and prosecution witnesses rejected that they organized deadly attacks on Abobo against unarmed civilians but on the contrary spoke in chorus of military operations against heavily armed groups that had taken over that neighborhood, which resulted in a massive displacement of its inhabitants;

4- The prosecutor omitted that there were attacks carried out in February and March 2011 in other parts of Abidjan, targeting populations. One such attack was called the massacre of Anankoua Kouté, named after the neighborhood where the crimes occurred.

---

[19] Prosecutor v. Gbagbo, Annex 3, ¶ 229.

5- The prosecutor saw as a footnote the attacks of those armed groups against the security forces.[20]

Regarding the March 2011 events, the prosecutor assumed that Abobo had a monolithic population, essentially composed of Muslim northerners and supporters of Alassane Ouattara. This assumption could not hold. Ivory Coast is the microcosm of a united Africa, and its cities are the reflection of this cosmopolitan essence. Echoing several other prosecution witnesses, Witness P-0330 could therefore assert: "There were all ethnic groups, but the predominant one is composed of...the people of the North, the North, first, of Ivory Coast, and beyond the north of Ivory Coast."[21] In the same vein, Witness P-0106, who disagreed with the simplistic view of the demographics in Ivory Coast, said that "Abobo is a large commune after Yopougon. There are all kinds of ethnicities there, all kinds of ethnicities that you want, they are in Abobo there...There are foreigners, there are Ivorians there."[22] Asked whether it was possible to determine or not the ethnicity of the people who died in Abobo during the conflict, P-0330 was clear: "I could not...I could not check. I could not verify since I told you earlier that in Abobo, we could find everyone. So, we could not specifically identify the ethnicity of the victims."[23]

The debate further deepened and revolved around the number of vehicles, the number of protesters, the number of crime-based witnesses, the number of shootings, the nature of the weaponry supposedly used during the incident, and the authenticity of tapes supposed to contain the recordings of the incident. Regarding the tapes, due to the counterattack of the defense, the prosecutor who initially brought 16 supposed videos of the incident had to drop more than ten of them and later relied on only one. In 2014, the defense brought to the attention of the court that 11 of these 16 videos "seem to show that it was a photoshop either because the shots were cut, or because the images have been inserted in one shot, or because the pictures were organized according to a different order, either because a soundtrack or a voiceover has been added, or because captions have been added."[24] The defendant lawyers also doubted the authenticity of the other five videos. In the Mid-Trial Brief, the prosecutor only mentioned one video out of the 16 initial ones.

Another debate followed suit about the authenticity of that single video. Another witness, P-0606, an expert in data analysis, at the request of the

---

[20] Prosecutor v. Gbagbo, Annex 3, ¶ 231.

[21] Prosecutor v. Gbagbo, Annex 3, ¶ 235.

[22] Prosecutor v. Gbagbo, Annex 3, ¶ 236.

[23] Prosecutor v. Gbagbo, Annex 3, ¶ 235.

[24] Prosecutor v. Gbagbo, ICC-02/11-01/11-637-Conf-Anx2-Corr2. ¶ 606. (2014).

prosecutor, concluded that the video was "allegedly" recorded on January 7, 2011, at 4:17 p.m., two months before the March 3 incident, but he could not specifically give the date when the footage was shot.

For the defense there was a strong possibility that attempts were made to provoke convoys by organizing rallies on their passage. They thought that perhaps there was one rally scheduled on January 7 and there was another one on March 3. They also insinuated that certainly there was no death or injury on that date because the witnesses were particularly few and incoherent and that soldiers shot in the air and not at defenseless women. For the prosecutor, the video was self-explanatory; for the defense, it did not prove the origin of the gunshots, and it did not show if the shots were fired at the women.

The defense lawyers argued that the video was suspicious and was not credible. No one was wounded, and all the dead were close to each other on a small perimeter. According to them, this spectacle destroys the argument that a heavy weapon was used. If it was a firing of a tank or a machine gun at a significant crowd, people would have been butchered, and bodies or parts of bodies would have been spread in different parts and directions, contended the defense.[25] Also, positions contrasted about the gender of the protesters. For the defense it was not an all-women rally, as there were men in their midst who were giving instructions to the women. Sirah Dramé, a local leader of Alassane Ouattara's party (RDR) in Abobo, who claimed to be the main organizer of the rally, was at the court as Witness P-0184. The defense rightfully exclaimed: "Where were the 3000 women protesters that the prosecutor said gathered to march?"[26]

For the sake of clarity and argument, it is important to recall the conflicting positions about the alleged video of the March 3, 2011 rally, which circulated widely on YouTube and on other social media. On the one hand, some Ivorians considered it unquestionably the absolute proof or evidence of the crimes committed by the Gbagbo defense and security forces. On the other hand, others, mostly in Gbagbo's camp, saw it as a "photoshop." Irrespective of what these two groups' positions were, other observers believed it was valid evidence that confirmed that women had been killed. But this does not resolve the mystery about the nature of the perpetrators of the crime. In Abobo, in a chaotic environment, there were several armed groups (some informal) with competing interests, and some "peaceful" protesters were armed. A careful analysis of the video showed that the videographer did not videotape the people on the ground from head to toe. His filming was fragmented, the images

---

[25] Prosecutor v. Gbagbo, Annex 3, ¶ 310.

[26] Prosecutor v. Gbagbo, Annex 3, ¶ 347.

were unclear, and it appeared difficult to those who watched the video to tell the disposition of the bodies and to check which body presented what type of injury.[27] Oddly enough, the main organizer of the rally, Sirah Dramé, was not videotaped and did not appear in the footage. During cross-examination, she could not tell the number of gunshots she claimed she heard. She said that all the images of the footage of the video were taken on March 3, 2011, while for the lawyers it was a compilation of images taken in different places.

In this regard, the testimony of Ate Kloosterman, Dutch forensic scientist and DNA expert affiliated with the Netherlands Forensic Institute (NFI), was crucial. He made a troubling revelation about the blood on an incriminating element, a T-shirt supposed to have belonged to one of the women victims who died in Abobo. That testimony delivered on Monday, May 29, 2017 cast doubt on the validity of the prosecutor's evidence in relation to that criminal incident, and it created a stir on social networks. During cross-examination, he confessed that he did not question the origin of the incriminating samples (hair, bones, teeth, and clothes, namely a T-shirt) provided to his center by the court, and he did not undertake an independent investigation to gather other potential pieces for DNA analysis. Pressured to disclose the procedures put in place to guarantee that the DNA samples of the victims he received from the ICC matched the samples coming from the victims' family members, the Dutch scientist said that this particular question should be addressed to the court and not to him. He added that his institute was not involved in the sampling and in the selection of pieces for the DNA analysis. In sum, the Netherlands Forensic Institute did not verify the authenticity of the samples provided by the court.

The findings of the scientist after he conducted several tests, including one on the T-shirt mentioned above, added more to the controversy and did not put the debate of the "dead women of Abobo" to rest: "We conducted the tests to determine whether there were traces of blood or not. We saw suspicious spots on the t-shirt, so we did the tests and all the tests were negative."[28]

Ate Kloosterman observed: "If a person wears a t-shirt it is expected that we can discover traces of the person's DNA on the t-shirt. So, we secured the item and after the tests we could not find any mark of human DNA on the t-shirt."[29] The state of the T-shirt supposed to have been extracted from a mass grave also added to the controversy. It appeared in impeccable condition and did not have any marks of dirt, wear or tear. Several supporters of the former Ivorian

---

27 Prosecutor v. Gbagbo, Annex 3, ¶ 63.

28 *RTI Bengue*, "(2e Partie) Procès: Gbagbo et Blé Goudé: 29 Mai 2017, Ate Kloosterman," YouTube video, May 29, 2017, https://www.youtube.com/watch?v=LZG7_aiySt4.

29 *RTI Bengue*, "(2e Partie) Procès: Gbagbo et Blé Goudé."

president thought that this answer confirmed their position according to which the red stain on the supposedly killed women was beef blood and not human blood and that there was no incident of any women who were killed in the first place and the media and Alassane Ouattara's strategists had staged it all. In the same vein, the testimony given by Professor Hélène Yapo Etté, the first female medical doctor in forensic in Ivory Coast was very significant. She worked on the exhumations of bodies of supposedly victims of post-electoral violence in order to investigate if they match with the people said to have been killed as reported by the relatives. She said that in most cases the bodies did not match with the victims said to be killed.

Regarding the March 17, 2011 incident, the prosecutor's line of attack was as follows: In the middle of the day, at least seven mortar shells were fired by soldiers from Camp Commando at the heavily populated area of Abobo, at several specific locations, including a market, a hospital, and private residences, killing more than 31 people, injuring more than 36 people, and destroying several homes, as well as a mosque. The prosecutor argued that P-0009 clearly stated that the military unit (BASA) was authorized to use 120 mm mortars on the orders of Laurent Gbagbo. The Office of the Prosecutor also added that the head of the army P-0009 had received a delegation of power from the former head of state of Ivory Coast for the purpose of using these mortars."[30]

Three of the prosecutor's witnesses' testimonies did not concord and lacked coherency. One said that he did not know anything about any shots; the other one did not remember the date when the shooting occurred; and the third gave a date of the shooting, March 4, which did not match with March 17. The prosecutor could not establish that a member of the military hierarchy and of the inner circle of the former Ivorian president gave the order to a soldier to use the mortar. The defense denounced the confusing use of the terms *requisition* and *delegation* by the prosecutor. With the alternative use of these words, he made it appear that the defendant took a specific decision on the use of the 120 mm mortars. In addition, the prosecutor suggested that the defendant gave a clear delegation of powers to his chief of the army as if he had signed a document for the use of these 120 mm mortars. The defense legal team argued that requisition involves delegation, and such a delegation never concerned the use of a specific weaponry but the overall decision-making capacity that now belonged to the command. In sum, there was no criminal intention in the requisition.[31]

---

[30] Prosecutor v. Gbagbo, ICC-02/11-01/15-1136-Conf-Anx1-Corr, ¶ 485 (June 13, 2018); Prosecutor v. Gbagbo, Annex 3, ¶ 446.

[31] Prosecutor v. Gbagbo, Annex 3, ¶ 452–453.

The chief of the army confessed that he authorized the use of the 120 mm mortar only once on February 25, 2011, as a test firing in the Banco Forest to find out or to make sure that it was not occupied by the rebels. The truth of the matter was that the rebels had taken control of the Banco forest. The prosecutor himself, who affirmed that the shootings of the mortar occurred during broad daylight, was unable to be specific about the time of their occurrence. The witnesses disagreed about the timing of the shooting, indicating different times and periods of the day. Those who said they heard the firing in the morning were P-0297, P-0105, and P-0294. Those who said they heard the mortar gun shooting in the afternoon were P-0106, P-0489, P-0363, P-0226, and P-0184. They also did not agree on the origin of the shooting of the mortar.[32]

A document entitled "Report on the Alleged Shelling Sites within Abidjan, the Ivory Coast Mission—Date 8-12 July 2013," drafted by Liam FitzGerald-Finch, was submitted to the court. It was believed to be a scientific analysis of the expert (Witness P-0411). During the cross-examination, he confessed that he was unable to determine whether a 120 mm mortar shell had fallen on each of the four sites he visited: "As I indicated in my report, and I have said it orally many times, in all these places there is not a single site that can confirm the use of a mortar of 120 mm heavy cased ammunition. It is the set of all the elements observed and that we could see after the lapse of a long period that allowed me to draw this conclusion. There is no specific site where…I can categorically say that it was a 120 mm mortar shell."[33]

During the cross-examination, P-0411 confessed that the impacts on two sites were compatible with the use of artisanal explosive devices and that he did not take any sample that would have made it possible to scientifically test the hypothesis of a mortar fire.[34] P-0411 wrote in his report that "the area of Camp Commando…was found to be a viable firing point for mortar systems and was well within the range parameters…for attacks on the subject areas visited."[35] But yet as the defense pointed it out, this statement was not based on facts, as he (the expert) was told during his investigation that there was not any 120 mm mortar at the Camp Commando and that he confessed during the cross-examination that firing could have come from any location in the vicinity of the camp.[36] The defense revealed methodological shortcomings of the

---

[32] Prosecutor v. Gbagbo, Annex 3, ¶ 461–462.

[33] Prosecutor v. Gbagbo, Annex 3, ¶ 499.

[34] Prosecutor v. Gbagbo, Annex 3.

[35] Prosecutor v. Gbagbo, CIV-OTP-0049-0048, p.0050 (June 12, 2014); ICC-02/11-01/15 ¶ 502 (September 28, 2018).

[36] Prosecutor v. Gbagbo, Annex 3, ¶ 505.

expert. He simply analyzed a bullet fragment that was given to him by the Office of the Prosecutor of the ICC, and he did not even go to the place where it was supposedly collected. Also, the cross-examination brought to light that the expert did not work autonomously and that there was a collusion of interests between the justice system of Ivory Coast and the Office of the Prosecutor, both which assisted him during his investigation.

During his visits, the expert was systematically accompanied by the prosecutor's substitute in Abidjan, by several representatives of the Ivory Coast Office of the Prosecutor, and heavily depended on them for all matters relating to his investigation: site identification, scientific measurements, collection of evidence, and exchange with the inhabitants, since he could not speak French.

Dr. Clark, who performed several autopsies, including those of the alleged victims of the mortar bombing of the Abobo market on March 17, 2011, wrote in his report submitted to the court: "Given that these were said to have been victims of a shelling attack, it was anticipated that most or all might have blast injuries from an explosive device and that residual shrapnel might be found in their remains. No shrapnel was found in any of them, however, albeit the only available means of detection was a metal detector."[37]The prosecutor's charge about the last incriminating incident stresses the fact that the day following Laurent Gbagbo's arrest, the forces of the deposed leader—composed of militiamen, mercenaries, and youths—executed 65 people and raped women in Yopougon.

Initially, while making the list of the alleged perpetrators of the April 12 incident, the prosecutor had added police officers to the groups of victimizers. Later, the police officers were dropped from the list, but according to the defense, the prosecutor was not able to clearly identify neither the authors of the alleged crimes nor the period. In addition, with the fall of Gbagbo, there was a situation of chaos and confusion in various parts of the country with the rebels who were seeking vengeance and who wanted to retaliate and looters who wanted to take advantage of the moment. Yopougon illustrated that scenario, and defenseless civilians were at the mercy of armed groups, mostly the rebels and mercenaries of both sides. In such an environment, it was practically difficult to be sure about the identity of the perpetrators of the crimes committed in Yopougon, argued the defense. Several events confirmed that Yopougon was no longer the exclusive haven of pro-Gbagbo forces and that

---

[37] Prosecutor v. Gbagbo, Dr. John Clark Testimony, https://www.icc cpi.int/sites/default/files/Transcripts/CR2018_03252.PDF.

recurrent incidents of conflicts between the security forces loyal to the former president and rebels and unidentified groups occurred.

On March 31, 2011 5,349 prisoners of the country's main prison (MACA) escaped, and many of them joined the rebels' ranks. Witnesses P-0010 and P-0046 confirmed that by March 2011, the rebels had already infiltrated Yopougon. P-0109 stated that Alassane Ouattara's forces renamed *Forces Républicaines de Côte d'Ivoire* (FRCI) had taken control of Yopougon at the time of President Gbagbo's arrest. It was also agreed that the Invisible Commando succeeded in penetrating Yopougon and was carrying out ambushes on the former Ivorian leader's forces. The United Nations mission in Ivory Coast reported crimes committed against pro-Gbagbo forces by pro-Ouattara forces and confirmed the existence of a pro-Ouattara military base in Yopougon when 300 alleged pro-Gbagbo youth were kidnapped and taken in a neighborhood called Gesco. The witnesses mentioned that there were intercommunity conflicts and gang fights.

During the entire trial and in the documents submitted to various chambers of the court, besides the four main ones chosen as "representative crimes" supposedly committed by the defendants because they alone were enough to establish the existence of contextual elements of crimes against humanity, the prosecutor still referred to 41 crimes, which included the four main ones. Consequently, the prosecution argued it was therefore unnecessary to prove the 41 other incidents. This position was rejected by the judges on December 16, 2013, pursuant article 61 (7) of the Rome Statute:

> The Appeals Chamber is not persuaded by these arguments. The Appeals Chamber notes that the factual allegations in question describe a series of separate events. Therefore, it is not immediately obvious that there is any distinction between the four Charged Incidents and the 41 Incidents in terms of their relevance to establishing an attack against a civilian population. The Appeals Chamber considers that the Prosecutor did not present any information or any other factual allegations that would provide a basis for making such a distinction or serve to explain the alleged link between the 41 Incidents and the four Charged Incidents.[38]

Despite the opposition of the judges to this methodological approach, the prosecution reiterated the same position and inserted it in the Mid-Trial Brief: the distinction of crimes, the notion of representativity of crimes, and the fact that the Office of the Prosecutor was not obliged to prove the criminal

---

[38] Prosecutor v. Gbagbo, ICC-02/11-01/11-572, Judgment on the appeal of the Prosecutor ¶ 46 (December 16, 2013).

responsibility of the defendants in each of the 41 or 34 criminal incidents, as the focus was on the four main ones. The defense replied, stating that the term "representative" has no legal meaning, and for each of the incidents, it has attempted to demonstrate that the accusations were biased, equivocal, unproven, unauthenticated, and unsubstantiated, as it did for the four main criminal incidents. According to the defense, for an attack to be part of a policy, it must have been carried out as part of an overall concerted plan and carefully organized according to a regular pattern.[39] The various cross-examinations considerably weakened the prosecution's case who, in ten years, has been insensitive to the suffering of other Ivorians, the parents of those who have been killed by Alassane Ouaatara warlords, namely the relatives of the massacred in Duékoué.

Myth of homogeneity of victimhood

One of the arguments of the Office of the Prosecutor was that it was fighting for the victims. Chief Prosecutor Fatou Bensouda expressed the claim as she vowed to continue to fight the perpetrators of crimes against humanity: "Indeed, the greatest affront to victims of these brutal and unimaginable crimes…women and young girls raped, families brutalised, robbed of everything, entire communities terrorised and shattered…is to see those powerful individuals responsible for their sufferings trying to portray themselves as the victims of a pro-Western, anti-African court."[40]

This statement presents an uniformization of victimhood or an image of homogeneity of victims. The prosecution of Gbagbo for his alleged crimes against a group does not soothe the pain of his own supporters who were also the victims of human rights abuses by Alassane Ouattara's camp since 2002. The victims in Ivory Coast are from a variety of groups involved in the conflict. There is a myth of homogeinity of victimhood which is highlighted in the following words: "For example, treating victims of the conflict as one actor group blurs their heterogeneity and suggests a sense of group belonging that does not always reflect social realities."[41] As the population of Ivory Coast in its diversity, as well as the victims of the conflict, are all stakeholders of the ICC,

---

[39] Prosecutor v. Gbagbo, Annex 3, ¶ 636.

[40] Smith, "New Chief Prosecutor."

[41] Netton Prince Tawa and Alexandra Engelsdorfer, "Acceptance of the International Criminal Court in Côte d'Ivoire: Between the Hope for Justice and the Concern of 'Victor's Justice,' in *After Nuremberg. Exploring Multiple Dimensions of the Acceptance of International Criminal Justice*, eds. Susanne Buckley-Zistel, Friederike Mieth, and Marjana Papa (Nuremberg: International Nuremberg Principles Academy, 2017). https://www.nurembergacademy.org/fileadmin/user_upload/Cote_d_Ivoire.pdf.

the prioritization of the pain of one group is injustice to the others. The ICC has not respected the pain and suffering of all parties. This also contributes to the conflicting views of several stakeholders about the court.

Laurent Gbagbo's trial, acceptance, and assessment of the ICC

In this section of the book, I intend to discuss the question of the perception and the acceptance of the ICC in Ivory Coast. Two researchers explored this issue during a three-month investigation conducted in 2016 in Ivory Coast. More than 50 people, Ivorians from diverse political backgrounds were interviewed, besides data collected from an analysis of the literature produced in the country. The outcome of the investigation revealed and confirmed the state of a highly divided Ivory Coast along political and ideological lines. The interviewees close to Alassane Ouattara said that the involvement of the ICC in the Ivory Coast was a positive sign for justice. Those close to Gbagbo denounced partial and selective justice and denounced the court as an imperialist tool used to break African nationalist leaders such as Gbagbo and Blé Goudé.[42] This leads to a disillusion and a decline of the acceptance of the ICC, as reflected by the following statement collected by the investigators:

> We officially exited from a decade of military confrontation that caused serious violation to human rights. We did and I agreed that the ICC intervenes to help Ivorians uncover the truth about what appended. The Court has launched a judiciary process, but it is only interested in crimes committed by the former ruling leaders. Finally, I am disappointed and disillusioned. The ICC gives us an unfinished and bitter taste of what international criminal justice can be.[43]

The above statement demonstrates the loss of credibility of the court. Several stakeholders have felt a repulsion towards the court and a public revulsion at it. As the trial proceeded as the case of the prosecutor weakened. In that context, the Trial Chamber I led by Cuno Tarfusser took the historical decision to pronounce the acquittal of the defendants.

Acquittal:
justice delayed but justice served or justice delayed but not served?

With regard to Laurent Gbagbo and Blé Goudé trial, after the court heard the prosecution witnesses, in the early weeks of the year 2018, Trial Chamber had

---

[42] Tawa and Engelsdorfer, "Acceptance of the International Criminal Court," 5.
[43] Tawa and Engelsdorfer, "Acceptance of the International Criminal Court."

asked the Office of the Prosecutor to produce a document (the Mid-Trial Brief) that would address the relevance of the testimonies in relation to the charges.

After the Mid-Trial Brief was produced and submitted to the judges, they turned to the legal defense teams to inquire about their onward game plan. The initial idea or reaction of the defense attorneys was to do some counter-investigation on the ground in Ivory Coast, for which they would need six to nine months—after eight years of prosecution investigation, legal procedures, and trial. The lead counsel of Laurent Gbagbo justified the estimate length of the counter investigation by the anticipated hurdles and difficulties his team may encounter on the ground in Ivory Coast under the government of Alassane Ouattara who has been putting in jail and silencing dissenting voices. In the course of this research I was informed that it was rather the judges of the Pre-Trial Chamber who suggested the lawyers that they should rather submit a request for dismissal instead of asking for more time to do the investigations on the ground.

On September 28, 2018, the legal defense teams therefore submitted confidently to the court a motion of the "No Case to Answer" requesting the dismissal of the case upon the secret suggestion of the judges of the Trial Chamber. They asked the judges to pronounce a total dismissal in the defendants' favor, their acquittal, and their immediate release.

The rationale of the "No Case to Answer" is threefold:

1. It is based on the assumption that the burden of proof is on the prosecutor;

2. The court shall honor its responsibility to protect the rights of the defendants;

3. The court should at any time respect the presumption of innocence of the defendants.

If the prosecutor fails to provide sufficient evidence for the conviction of the accused after she presented her evidence, and after hearing the testimonies of the witnesses, there was no need to continue the trial. The ICC Trial Chamber decided on January 15, 2019 to drop all charges against Laurent Gbagbo and Blé Goudé. The dissenting opinion emanated from Herrera Carbuccia. The two other judges who represented the majority were Cuno Tarfusser, president of the chamber, and Geoffrey Henderson.

In an oral decision, the court concluded that the prosecutor failed to demonstrate that Gbagbo has put in place a Common Plan with his inner circle to remain in power at all costs. The majority considered that the prosecutor could not demonstrate that the defendants gave speeches to incite violence against civilians. Therefore, they decided on their immediate acquittal:

In particular, having thoroughly analyzed the evidence, the Chamber concluded by majority that the Prosecutor has failed to demonstrate several core constitutive elements of the crimes as charged, including the existence of a "Common Plan" to keep Mr. Gbagbo in power, which included the commission of crimes against civilians "pursuant to or in furtherance of a State or organisational policy"; and the existence of patterns of violence from which it could be inferred that there was a "policy to attack a civilian population..." The Chamber decided that, accordingly, there is no need for the defence to submit further evidence.[44]

The improbable trial of the defendants led to an unanticipated outcome for those who had not watched closely the evolution of the debates, testimonies, and cross-examinations. Let it be recalled that the Pre-Trial Chamber had adjourned the confirmation of charges. It was that ray in the jumble of obscure incongruities that foreshadowed an eventual failure of the prosecution. That ray is the primary key to understand and to decipher the decision of the acquittal. The prosecutor Bensouda was asked to further, to extend and expand her investigation along six axes. Here I will recall only three of those axes: one, three, and four. The prosecutor was asked to give more details on the pro-Alassane Ouattara's forces activities and on how their activities played out in the overall military confrontation (axis 1). The prosecutor was urged to provide specific information on meetings during which the Common Plan was adopted (axis 3). The prosecutor was asked to demonstrate for each of the 45 incriminating incidents that the perpetrators of crimes acted knowingly according to the Common Plan (axis 4).

Fatou Bensouda has been consistent about her prosecutorial rationale and strategy. Despite these injunctions along the six axes, she sought to exculpate the pro-Alassane Ouattara's forces and had not given a convincing answer to the recommendation in axis 1. She has not been able to demonstrate the existence of the Common Plan let alone to give details of the meetings during which the so-called Common Plan was adopted (axis 3). With regard to the axis 4, she opted to make a differentiation of crimes between what she called main crimes or core rimes also labeled representative crimes and the other crimes she presented as secondary crimes. She did not bother neither to elaborate nor to demonstrate the criminal responsibility of the defendants on the secondary crimes, thus failing to give a conclusive answer to axis 4.

The news of Gbagbo's acquittal shocked and shook the globe, making headlines on all—if not on the most important—news organizations of the

---

[44] *Prosecutor v. Gbagbo*, ICC-02/11-01/15, Trial Chamber Oral Decision (January 15, 2019).

world. The very western media which had demonized and vilified him echoed the news of his acquittal. As the first former head of state to be brought before the court, he was then the first former head of state to be acquitted, leaving many of his detractors in disbelief and shock. One can therefore say: "It was justice delayed but justice served, just for a moment."

The news of his release led to spontaneous rallies and processions of singing and dancing in various parts of Ivory Coast. It galvanized the Pan-African revolutionary movement. It convinced many of the possibility of winning battles against neo-colonialism and the Wheel of Imperialism. The government of Ivory Coast issued a communique in which it declared that it hoped the acquittal of Gbagbo would contribute to peace, and it announced that it would provide more financial support and assistance to the victims of the electoral crisis.[45]Immediately after the pronouncement of the acquittal, Fatou Bensouda, the prosecutor, submitted a request to the judges to ask them to put a set of binding conditions on the freedom of the newly acquitted, pending the written decision after which she could appeal the acquittal. Her request was based upon article 81(3) (c) of the Rome Statute, which disposes:

> c.   In case of an acquittal, the accused shall be released immediately, subject to the following:
>
> > i.   Under exceptional circumstances, and having regard, inter alia, to the concrete risk of flight, the seriousness of the offence charged and the probability of success on appeal, the Trial Chamber, at the request of the Prosecutor, may maintain the detention of the person pending appeal;
> >
> > ii.   A decision by the Trial Chamber under subparagraph (c) (i) may be appealed in accordance with the Rules of Procedure and Evidence.[46]

Her rationale was summed up in the following lines:

> The prosecution submits that pursuant to article 81 (3) (c) (i), there are exceptional circumstances for maintaining both Accused's detention appeal. There is a concrete risk that the Accused will not appear for the continuation of the trial if the Prosecution's appeal against the Decision

---

[45] Côte d'Ivoire Government Communiqué, "Acquittement et Libération de Gbagbo et Blé Goudé: Le Gouvernement prend note et formule un souhait," Linfodrome, January 16, 2019, http://www.linfodrome.com/actualites-gouvernement-ivoirien/45012-acquittement-et-liberation-de-gbagbo-et-ble-goude-le-gouvernement-prend-note-et-formule-un-souhait.

[46] International Criminal Court, Rome Statute.

is successful. In addition, the offences charged in this case are very serious. There is also a probability that the Prosecution will succeed on appeal. However, the Prosecution would not oppose release if the flight risk can be mitigated by imposing a series of conditions in relation to the release of the Accused, including that they be released to a State Party to the Rome Statute other than Côte d'Ivoire. Conditions should also be imposed to preserve the integrity of the continued proceedings.[47]

This request was rejected, and Fatou Bensouda's office resubmitted it to the Appeals Chamber, who agreed on January 18, 2019, to analyze it; and a hearing to this effect was scheduled for February 1, 2019. In the meantime, the decision of their immediate release and acquittal was suspended. The decision implied that the two defendants were to be kept in the custody of the ICC until the prosecution's appeal against their release was heard. The suspended acquittal and the dissenting opinion about the suspended acquittal both drew from Article 81 (3) (c). All parties used it to justify their respective positions. Legal experts starting with those at the ICC had dissenting interpretations of the Treaty of Rome article 81(3)(c). Irrespective of the competing positions it was undeniable that the principle or the main idea in the acquittal and in the article mentioned above was freedom. Detention and the imposition of conditions are exceptions, which can only be authorized in exceptional circumstances that could be a risk of escape or the gravity of the crime, or in the anticipation that the appeal is likely to result in a conviction of the acquitted as the prosecutor said it.

In light of this article, what could have been the exceptional conditions that would justify the custody of Gbagbo and Blé Goudé after the decision of acquittal before a court located in a European city? Why would the court not decide that they stay in any place in The Hague for two weeks till the February 1, 2019 hearing? What could be the risk of flight of two famous detainees from a European country who must go through the security checkpoints of any international European airport? The seriousness of the offense could not be a serious argument either in this case because the Trial Chamber, while making the decision to acquit, argued that the prosecutor did not present qualitative and substantial evidence to sustain her case against the defendants whose presumption of innocence was denied all that time during the time of their illegal detention.

Critics and observers were curious to see the eventual fate of the two acquitted freedom. One wondered if Laurent Gbagbo, whose provisional release was rejected thirteen times, would remain in preventive detention contingent upon the appeal. The day finally came on February 1, 2019. After hours of deliberation, the majority of the Appeals Chamber, 3/5, suspended the

---

[47] Prosecutor v. Gbagbo, ICC-02/11-01/15, Office of the Prosecutor, ¶ 3 (January 15, 2019).

decision of the immediate acquittal of Laurent Gbagbo and Blé Goudé, who should be given freedom with a set of conditions provided that a country which complies with the ICC rules and regulations was willing to host them. The judges who constituted the majority were Chile Eboe-Osuji (president), Solomy Balungi Bossa, and Luz Del Carmen Ibanez Carranza. The dissenting opinion was expressed by Judges Howard Morrison and Piotr Hofmański. The Appeals Chamber February 1, 2019 decision of acquittal rejected the unconditional release and ordered the conditional release. It was now clear that they would no longer remain in preventive detention but in freedom with binding conditions subject to change. In other words these binding conditions could be tightened or lightened depending on the circumstances.

The binding conditions were as follows: they were not allowed to travel outside The Hague without the permission of the court; they should give their passports to the Registry of the international court; they had to report to the ICC regularly; they were forbidden to contact the witnesses and to speak publicly on the court case; they should sign a written document in which they commit to abide by all instructions and orders of the court, including appearing at the hearing when it is ordered, and agreeing that the proceedings before the Appeals Chamber may continue, if they do not appear before the court when ordered.[48]

The decision of acquittal did not automatically end the trial insofar as the possibility of appealing the judgment remained. The Appeals Chamber may confirm the decision of acquittal of the Trial Chamber or may decide of another trial and in the case of the latter, the accused had to be ready to answer charges. Despite being not only presumed innocent but also recognized innocent, they have been placed in an amphibian state of neither detainee nor free.

It was becoming clear that the impotence of the prosecutor was becoming more patent. She was running out allies. She was running out of options. She was running out of time. Time has exposed her deceit. The case was no longer defensible. She was given two chances for two trials and the result was the same: The Prosecutor was unable to demonstrate that Laurent Gbagbo put together a common plan to remain in power and that he has committed crimes against humanity.

It was also obvious that she had exhausted her cards and that her chances of success in the event of another trial were used up as she failed to convince the

---

[48] Prosecutor v. Gbagbo, ICC-02/11-01/15, Judgment on the Prosecutor's appeal, February 1, 2019, https://www.icc-cpi.int/CourtRecords/CR2019_00611.PDF.

judges of Laurent Gbagbo's guilt, after eight intense years of investigations and hearing.

Two fundamental human rights denied to the accused Laurent Gbagbo and Blé Goudé were at stake: the right to the presumption of innocence and the right to freedom. The premise of the right to the presumption of innocence is that anyone prosecuted is considered innocent until proven guilty. Freedom is the general rule and preventive detention is the exception. Noting that the defendants were cleared of all charges, logic would recommend they regain their right to freedom. Keeping the acquitted in the bonds of detention is a double violation of their right to the presumption of innocence and of their right to freedom.[49]

The ICC stakeholders were watching to see where the two defendants would remain before appearing in court for the appeal trial in the event that the prosecutor's appeal was granted and taking into account the fact that they were going to be kept out of the bonds of preventive detention. The prosecutor did not want the accused to go back to Ivory Coast. The Appeal Chamber did not grant her that wish. In their decision, it was clear that their return to Ivory Coast pending trial and in binding conditions became a possibility. But for this to happen, two conditions were to be met. On the one hand, the ICC must grant the authorization; on the other hand, the government of Ivory Coast must be willing to see them return to Ivory Coast. The chances of such a scenario were very slim because the Ivorian government did not want the newly freed men to return to Ivory Coast.

However, the tide was turning against the prosecutor and the government of the Ivory Coast. Belgium accepted to welcome Gbagbo immediately because his second wife, Nady Bamba, was living there with their son who was born in 2002. On October 30, 2019, Blé Goudé was still in The Hague in a hotel room paid for by the court.

The Pre-Trial Chamber had exposed the weakness of the prosecutor's evidence at the stage of the confirmation of the charges hearing. The Trial Chamber just confirmed the emptiness of the case. The verdict of acquittal restituted and re-established the historical truth about the trial and exposed the manipulative machinery of Françafrique and neo-colonial forces. They had pronounced the

---

[49] Oulaye Hubert discussed the right to the presumption of innocence, the right to freedom, the hybrid state of the accused, and the weakness of the prosecutor case as exposed by the Pre-Trial Chamber in the early stage of the trial, during a conference he delivered on May 31, 2019 in Ivory Coast. It was on the birthday of the former president of Ivory Coast. The topic was "Laurent Gbagbo Acquitted but Forbidden to Return to Ivory Coast."

condemnation of Laurent Gbagbo even before the beginning of the trial. The neo-colonial forces could not anticipate the Pan African resilience and revolt.

Reactions to acquittal

The news of the acquittal of the former president of Ivory Coast gave rise to dissenting views across the globe. Laurent Gbagbo's trial, which was the hallmark of the controversy surrounding the ICC, represents several symbols. The acquittal of the former Ivorian president is a landmark in international justice that set a huge blow to the International Criminal Court. This setback in Gbagbo's trial is the illustration of the court's unsatisfactory results in most cases. Several stakeholders argued that the acquittal of Ivory Coast's former president would damage the credibility of the court. This view is summed up in the title of an article published by the BBC, "Laurent Gbagbo Case: Ivory Coast Leader's Acquittal Rattles ICC foundations," written by Anna Holligan. The author of the article reported the views of Mark Kersten, who expressed the concerns of that category of stakeholders: "Whenever a case involving mass atrocities essentially collapses at the ICC, it does damage to the perception of the court as a credible and effective institution of international justice. The ICC needs wins and it's racking up losses."[50]

On Twitter, several questioned the professionalism and the efficacy of the court and ridiculed the Office of the Prosecutor, seen as an office that has more terminations and acquittals than convictions.[51] Another stakeholder, Phil Clarke of the School of Oriental and African Studies at the University of London, argued that the ICC is performing worse than he anticipated, unable to prosecute deposed presidents after failing to convict sitting governments' leaders and officials.[52] The weakness of the case against Laurent Gbagbo has done considerable damage to the credibility of the ICC.[53]

---

[50] Anna Holligan, "Laurent Gbagbo Case: Ivory Coast's Leader Acquittal Rattles ICC Foundations," BBC, January 15, 2019, https://www.bbc.com/news/world-africa-46874517.

[51] Barrie Sander (@Barrie_Sander), "Emerging narratives in the lead up to and aftermath of today's #ICC majority decision to grant the defence's "no case to answer" motion to acquit #Gbagbo & #BleGoudé," Twitter, January 15, 2019, https://twitter.com/Barrie_Sander/status/1085140840199213057.

[52] Phil Clark (@philclark79), "In my book Distant Justice I argue the #ICC is fundamentally unable to prosecute cases of sitting govt officials," Twitter, January 15, 2019, https://twitter.com/philclark79/status/1085119561157042176.

[53] Laurent Bigot, "La faiblesse du dossier contre Laurent Gbagbo a fait un tort considérable à la crédibilité de la CPI," *Le Monde*, October 1, 2018, https://www.lemonde.fr/afrique/article/2018/10/01/la-faiblesse-du-dossier-contre-laurent-gbagbo-a-fait-un-tort-considerable-a-la-credibilite-de-la-cpi_5362813_3212.html.

The general observation is that several stakeholders in the Western world have lamented the acquittal and expressed disappointment over the decision of Laurent Gbagbo's release. Few have denounced his unnecessary and unjust incarceration, including that of Blé Goudé, as if all those who denounced the acquittal agreed with their preventive imprisonment and wished that they stay in prison even if the case was not solid.[54] Several opinion leaders attributed what they perceived as the failure of the prosecution to very long and inefficient procedures, as in the case of Jean-Pierre Bemba or Laurent Gbagbo. Ismaïl Diallo, interviewed by Eric Manirakiza, of Voice of America (VOA) spoke of the "double failure, bitter failure" of the ICC for having kept in detention for several years the former Congolese vice president Jean-Pierre Bemba, the former president of Ivory Coast Laurent Gbagbo, and Charles Blé Goudé. He argued that it is not a question of performance or efficiency but rather the political interference that remains the main driver of the inefficiency of the court, thus making it a political instrument used by the most powerful nations:

> What are we going to do with Gbagbo's eight years behind bars, years of Bemba behind bars, just excuses, we've made a mistake, excuse us…There was a military operation led by France against Laurent Gbagbo, there was an abduction by the French troops of Laurent Gbagbo…There was a forced transfer of Gbagbo to the ICC. People can speculate anyway they like. There was no justice. It's not the weakness of the accusation or the prosecution, it's the whole system. The reality is that it was the politics of the strongest.[55]

Some Africanists found in the acquittal of Laurent Gbagbo the argument they have been waiting for to dismiss the accusation against the ICC as a tool of neo-colonialism: "The decision demonstrates the Court's integrity to grant no case to answer motions, making it harder to depict it as a biased weapon of neo-colonial justice."[56]

This observation cannot be convincing and feeds into the insensitivity of a number of scholars in the West. What cannot be erased before the acquittal is that the ICC decided to do a selective prosecution focusing on the crimes allegedly committed by Laurent Gbagbo's forces, ignoring those committed by Alassane Ouattara's forces. What cannot be erased is the fact that the ICC found Laurent Gbagbo guilty even before the beginning of the trial. What cannot be ignored is the ICC refusal to release him on bail 13 times, denying him the

---

[54] Megan Fairlie voiced this view at a conference, "The International Criminal Court and the Community of Nations," University of Georgia School of Law, Athens, Georgia, March 8, 2019.

[55] Eric Manirakiza, "La CPI, 'un instrument politique'," VOA, January 16, 2019, https://www.voaafrique.com/a/la-cpi-un-instrument-politique-analyste/4746165.html.

[56] Sander, "Emerging narratives."

presumption of innocence. The truth of the matter is that the ICC has operated for ten good years as a legal instrument in the hands of France and the United Nations against the former president of Ivory Coast.

The chart below shows the outcomes of all the cases.[57]

International Criminal Court Cases

There have been twenty-seven cases before the ICC. Seven have resulted in acquittals or no charges, while four have resulted in reparations or imprisonment.

Case start	Country	Person charged	Status
2018	Mali	Al-Hassan	Pretrial
	CAR	Yekatom and Ngaissona	Pretrial
2017	Libya	Al-Werfalli	Pretrial
2015	Mali	Al-Mahdi	Reparations, prison sentence
	Kenya	Gicheru and Bett	Pretrial
2013	Kenya	Barasa	Pretrial
	CAR	Bemba et al.	Appeals final, prison sentence
	Libya	Khaled	Pretrial
2012	Ivory Coast	Simone Gbagbo	Pretrial
	Sudan	Hussein	Pretrial
	DRC	Mudacumura	Pretrial
2011	Ivory Coast	Laurent Gbagbo and Ble Goude	Acquittal
	Kenya	Kenyatta	Charges withdrawn
	Libya	Qaddafi	Pretrial
	Kenya	Ruto and Sang	Charges vacated
2010	DRC	Mbarushimana	Charges not confirmed
2009	Sudan	Abu Garda	Charges not confirmed
	Sudan	Al-Bashir	Pretrial
	Sudan	Banda	Trial
2008	CAR	Bemba	Acquittal
2007	Sudan	Harun and Ali Kushayb	Pretrial
	DRC	Katanga	Reparations, prison sentence
	DRC	Ngudjolo Chui	Acquittal
2006	DRC	Lubanga	Reparations, prison sentence
	DRC	Ntaganda	Trial
2005	Uganda	Kony et al.	Pretrial
	Uganda	Ongwen	Trial

Sources: International Criminal Court; CNN.

COUNCIL on
FOREIGN
RELATIONS

Figure 3: International Criminal Cases.
Source: Council on Foreign Relations, February 23, 2021

---

[57] Felter, "The Role of the International Criminal Court."

It is worth noting that the ICC is experiencing a crisis of legitimacy, which is a deficit of social acceptance and recognition of the court because of the discrepancy between the premises of its foundation, the promises of its existence, and its actual performance, namely regarding Laurent Gbagbo's trial.

In line with the solution proposed by Reus-Smit, it is therefore imperative that the court embark on a remedial recalibration and a self-redemptive undertaking: "To reconstitute its legitimacy, an actor or institution must, first, recalibrate the relationship between its social identity, purposes, and practices, and the prevailing social norms that define the parameters of rightful agency and action; and, second, realign its realm of political action with its social constituency of legitimation."[58] The court is conscious of its image and has alternated public relations projects and self-studies. One of the most recent is Strategic Plan 2019–2021, produced by the Office of the Prosecutor; this department acknowledged its shares of failures while it claimed to have had successes and vowed to shift its prosecutorial strategy:

> The Strategic Plan 2019–2021 also coincides with a period of mixed results in court as well as unprecedented external challenges. Despite a number of successes in court during 2016–2018 (e.g., Al-Mahdi case, Bemba et al. case), and the best efforts of dedicated and able staff of the Office, there have also been significant setbacks (Ruto & Sang case, Bemba main case, Gbagbo & Blé Goudé case). Different factors have caused these unsatisfactory outcomes, including the residual effects of the Office's previous strategy prior to 2012; the need to further strengthen the present strategy; cooperation and security challenges, and the lack of judicial clarity and certainty. While some of the factors affecting performance are outside its control, the Office remains fully committed to learning from all its experiences, both in terms of successes and failures, and to taking all available measures within its control to improve its final outcomes in court during the 2019–2021 period. This Strategic Plan 2019–2021 is intended to mark the path toward that goal.[59]

The Office of the Prosecutor set four strategic goals for "Improving performance in relation to the Office's core activities: to achieve a high rate of success in court; to increase the speed, efficiency and effectiveness of preliminary examinations, investigations and prosecutions; to develop with States enhanced strategies and methodologies to increase the arrest rate of

---

[58] Christian Reus-Smit, "International Crises of Legitimacy," *International Politics* vol. 44 (2007): 167.

[59] Office of the Prosecutor, "Strategic Plan 2019–2021," International Criminal Court, July 17, 2019, p. 4, ¶ 3. https://www.icc-cpi.int/itemsDocuments/20190726-strategic-plan-eng.pdf.

persons subject to outstanding ICC arrest warrants; and to refine and reinforce its approach to victims, in particular as regards victims of SGBC and crimes against or affecting children."[60] The Strategic Plan 2019–2021 represents a paradigm shift. The prosecutor aims at putting more focus on narrower cases, on cases that involve less high-level accused. So far it has put emphasis on high profile officials at the head of chains of command:

> However, building on Strategic Plan 2016–2018 and its Policy Paper on Case Selection and Prioritisation, during 2019–2021 the Office will give increased consideration to the possibility of bringing cases that are narrower in scope, insofar as they focus on key aspects of victimisation, particular incidents, areas, or time periods, or a single accused. In particular, when appropriate, the Office will consider bringing cases against notorious or mid-level perpetrators who are directly involved in the commission of crimes, to provide deeper and broader accountability and also to ultimately have a better prospect of conviction in potential subsequent cases against higher-level accused. The Office will also emphasize evidential strength in its selection of suspects and charges, opting where appropriate for narrower but stronger cases over broader cases with higher risks of evidentiary weaknesses.[61]

Even though the Office of the Prosecutor was conducting self-studies, it was not willing to give up and to give in in the case of Laurent Gbagbo's trial. Fatou Bensouda could not accept that this trial could end with a No Case to Answer. She rather fights for a mistrial as she was adamant to see the trial continue.

---

[60] Office of the Prosecutor, "Strategic Plan 2019–2021," p. 3.

[61] Office of the Prosecutor, "Strategic Plan 2019–2021," p. 20.

The decision, the prosecutor's appeal, and the Appeals Chamber's judgement

The written version of the oral decision pronounced on January 15, 2019 to acquit Laurent Gbagbo and Blé Goudé was made public on July 16, 2019, three days before the beginning of the judicial recess. It included the majority opinion of Trial Chamber I, by the presiding Judge Cuno Tarfusser and Judge Geoffrey Henderson, alongside the dissenting opinion of Judge Herrera Carbuccia. The ICC prosecutor Fatou Bensouda asked for an extension of the deadline for appeal until October 10, which would give her office enough time to read the 1,366 pages written by the three judges of the Chamber I, after which she could assess whether she would appeal the decision. Based on the pattern the prosecutor Fatou Bensouda has displayed throughout the eight years of trial, the idea that she was going to give up was unthinkable. There was a widespread anticipation that she would appeal. She finally appealed the chamber-written decision, called "The Decision" in October 2019.

The appeal was made in two stages: first, a notification of the grounds for appeal was filed, then a detailed brief to explain them. The prosecutor requested an extension of time for each of these two steps. She obtained a period of thirty days instead of the fifty-five she requested for the notification. As for the brief, she was granted ninety days instead of the 145 she requested. She had sixty days starting from July 16, 2019, to present the grounds for appeal and three months to file her submission. In other words, the Appeals Chamber should have received the grounds and the prosecution's appeal brief no later than mid-October.

The decision

The majority opinion of Trial Chamber I presented a detailed analysis of the evidence for the accused's acquittal in a 966-page document titled "The Reasons," written by Judge Geoffrey Henderson (Annex B). Judge Cuno Tarfusser also wrote a separate document of 90 pages, in which he presented his reasons and further reflections on the case (Annex A). Judge Herrera Carbuccia outlined her dissenting opinion in 307 pages (Annex C).

Majority opinions

The presiding judge Cuno Tarfusser, who had been the dissenting voice for the last three times when the majority refused to release the defendants on bail seized the opportunity to address some theoretical issues related to the court methodology, the procedures, and the hermetic judicial language coupled with the propensity to write voluminous documents incomprehensible to the common man, the very stakeholder for whom the court had been put in place. As an illustration of his point, he mentioned voluminous documents produced by the prosecutor and arguments for the acquittal called "The Reasons" produced by the other member of the majority, Geoffrey Henderson.

Judge Cuno Tarfusser expressed his disapproval of the way the ICC conducted its activities. He also lamented the trial's lack of direction. One of the elements he mentioned to sustain his position was the lengthy documents that the court produced which are incomprehensible to the common stakeholder. As an illustration, he referred to the document produced by Judge Henderson, which details the reasons of the acquittal of the accused. The Reasons is a 966-page document that explains the factual and legal findings which motivated the decision of acquittal and the dropping of all charges against the accused. He also criticized the prosecutor's performance at both the investigation and prosecution stages, as well as that of the defense. The presiding judge also devoted some lines to criticism of the performance of both legal defense teams who contributed to the elasticity of the trial. He lamented the time wasted by the legal defense teams to pinpoint the incongruencies and the flaws of the prosecution. He considered that they should have been motivated by a sense of urgency to at least appeal the decision of the refusal to grant a release on bail to the accused. Regarding the prosecution, he argued that the Office of the Prosecution's performance was far from being satisfactory and raised the question of the lack of professionalism in that department of the ICC. In gathering her incriminating documents, the prosecutor presented photocopies of documents whose originals were either misplaced, destroyed, or altered. The choice of making photocopies resulted in the alteration and the loss of content of these documents, as sentences were cut,[1] and in waste of time and resources that could have been avoided if the prosecutor had decided to use the originals of the documents. The image of the 120 mm mortar, a weapon carried by BASA and believed to have been used during the March 17 incident, was also problematic. It was a picture downloaded from the internet by the investigator,

---

[1] Prosecutor v. Gbagbo, ICC-02/11-01/15, The Decision: Opinion of Judge Cuno Tarfusser, ¶ 91 (July 16, 2019).

who did not see the weapons while in Ivory Coast. He did so at the request of one interviewee.

Judge Cuno Tarfusser also addressed the burning critical issues about the accessibility and relevance of evidentiary elements, and the comprehensibility of the court. All these affected the sustainability and legitimacy of the ICC. Several testimonies went beyond the scope of the charges and lacked consistency, coherency, clarity, and above all, relevance in relation to the prosecution's case.

When the presiding judge referred to the case, he aimed not only at demonstrating that the documents and testimonies lacked substance but also at discussing the lack of professionalism of the prosecutor, who did not filter the testimonies or organize them. Witnesses followed each other in the courtroom in an unorganized manner. They could have been regrouped according to issues and events. The questions should have been more relatable to the relevant points, and the Office of the Prosecutor could have used what it had used in the past in order to avoid the unnecessary redundancy of the in-court discussions, the "in-depth analysis chart."[2] A sound preparation would have avoided the waste of time and the lengthy discussions in the courtroom. Judge Cuno Tarfusser argued that if the prosecutor had vetted the witnesses, only those with relevant testimonies would have been selected and would have appeared in court. It took 12 days to interrogate the prosecution's expert witnesses. Seven out of twelve gave inconclusive testimonies, weakening the prosecutor's case. The DNA analysis appeared to be inconclusive. Only three out of the 16 women supposedly killed during the March 17 incident whose remains were analyzed matched with relatives. Among the bones that were analyzed, there was one that was from a man.[3]

Some foreign nationals who served as translators, who were not fluent enough in French, gave wrong interpretations of some sentences and phrases when they were conducting interviews of witnesses which the prosecutor used as evidence. Suffice it to mention that a crowd chant "Sarkozy Assassin, Sarkozy Assassin..." which means (Sarkozy, Assassin, Sarkozy Assassin) was translated as "Assassinate Sarkozy, Assassinate Sarkozy."[4]

Judge Cuno Tarfusser in his opinion seized the opportunity to expose his views on the proceedings of the trial; the exceptional weakness of the evidence, which was unsubstantiated and unauthenticated; the unnecessary length of the trial; and the mounting documents submitted to the court. He conducted a

---

[2] Prosecutor v. Gbagbo, Opinion of Tarfusser, ¶ 22.

[3] Prosecutor v. Gbagbo, Opinion of Tarfusser, ¶ 33.

[4] Prosecutor v. Gbagbo, Opinion of Tarfusser, ¶ 24 (iii).

theoretical and philosophical debate about the legitimacy and the sustainability of the international justice system. The prosecution witnesses have destroyed the narrative and the theory of the prosecutor, he argued, because there was a discrepancy between the narrative as presented by the prosecutor and the historical truth that emerged through the hearing and the prosecution's own witnesses. He concurred with "The Reasons" and referred to that gap as an "overall disconnect"[5] between the narrative of the prosecutor and the testimonies heard in the courtroom. Cuno Tarfusser considered that the evidence of the prosecutor was based on anonymous hearsay and unsubstantiated evidence and would not have passed the level of admissibility in any court.

Among the court practices of which Cuno Tarfusser disapproved was the propensity of judges, prosecutors, and defense teams to produce lengthy written documents with abundant footnotes in incomprehensible and complex judicial jargon that was seldom decipherable. This makes it difficult for readers to locate core evidence, key findings, and relevant information in these voluminous documents. This practice, he stated, undermines the accessibility, the comprehensibility, and the overall legitimacy and sustainability of international justice.

In the same vein, several other aspects caught his attention: the volume of questions, the multitude of repetitions, asked and reiterated over and over about incriminating incidents as if they alone could suffice to establish the penal responsibility of Laurent Gbagbo.[6] The refusal of the prosecutor to take into account the historical background and the contextual environment of the commission of crimes and the occurrence of incriminating events was perceived by the majority as a serious shortcoming and flaw.

The court is victim of the tradition of extended courtroom discussions that prevents the possibility of the "expeditiousness" of trials in the field of international justice. These discussions are often too academic and put a huge gap between the court and the people it wants to serve and are an obstacle to the accessibility of the international criminal justice.[7] The time period between the verdict of the Pre-Trial Chamber and the beginning of the trial per se before Trial Chamber I was unnecessarily long, 16 months in the case of Laurent Gbagbo and 13 months in the case of Blé Goudé.[8] Tarfusser buttressed that

---

[5] Prosecutor v. Gbagbo, ICC-02/11-01/15, The Decision: The Reasons by Judge Geoffrey Henderson, ¶ 865, (July 16, 2019).

[6] Prosecutor v. Gbagbo, Opinion of Tarfusser, ¶ 17.

[7] Prosecutor v. Gbagbo, Opinion of Tarfusser, ¶ 18.

[8] Prosecutor v. Gbagbo, Opinion of Tarfusser, ¶ 19.

some of the documents contained repeated and overlapping footnotes, and revealed a lack of correspondence between the referenced parts of them and the footnotes. Other footnotes even contradicted some reference information contained in the body of the documents, and some paragraphs were repeated.

The court registered abundant written documents, videos, pictures, statements both from the prosecution and from the two legal defense teams. Regarding the prosecutor who had the burden of proof, Judge Cuno raised the question of the relationship between the size of voluminous incriminating documents (the quantity of evidence) in relation to the quality of evidence. According to the presiding judge, the validity of evidence is not measured by the quantity of witnesses and by the volume of incriminating charges but rather by the quality of evidence: "A mass of papers, pictures, videos, and other documentary items, or a legion of witnesses, does not make a trial complex, any more than the number of pages or the type of graphics make a book a good or a bad one; what matters is obviously the content and the quality of the material, as well as its relevance to the issue at stake."[9]

He began his opinion by underlining that the burden of proof was on the prosecutor, who failed in several aspects. For Cuno Tarfusser, the charges should not even have passed the Pre-Trial Chamber, because as a general rule a trial should not proceed if the prosecutor is unable to establish the link between the contextual environment that favored criminal acts and the accused. He had held this position since the time he was involved in the case of Abu Garda. This explains why the majority applied the "No Case to Answer" standard in their final pronouncement.

In the eyes of the majority, one of the fundamental shortcomings of the prosecutor's case was the presentation of an unbalanced narrative based on a unidimensional view of the role of nationality, ethnicity, and religion in Ivory Coast in general and during the post-election crisis. For the presiding judge of the Trial Chamber I, the depiction of an Ivory Coast in which a line can be drawn between pro-Ouattara and pro-Gbagbo, Muslims and Christians, people from the south and people from the north, was destroyed by the witnesses from diverse ethnic groups and religions:

> Day after day, document by document, witness after witness, the "Prosecutor's case" has been revealed and exposed as a fragile, implausible theorem relying on shaky and doubtful bases, inspired by a Manichean and simplistic narrative of an Ivory Coast depicted as a "polarized" society where one could draw a clear-cut line between the "pro-Gbagbo," on the one hand, and the "pro-Ouattara," on the other

---

9 Prosecutor v. Gbagbo, Opinion of Tarfusser, ¶ 35.

hand, the former from the South and of Christian faith, the latter from the North and of Muslim faith; a caricatured, "one-sided" narrative, "built around a unidimensional conception of the role of nationality, ethnicity, and religion (in the broadest sense) in Côte d'Ivoire in general and during the post-electoral crisis.[10]

The court refused to go along with the prosecutor, who wanted the judges to accept at face value the label pro-Gbagbo, of which she failed to demonstrate the affiliation and identification of the membership. The witnesses, especially P-0009, rejected the narrative of the existence of parallel forces endowed with secret missions other than the mere execution of the duties of security forces in a republic.

Regarding Blé Goudé, the majority acknowledged that he was a staunch supporter of the former president and claimed not to have found a single witness who could demonstrate that he had conducted violent rallies against civilians; instead, his speeches contained strong content for peace. He had not presided over militia groups such as the GPP.

In "The Reasons," as set out in Annexes A and B, the majority laid out and further developed details of the motivations that sustained all the points raised in the oral decision. According to the majority, the prosecutor had not demonstrated that there was a Common Plan masterminded by Laurent Gbagbo that would keep him in power and in the name of which the commission of crimes against civilians was planned and executed.

They argued that the prosecutor failed to substantiate the allegation of the existence of a policy aimed at attacking a civilian population, based on the recurrent modes of operation alleged to have been the result of the violence and other indirect evidence referred to in support of this allegation. The prosecutor had not shown that the crimes as alleged in the charges were committed pursuant to or in pursuit of a state policy or organization aimed at attacking the civilian population. She failed to demonstrate that public speeches by Laurent Gbagbo or Charles Blé Goudé constituted ordering, soliciting, or encouraging the commission of the alleged crimes and that any of the accused contributed knowingly or intentionally to the commission of such crimes.

She had not considered some essential information, thus making it difficult to fully understand what happened. The majority found that what emerged from the evidence appeared to be significantly different from the picture painted by the prosecutor and added that the evidence produced, mostly the

---

[10] Prosecutor v. Gbagbo, Opinion of Tarfusser, ¶ 12.

circumstantial evidence, was too weak to support the deductions and inferences that the prosecutor was asking the chamber to make.

The majority acknowledged that crimes were committed in the analysis of the major criminal incidents presented by the prosecutor but decided to focus instead on whether it was possible to establish who was criminally responsible for these crimes. In that regard, the available evidence did not support the allegation that the crimes in question were the result of a policy aimed at targeting persons considered to be political opponents. Moreover, they were not convinced that the evidence the prosecutor relied upon was sufficient to establish the existence, in the context of the commission of crimes, of a recurrent procedure from which could be deduced the existence of such a policy. In addition, in his concurring opinion, Judge Tarfusser stressed certain features of the case, including certain procedural facts that occurred prior to the commencement of the trial.

The majority judges also debated the role of the Invisible Commando. They stated the prosecutor failed to elaborate on the Invisible Commando for fear of weakening her thesis, even though it was widely mentioned by the army officers during the hearing, her key witnesses. For the judges, the evidence showed that the Ivorian forces faced an urban guerrilla warfare and therefore were in a rather defensive position. They echoed the testimonies describing tanks of the French army firing at the Ivorian soldiers and depositions indicating that Abidjan was under assault by Alassane Ouattara's forces. They also added that the United Nations has been at times partial, favoring Alassane Ouattara and his forces.

Judge Tarfusser also denounced the flaws of the investigation during which there was a clear collusion between the Ivorian authorities, the Office of the Prosecutor, and some investigators who do not speak French well. As an illustrative example, Judge Cuno mentioned the fact that the prosecutor had established first contacts with certain witnesses even before the ICC prosecutor obtained the legal authorization to investigate, on October 3, 2011. He did not overlook the strategic support of France, which enabled the Office of the Prosecutor to issue a speedy arrest warrant against the former president, two months later. They also wondered about the forces involved, suggesting that there was nothing in the case to show that he [Laurent Gbagbo] would have set up a parallel command within his forces to target civilians, pro-Ouattara supporters, and militants during the trial as pointed out by General Mangou.

One criminal incident that was listed by the prosecutor as one of the four main incriminating incidents was discussed by Judge Cuno: the April 12 incident. The presiding judge asked how the prosecutor could put criminal responsibility for such an incident on the accused, which occurred one day after his fall and capture. Moreover, Blé Goudé had been in hiding for most of

April. In sum, the majority concluded that the former president was not in control of the situation, which was anarchic and chaotic in Abidjan and in the countryside, and did not put into place parallel forces.

His troops were under repeated military assaults by several armed groups that were working in a coordinated way to take hold of Abidjan after conquering the interior of the country: the rebel forces called *Forces Nouvelles* since the Marcoussis Agreement, the Invisible Commando, the United Nations Mission forces, and the French troops. The last two had lost their position of impartiality and fully supported Alassane Ouattara's forces, represented by the first two. Speaking of operations by rebel forces, it was evident, substantiated, and demonstrated that Laurent Gbagbo's forces were not the sole forces operating in Abidjan, where the pro-Ouattara troops continuously conducted military expeditions while the civilians, through rallies, were suspected by the Gbagbo supporters to be in a permanent state of uprising.

The majority used one video as an exculpatory document in which Alassane Ouattara's soldiers were urged to use their weapons for the December 16 rally. The prosecutor fell into the trap of redundant references to events, failing to demonstrate the criminal responsibility of the accused. Judge Cuno Tarfusser contended that the prosecutor and the Pre-Trial Chamber's decision to make a distinction between the core crimes referred to in various terms as representative crimes, essential facts, material facts, evidence, and secondary incidents was susceptible to creating legal confusion insofar as the prosecutor had claimed that the core crimes were sufficient to establish the criminal responsibility of the accused and did not feel therefore the need to demonstrate the evidentiary essence of the secondary incidents. She repeated this line of argument in several documents she submitted to the court.

Consequently, in light of the fact that the incidents were not essential to the scope of the trial and the charges, the presiding judge contended that they should not have been subject to discussion in the courtroom. He added they should not have accepted witnesses brought into the courtroom to testify on these incidents. This contributed to prolonging the proceedings of the trial. As an illustration he mentioned the December 1 and 2 incidents at the RDR headquarters in Wassakra, which registered four testimonies, P-0046, P-0011, P-0440, and P-0009.[11]

For the presiding judge, the distinction of the crimes was a mistake. All crimes should be considered equal if mentioned as part of the charges, and each needed to be proved.[12] This was reiterated by "The Reasons," which stated: "[i]t

---

[11] Prosecutor v. Gbagbo, Opinion of Tarfusser, ¶ 43, 44, 45, 46.
[12] Prosecutor v. Gbagbo, Opinion of Tarfusser, ¶ 47.

is not entirely clear how the evidence for the 20 uncharged incidents is capable of corroborating the evidence for the five charged incidents. They are all discrete events that took place at different times and places and involved different alleged perpetrators."[13]

The majority rejected the idea that Laurent Gbagbo had used incendiary words and speeches. In order to sustain this point, Cuno Tarfusser recalled that the former president had made a proposition to recount the votes, which was rejected by the international community. It was an act of good faith that showed his commitment to peacefully resolving the electoral stalemate. He maintained that the requisition and curfews recommended by the military officials were tension-deterrent mechanisms and could not be perceived as tools for the indiscriminate killing of the civilians.

The debate about the results of the election caught the attention of the majority only to say that the FDS made a choice to defend the institutions of the republic and its president, Laurent Gbagbo, duly recognized as president according to the Constitutional Council. The evidentiary assessment and the legal rationale of the acquittal were highlighted in the written decision. The legal standard used for the acquittal is called "No Case to Answer." The No Case to Answer motion is a judicial action in the course of the proceedings whereby a court must decide whether the legal action should proceed after an analysis of the elements gathered by the investigation or the prosecutor. In this case there is no need for the defense to present the elements of defense.

During the proceedings, there was a debate about whether the trial should be stopped in light of the weakness of the evidence, of the doubt cast on the validity and reliability of the supposedly incriminating evidence, or whether it should proceed. The deputy prosecutor Eric MacDonald, who wanted the trial to proceed till the end, rejected the idea of No Case to Answer, arguing that the Rome Statute did not provide for such a legal standard. He elaborated his thoughts as follows:

> [I]n deciding whether any Trial Chamber could reasonably convict, this Chamber will also refrain from engaging in a sort of evaluation of the credibility and reliability of the evidence, testimonial or documentary, that is would at the end of the trial when assessing the weight of the evidence to determine guilt or innocence. This is because...the trial proceedings have not yet reached the stage of deliberations envisaged by article 74 of the Statute. Were the Chamber to weigh credibility or reliability at this stage of the process, then we would no longer be dealing with no case to answer motions, but something else, for which

---

[13] Prosecutor v. Gbagbo, The Reasons, ¶ 1388.

there is no precedence and no jurisprudence and that in our submission would not fit within the procedural structure of the Statute.[14]

After the prosecutor had exhausted all her supposedly evidentiary documents and after hearing all the prosecution witnesses, the majority decided to apply the No Case to Answer legal standard on January 15, 2019, during the oral pronouncement of the verdict. Knowing that any trial can end with either an acquittal or a conviction, the majority therefore based its decision on the evidentiary standard set forth in Article 66 (3): "[i]n order to convict the accused, the Court must be convinced of the guilt of the accused beyond reasonable doubt."[15]

In the process of demonstrating her narrative about the Common Plan, the prosecutor based her arguments on indirect evidence and anonymous hearsay and prosecution testimonies that were more exculpatory than incriminating; and, more important, there was no single document that could confirm the existence of a Common Plan. The Office of the Prosecutor stuck to its case theory in presenting documents, even though these documents were suspicious and lacked validity. A case in point is CIV-OTP-0045-0359,[16] which supposedly emanated from Laurent Gbagbo, whose content was the declaration of Abobo as a war zone. P-0009, who claimed to have never seen the document, bluntly added it was not a serious document. But yet, the prosecutor still continued to believe in its authenticity.[17] The majority opinion noticed that in the three-year hearings, the prosecutor never amended nor adjusted her narrative.

The prosecution case was built around another allegation: Laurent Gbagbo's forces were solely and exclusively responsible for the electoral violence and they, alone, committed crimes deemed worthy of prosecution. Therefore, she refused to consider the activities of pro-Ouattara forces, namely the Dozos and the Invisible Commando, who committed various human rights violations. These groups, particularly the soldiers of the latter, carried out assaults with tanks and heavy weaponry, using camouflage techniques by mixing themselves with civilians. Such techniques qualified as "terroristic" and "nonconventional" contributed to outplay the FDS, who did not know how to react to such

---

[14] Prosecutor v. Gbagbo, ICC-02/11-01/15-T-221-Red2-ENG, Transcript of the Hearing, ¶18 (October 1, 2018).

[15] International Criminal Court, Treaty of Rome, Article 66 (3).

[16] Prosecutor v. Gbagbo, ICC-02/11-01/15, Document, CIV-OTP-0045-0359.

[17] Prosecutor v. Gbagbo, Opinion of Tarfusser, ¶ 100.

warfare.[18] The prosecutor, knowing that the Invisible Commando would destroy her narrative, decided to ignore it and to tone down its impact on the intensification of violence in Ivory Coast. Also, the presiding judge mentioned another mistake made by the prosecutor, that of ignoring the fact that the uniforms of soldiers and of CECOS were stolen and worn by individuals who could be rebels or mercenaries, as both camps resorted to mercenaries. The prosecutor could not distinguish who were committing some of the crimes of which she accused the defendants.[19]

In his opinion, Cuno Tarfusser rebutted the idea painted by the prosecutor of the army of Ivory Coast under Gbagbo as being ethnic, and added that it was instead socially and ethnically diverse. He expressed his disapproval of the Appeals Chamber, who turned the majority acquittal decision into a liberty with constraining conditions not under any condition provided for by the Rome Statute in Article 81 (3)(c). He argued that he could not understand such a decision toward the accused, who had been cleared of all charges by Trial Chamber I in light of the weakness of the prosecution and the unreliable, unsubstantiated, inauthentic biased evidence. The flight risk evoked by the Appeals Chamber could not be a solid reason, he contended. In sum Cuno Tarfusser declared:

> Whilst I am sympathetic to their [Ivorians of all political allegiances, ethnical origins, or religious faith, both in Abidjan and in other parts of the country] grief and sorrow, as well as conscious of the lasting consequences of these traumas on their ongoing lives, it remains my duty not to let this kind of compassion interfere with my professional and ethical obligations as one of the judges in charge of adjudicating this case. It is not for a criminal trial to judge the history of a country or to challenge the political decisions taken by its leader(s); nor is it to judge on political responsibilities, or to side with one or the other side of parties in conflict. Instead, it is for any criminal trial to ascertain the criminal responsibility of those individuals the Prosecutor has identified as responsible for facts and conducts alleged to be criminal. Such ascertainment must remain exclusively based on the evidence gathered by the Prosecutor during the investigation and submitted to the Chamber. If this evidence is judged as insufficient to reach the conclusion that the accused is criminally responsible, the accused must be acquitted. This, and only this, is what has been done in this case.[20]

The bulk of the arguments that constituted the rationale of the acquittal was contained in the Reasons written by Judge Henderson. In his preliminary

---

[18] Prosecutor v. Gbagbo, Opinion of Tarfusser, ¶ 104.

[19] Prosecutor v. Gbagbo, Opinion of Tarfusser, ¶ 113.

[20] Prosecutor v. Gbagbo, Opinion of Tarfusser, ¶ 124.

remarks, Judge Henderson disputed that the court would cease to be a court if it were to satisfy humanitarian and political goals. He furthered his assessment by arguing that it was not the mission of the court to rescue the prosecutor, who bore the burden of proof and who was not able to support her narrative with qualitative and substantive documents. Judge Henderson contended that the written decision of the acquittal would have been hundreds of pages shorter if the prosecutor had not inserted numerous hearsays in her 4,610 evidentiary documents she submitted to the court. He argued that he felt obliged to explain and articulate every segment of the decision.

Just in the beginning, Judge Henderson admitted that the document "The Reasons" explained the reasons why he sided with Judge Cuno Tarfusser to acquit the defendants: "What follows are my written reasons for joining Judge Tarfusser in deciding to end the case against Mr Laurent Gbagbo and Mr Charles Blé Goudé and to acquit them of all charges of crimes against humanity. This is not a decision that I have reached lightly."[21] This confession was used by the prosecutor as one of the points of her appeal against the acquittal of the accused.

The majority questioned the authenticity of several documents, namely the archives of the *Gendarmerie Nationale* and the documents taken from the presidential palace after the fall of Laurent Gbagbo. Signatures at the bottom of the pages of the archives of the *Gendarmerie Nationale* were either inauthentic or were not those of the actual authors of the documents.[22] Similarly, there was some suspicion about the documents taken from the presidential palace after the downfall of Laurent Gbagbo, which were submitted to the court by the prosecutor. The ICC investigators who, with the help of the UN mission, supposedly collected the documents from the presidential palace were told by the Ivorian authorities that the documents were untouched. The judges could not be convinced about the veracity of such assertion because, as the reports indicated, they were moved several times from one location to another. As a result, the majority cast doubt about their authenticity:

> As these examples show, there were pervasive problems affecting a considerable number of documents that made their authenticity questionable. It is probably fair to say that a majority of the documentary exhibits that were submitted by the Prosecutor in this case would not pass even the most rudimentary admissibility test in many domestic systems. This does not mean, of course, that they should, therefore, automatically be excluded from this Court as well, but it would equally be a mistake to pretend that these problems do not exist.

---

[21] Prosecutor v. Gbagbo, The Reasons, ¶ 1.

[22] Prosecutor v. Gbagbo, The Reasons, ¶ 33.

This is especially true in a case like the present one, where much of the evidence was essentially provided by the current government, which was headed by political opponents of the accused. Indeed, under these circumstances, the Chamber would have expected the Prosecutor to take further steps to ensure that important documentary evidence was properly and demonstrably authenticated before being submitted for the Chamber's consideration.[23]

Moreover, the fact that the documents were provided to the Office of the Prosecutor by the Ivorian government threw a stain on their credibility, the majority opinion argued. Judges Henderson and Tarfusser also questioned the choice made by the prosecutor to submit recorded testimonies to the court in light of the fact that several witnesses changed their narrative during cross-examination. The selectivity in the gathering and collection of information was also problematic in the eyes of the judges, who claimed that the prosecutor did not commit to collect all evidentiary elements but only the ones that supported her narrative. Furthermore, she had not vetted the testimonies and the evidentiary documents.

The majority opinion contended that voluminous evidence was based on hearsay and could not be evaluated because of the unknown nature of the origin and of the source of information, and therefore lacked probative value. Also, there was serious contention between the judges and the Office of the Prosecutor about the criteria that determine the relevance and the credibility of evidence. The majority opinion claimed that that credibility and reliability of evidence could not be measured by disclosure of the source of information but rather by the reliability of the process through which the source obtained the information.

In addition, the majority maintained that the duplication of items of evidence did not reinforce the case and did not have corroborative value. The prosecutor's theory and narrative were discussed after it was summarized at length in five pages (37–42) and in 11 paragraphs. The main problem the judges had with the prosecutor's narrative was that she presented a one-sided misleading version of the events that did not reflect the full picture and the reality of what actually happened. The majority judges contended that Fatou Bensouda alluded to historical events that occurred in Ivory Coast, but she did not draw the legitimate, expected deductions and conclusions from them: the 2002 coup d'état; the presence of the Invisible Commando in Abobo during the post-electoral stalemate; the interference of the UN mission, which sided with Alassane Ouattara's rebels; and the hegemonic role of France, perceived by an

---

[23] Prosecutor v. Gbagbo, The Reasons, ¶ 36.

important part of the Ivorian population as neocolonialist. Regarding the 2002 failed d'état, the majority judges wrote:

> This reality obviously had significant consequences for Mr Gbagbo's position as elected president of Côte d'Ivoire. Mr Gbagbo was never a "normal" president in a "normal" situation. Almost from the beginning, his presidency was embattled and from 2002 onwards he was never able to exercise his constitutional role in a regular manner. In fact, even though the available evidence is far from complete, one gets the impression that Mr Gbagbo's regime was under quite severe strain and pressure for most of the time he held office. Indeed, because of the rebellion, Mr Gbagbo lost control over half the country and a significant portion of the state's armed forces had defected—with their equipment—and was committed to overthrowing him. This must inevitably have informed a number of the choices and decisions he made during the post-electoral crisis.[24]

The prosecutor repeatedly referred to Alassane Ouattara's forces, namely the Invisible Commando which operated in Abobo, but failed to logically interpret the urban guerilla warfare they launched against the former president's regime, which could not claim to be in total control of Abidjan, let alone the entire country. The prosecutor, the judges stressed, overlooked the perception of the supporters of the former Ivorian president in the face of threats, assaults, and pressure. They considered that the maintaining of Laurent Gbagbo in power was an imperative in their struggle for self-determination against all of these forces:

> More generally, the Prosecutor's narrative ignores the fact that the accused and many of their supporters seem to have considered the survival of Mr Gbagbo's regime as a precondition for the continued emancipation of Côte d'Ivoire from the economic and political influence of the former colonial power, France. Regardless of whether or not this view was justified, it undeniably existed and may have gone a long way to explaining a lot of the accused's choices, rhetoric, and conduct.[25]

As a consequence, the existence of the militia and self-defense groups that committed to defend Laurent Gbagbo could be seen, according to the judges, as a logical response in a context of insecurity with the continuous depletion of the security forces.[26] Thus Judge Henderson concluded that the situation in Ivory Coast was more complex than the mere depiction made by the

---

[24] Prosecutor v. Gbagbo, The Reasons, ¶ 67.

[25] Prosecutor v. Gbagbo, The Reasons, ¶ 70.

[26] Prosecutor v. Gbagbo, The Reasons, ¶ 71.

prosecutor, which appeared to be simplistic. He therefore dismissed her evidentiary approach, using several metaphorical expressions to describe the prosecutorial strategy such as "the cart before the horse," "cat mouse," and "everything proves everything."

The majority opinion contended that the prosecutor put the cart before the horse. Since the beginning, for Fatou Bensouda, Laurent Gbagbo was guilty, and later she attempted to find evidence to sustain her case. She presented a narrow, selective, partial perspective of the political situation in Ivory Coast and failed to provide a broader contextual environment, which would have brought more clarity to the case. Henderson rejected the prosecutor's approach, in which everything proves everything. He rebutted the prosecutor's argument that the court had not taken into account certain evidence, stating that the prosecutor should not have hidden any relevant evidence and any evidentiary item.

According to the majority opinion, the documents supposedly retrieved from Simone Gbagbo's room, the training of the youth in the Banco Forest, the support of Blé Goudé, and the loyalty of the FDS to Laurent Gbagbo presented by the prosecutor as incriminating elements in the execution of the Common Plan did not establish any criminal intention, let alone the desire to commit crimes against civilians. The decision to acquit was the result of an assessment of the evidence, which appeared insufficient to the judges, who argued that they had not addressed the moral and political responsibility of the accused.

In assessing the documents, the judges considered other pieces of evidence on record that the prosecutor had ignored in order to stick to her line of attack and to her narrative. He thought that asking the defense, as recommended by the prosecutor and the dissenting judge, to demonstrate the insufficiency of the evidence would not meet the goals of fairness and expeditiousness of the trial. The prosecutor saw criminal intention in the requisition, contrary to the view of the majority judges, as for her it was not even necessary. She added that it must be reprehensible in light of the previous requisitions of 2000 and 2004, which were followed by perpetration of acts of violence by alleged supporters of Laurent Gbagbo against those of Alassane Ouattara.

The question about who won the election was also addressed by the majority judges. They shared the prosecutor's position who said that it was not relevant to open the debate in court about the outcome of the Ivorian 2010 presidential election, but they disagreed with her when she contended that the former president of Ivory Coast was willing to kill civilians to remain in power at any cost.[27]

Regarding the meetings held at the presidential palace between the former Ivorian president and several officers and leaders of the *Galaxie Patriotique*, Judge Henderson conceded that he could agree with the prosecutor who contended that their objective was to prepare nefarious actions against civilians, in so far as it was impossible to know their content and resolutions. Also, some documents—the minutes of meetings, like that of December 3, perceived by the prosecutor as evidence of the execution of an aspect of the Common Plan—were neither on letterhead nor signed.[28] The testimony of Mangou, who revealed in court that he and his family were victims of military assaults after he had told the former president to resign, was used by the judges to demonstrate that the theory of the existence of the Common Plan was not tenable, as the prosecutor had mentioned him as one of the pillars of that Common Plan. Under pressure, with cracks in their midst, and with loyalty failing and fading, it was a challenge for the various groups of the security forces and the members of the inner circle of the former Ivorian head of state to work in a coordinated way. Suffice it to mention the following words of General Detoh Letoh's testimony, which revealed divergence among the officers:

> Dogbo Blé said that he wanted to pursue the battle of Abidjan. It was that day when I learned that there was the battle of Abidjan. So I took the floor at that moment and I asked Dogbo Blé which battle he was talking about, because from a military perspective we had had covered 600 kilometres to arrive at Abidjan. We had people who were on the frontline. And for several days all the elements who had been at the frontline had retreated...On that day I told them, "If you want to carry out the battle in Abidjan, how are you going to do that? Because we are not in control of Abobo. We are not in control of Koumassi or Adjamé..." I did not think that we could start a battle in Abidjan, that it was not possible. He got angry on that day...He told me that I was one of those who were demoralising soldiers and that we did not want the battle of Abidjan to continue. I told him that he was a chief of corps. I was a commander in the army, and I did not have any direct relationship with him. When I wanted to talk to my troops, I would talk to the battalion commanders; and to my general staff at best. I do not talk to a soldier, a soldier with whom I do not even have any contact, to tell them not to take part in the battle of Abidjan.[29]

---

[27] Prosecutor v. Gbagbo, The Reasons, ¶ 301.

[28] Prosecutor v. Gbagbo, The Reasons, ¶ 325.

[29] Prosecutor v. Gbagbo, The Reasons, ¶ 450.

The statement above consolidated the idea the majority judges had about the dysfunctionality of the chain of command. As a consequence, as their opinion put it, several officers may have conducted some operations on their own without receiving clear instructions from the former president and from the leaders of the inner circle. Moreover, they [the judges] were not convinced about the involvement of Laurent Gbagbo himself in the actual military operations of the FDS, even though he was the commander in chief. Even Simone Gbagbo's aide de camp, one of the most loyal of the regime, who had under him well-equipped soldiers and mercenaries and who was at odds with several high officials, could not be perceived as someone willing to kill civilians just in the name of his loyalty to the presidential couple.

The issue of the financing of the patriotic groups, including the Agoras and Parlements by the presidency, which the prosecutor used in her narrative, was also addressed by the judges. For them, there was no document that could show the reasons for the distribution of that money and how it was used and for what purpose it was provided in the first place. Some of the receipts presented as incriminating documents in this regard were not stamped, were not on letterhead, and did not match some other official receipts of the presidency. The majority judges of the Trial Chamber concluded that nothing suggested that the sums of money that the leaders of the *Galaxie Patriotique* were receiving were for the execution of the Common Plan, as nothing on the receipts indicated the intended purpose of the money. They also rejected the idea according to which the rise of the *Galaxie Patriotique*, which was a reaction to the upsurge of the rebellion, was a part of a preconceived strategy for Laurent Gbagbo to remain in power as soon as he took office in 2000.

Judges Henderson and Cuno conceded that there were attempts to integrate into the security forces new recruits from some of the self-defense groups such as the GPP and from other patriotic groups. However, based on the evidentiary documents, they could not be certain about the scale of the recruits and could not be convinced that the primary objective of the integration of these new elements in the Ivorian army was for the killing of civilians.

The majority judges denounced the prosecutor's one-sided depiction of the use of mercenaries in the Ivorian conflict. She presented the situation as if the Gbagbo regime was the only side to have used mercenaries, namely Liberians, while evidence supported that both sides having recruited and financed Liberian mercenaries. Based on the evidence, they could not confirm that the Liberian mercenaries who operated on the side of the former Ivorian president were actually integrated in the Ivorian forces or where they were coming from: if they were already in the country or if they were coming from Liberia, as Ivory Coast and Liberia share in common a number of ethnic groups.

Even though Blé Goudé was the leader of the *Galaxie Patriotique*, no evidence proved that he had effective authority over militia groups and self-defense movements. Therefore, he could not be held responsible for the actions of these groups. The judges could not agree with the prosecutor who argued that the substantial weapon cache at the presidential palace served to sustain the Common Plan and was for criminal purposes. Instead, they believed it was a normal reaction for a leader who was facing violent opposition that had put him under perpetual threat and pressure since 2002. The judges maintained that the reports provided by the UN mission and the French Licorne mission in Ivory Coast, which did not contain an inventory of the weapons and the ammunitions discovered at the presidential palace, did not have substantial evidentiary weight. The chamber could not conclude that the Gbagbo regime had deliberately hidden these weapons and intended to distribute them for the commission of criminal acts with the goal of keeping him in power.[30] The available evidence did not confirm the assertion of the prosecutor, who said that the parallel structures were at times better militarily equipped than the official units of the army.

With regard to the public expressions of the Common Plan, the prosecutor relied on videos that contained speeches of prominent leaders of the Gbagbo regime in order to sustain her allegations. However, the majority judges remarked that the prosecution had taken several speeches out of context and even that some contained calls for peace. The prosecutor then asked the court to ignore the excerpts that call for peace and focus only on the other parts that were incriminating in her view. The judges refused her request and stated that she did not expose and decipher the supposed code Blé Goudé was accused of using in order to convey his messages.[31]

Contrary to the allegations of the prosecutor, the majority opinion noted that there were recurrent calls for dialogue and peace in the speeches delivered by the officials of the former regime while addressing Alassane Ouattara and his supporters, who were seen as instruments in the hands of neocolonialist forces. The accused delivered multiple speeches in which they vowed to fight for the unity of the Ivory Coast; they called their supporters not to attack the civilians who either voted for Alassane Ouattara or supported him.

The question of the supposed blockade of the Golf Hotel was addressed. The court considered that posting a checkpoint to monitor the movements of armed officers who were in the Golf Hotel was not synonymous with blockade, as the objective was not to deprive the hosts of the hotel from food. The

---

[30] Prosecutor v. Gbagbo, The Reasons, ¶ 885.

[31] Prosecutor v. Gbagbo, The Reasons, ¶ 960.

majority rejected a document supposedly taken from Laurent Gbagbo's bedroom, which is believed to contain information and instructions about the blockade. It did not contain any sort of stamp or signature and was rejected by the court. Consequently, it did not have probative value, and its source could not be verified.[32]

Judge Henderson recalled a portion of General Mangou's testimony, in which the army officer told the court he reported to president Laurent Gbagbo an exchange he had with General Palasset, Head of Licorne mission, who prohibited him from chasing and pursuing Alassane Ouattara's soldiers who came from the Golf Hotel and who retreated to that hotel after being stopped by some elements of FDS. The French general had told the chief of the Ivorian army that attacking the Golf Hotel was synonymous to attacking France. The response of Laurent Gbagbo, who told Mangou to instruct his soldiers not to move and not to attack the Golf Hotel, demonstrated that he did not have any criminal intention against the hosts of the hotel and that there was no blockade against that facility.[33]

The prosecutor was not able to convince the court that the checkpoint put in front of the Golf Hotel to monitor the movements and actions of Alassane Ouattara closest had a hidden motivation, namely the repression of the December 16, 2010 so-called peaceful demonstration at the national television. In her narrative she established a causal relation between the checkpoint and the repression of the December 16 rally. The majority judges rejected this idea because the checkpoint had been set up way before the December 16 rally.[34]

Judge Henderson devoted most of the second half of the "Reasons" on the four representative crimes chosen by the prosecutor to sustain her narrative against the accused. He disagreed with the prosecutor, who claimed that the December 16 rally was peaceful: "In addition, a point that the Prosecutor seems to ignore is that it can be noted at the very least the FDS had reasons to believe there would be armed opposition amongst the demonstrators. In this regard, reference is made to the FDS deaths that occurred on the day of the march (16 December 2010) and FDS intelligence pertaining to the march, the evidence of which will be set out below."[35]

Furthermore, the prosecutor's allegations that the members of the inner circle and Laurent Gbagbo were communicating among themselves in a coordinated way for the commission of crimes against civilians were unpersuasive. The

---

[32] Prosecutor v. Gbagbo, The Reasons, ¶ 1082-1083.

[33] Prosecutor v. Gbagbo, The Reasons, ¶ 1108.

[34] Prosecutor v. Gbagbo, The Reasons, ¶ 1081-1083.

[35] Prosecutor v. Gbagbo, The Reasons, ¶ 1159.

judges wondered whether Laurent Gbagbo used disproportionate military means against the December 16 marchers or whether it was reasonable for the former Ivorian president to allow Alassane Ouattara and his supporters, who were willing to take over the country, to have a free ride. Judges Cuno and Henderson, based on the available evidence and the findings of the cross-examinations, claimed that the decision to prohibit the December 16 rally and the measures taken to enforce it did not have criminal intention. They concluded: "Although the available information is limited and fragmented, it does not seem to support the conclusion that the decision to deploy the armed forces was exaggerated. Indeed, the fact that there were a number of incidents in the morning of the march where members of the FDS were killed or injured by armed individuals in civilian clothing is likely to have raised the level of concern among the units deployed throughout the city."[36]

Analyzing the contextual environment of the operations of the FDS in Abidjan and mainly in Abobo, the judges asserted that the prosecutor's stance was partial and one sided because she downplayed the activities of the Invisible Commando and those of Alassane Ouattara's armed groups. In addition, they contended that these forces blended with the civilian population and the reaction of the FDS to such a situation might make one think that the former Ivorian president forces were targeting civilians, which was not the case:

> Presumably, this is because the Commando Invisible blended in with the civilian population in Abobo. The Prosecutor's position on this point is untenable. To the extent that there is information in this regard, it is quite clear that the targets of the use of lethal force by the FDS were the members of the Commando Invisible. The fact that civilians in Abobo were at risk of being confused with the enemy by the FDS does not make them the targets of the FDS as such.[37]

According to the prosecutor, the army took over the security operations after the failed police operations of January 11, 2011 thus leading to the intensification of violence and the death of civilians. The majority opinion dismissed such narrative in light of the army officers' testimonies and the available evidence. Suffice it to mention with regard to the civilian casualties the United Nations Mission Weekly Situation Report of January 18, 2011, which reported that 50 people were killed in Abobo as a result of the clashes that occurred from the 11th to the 18th of January, 2011 between the supporters of both Alassane Ouattara and Laurent Gbagbo. The majority opinion argued that

---

[36] Prosecutor v. Gbagbo, The Reasons, ¶ 1213.
[37] Prosecutor v. Gbagbo, The Reasons, ¶ 1222.

the content of that report could not be credible and reliable, as it was based on hearsay.[38]

The discussion about the intensification of military operations led to Abobo being treated as war zone, according to the prosecutor. The former Ivorian president rejected the suggestion made to him by General Mangou, who advised him to treat Abobo as a war zone. Despite his rejection, the prosecutor presented to the court two military official documents, as evidence BQI and FRAGO 69, which referred to Abobo as a war zone. She would later contradict herself when she claimed that the fact that the former president had not declared Abobo a war zone indicated his lack of concern for the lives of civilians who were at the mercy of his mortar shells.[39]

Several claims were made by human rights organizations and the UN mission about the murder of Alassane Ouattara's supporters in that neighborhood. And the majority was categorical: "In short, even if the poor quality of the evidence relating to the FDS killings in Abobo during this period was disregarded, there would still be no evidence to connect the perpetrators of the alleged crimes and the FDS high command, let alone M. Gbagbo himself."[40] Similarly, the majority opinion considered that the responsibility of Laurent Gbagbo could not be established in the firing of mortar shells in Abobo. General Mangou himself, in his testimony, clearly stated that the firing in the Banco Forest was a test and that the army was not responsible for the ones in Abobo. Based on this evidence, the court established that the mortar shells were not purposely fired at civilians.

In addition, the fact that the former president gave instructions to his officers to minimize the civilian casualties in Abobo demonstrated that civilians were not the targets of the military operations of his officers.[41] While analyzing the representative incidents, the majority judges wanted to find out the rationale of the perpetrators of the crimes and their identity; in other words if they were pro-Gbagbo and if the victims were civilians and pro-Ouattara.[42] Furthermore, they sought to demonstrate that being pro-Gbagbo was not sufficient and that the commission of crimes was to be intended to consolidate the Common Plan. As the prosecutor could not establish that the alleged crimes were part of an overall strategy of a Common Plan, the judges, therefore, rejected the criminal responsibility of the accused.

---

[38] Prosecutor v. Gbagbo, The Reasons, ¶ 1296.

[39] Prosecutor v. Gbagbo, The Reasons, ¶ 1363.

[40] Prosecutor v. Gbagbo, The Reasons, ¶ 1323.

[41] Prosecutor v. Gbagbo, The Reasons, ¶ 1375.

[42] Prosecutor v. Gbagbo, The Reasons, ¶ 1391.

Regarding the casualties of the December 16 incident, Judge Henderson underlined that the number of persons supposedly killed changed in the various documents presented by the prosecutor, from 45 to 24.[43] This cast doubt on the reliability of the information about the casualties. Judges Tarfusser and Henderson maintained that the narrative about the December 16 incident was different from other incidents, such as those of Abobo and Yopougon, which were less difficult to assess. The story of the December 16 incident was provided by a single individual who could not provide an expansive and comprehensive account of what happened. They rejected the idea that any person believed to be from the north, Muslim, and an alleged supporter of Alassane Ouattara killed around the December 16 date was involved in the march and therefore was victim of the security forces' repression. In addition, they could not see any probative value in the incriminating documents, which put emphasis on the list of people who were allegedly killed, and omitted to mention the perpetrators of the killings.

Regarding the second incident, which occurred from February 25–28, 2011 in Yopougon I, between the youth of Yao Sehi (pro-Gbagbo) and those of Doukouré (pro-Ouattara), the majority opinion stated that the violent conflicts started after pro–Ouattara supporters burned minibuses, *gbakas,* and that they might not even be related to the speech Blé Goudé delivered on February 25, 2011 at Le Baron, which did not contain any word that could incite violence. The former, those of Yao Sehi, were supposedly backed by the police according to witnesses and to the prosecutor. The contradictions in the testimonies of the witnesses who gave their accounts of the incident served to weaken the prosecutor's narrative. One of the witnesses initially said that it was the police who backed the pro-Gbagbo supporters and later adjusted his testimony and said it was a militia and not the police anymore. The prosecutor asked the court to consider this as a minor mistake, which the judges rejected. The contradicting narratives of the testimonies cast doubt on their reliability:

> In particular, the formation of the two groups being physically separated, with the Police in the middle and firing at the inhabitants of Doukouré, as P-0442 described it, is hardly compatible with P-0436's narrative, according to which the pro-Gbagbo people had already infiltrated Doukouré and were looting, before the Police intervened and used lethal force. Moreover, if the inhabitants of Doukouré had had the Police in front of them and one of the two groups of pro-Gbagbo youth behind (as P-0436 described it), the Police shooting, which P0442 claimed was directed at Doukouré inhabitants, would have been likely

---

[43] Prosecutor v. Gbagbo, The Reasons, ¶ 1419.

to hit the pro-Gbagbo youth behind them as well, as the latter would have found themselves in the same line of fire.[44]

With regard to the roadblocks, the majority indicated that there was not a uniform and common *modus operandi* in their management. Even though they were established against unmasked pro-Alassane Ouattara's infiltrators, some of the vigilantes were more concerned about extorting money from those who had to go through them while others were sticking to the primary mission of their erection, which means checking IDs. A witness P-0047 claimed that he went through some of the checkpoints even though the vigilantes knew he was from the northern part of the country after he disclosed his identity but yet they let him go after he paid some money.[45] The "Reasons" indicated, based on the available evidence, that the pro-Ouattara youth also erected some for security reasons.

Judge Henderson claimed that not all murdered around February 25, 2011 were because of their political affiliation. The prosecutor could not establish such evidence. As an illustration, the majority mentioned the name of Siaka Bakayoko, the only one to have been killed by a grenade thrown at him by the police.[46] The case of Modibo Kamara was also of interest. His death was reported by the Malian Council, "Conseil des Maliens." He was burned alive on February 25 not far from a police station, the *16e Arrondissement*. Due to the absence of strong evidence, the judges could not agree with the prosecutor that he was killed by pro-Gbagbo supporters because he was a Malian.[47]

The methodology to debunk the narrative of the prosecutor was applied to the third incident, the women's march. Judge Henderson affirmed that it was impossible to know who fired the shots at the women but concurred after watching videos of the incident that BTR 80 opened fire at a group of people among whom some were male. He added that there was no evidence to affirm that the convoy, who was unaware of the march, had deliberately decided to shoot at unarmed women.

As to the shelling of Abobo of March 17, 2011, the majority judges agreed that there was evidence of several explosions heard and witnessed by several people that came from mortar shells. It was not clear if they were 120 mm, 81 mm, or 60 mm mortars. But they could not agree with the prosecutor that the order to use them came directly from the former president Laurent Gbagbo himself, in

---

44 Prosecutor v. Gbagbo, The Reasons, ¶ 1665.
45 Prosecutor v. Gbagbo, The Reasons, ¶ 1721.
46 Prosecutor v. Gbagbo, The Reasons, ¶ 1744.
47 Prosecutor v. Gbagbo, The Reasons, ¶ 1749.

the absence of a substantive evidentiary document. After the investigations of officers as reported by the UN mission, the mortars used were within the range of 81 mm, and six shells were shot. The UN document, argued the majority judges, could not be a reliable source as it could not determine the origin of the firing.[48] Thanks to the cross-examination, it was established that the shells were aimed at a military target, the Invisible Commando, whose members were at the site of the market. Henderson questioned how mortar shells launched from a military base to a public place could spare the pro-Gbagbo and kill exclusively the pro-Ouattara supporters: he dismissed the idea that the firing of the mortar shells was intended to target civilians and to target them because they could be Dioulas.

The last incriminating incident is that of April 12, 2011 in Yopougon in a context of lawlessness after the fall of former president Laurent Gbagbo. Judge Henderson used it to deconstruct completely the theory of the Common Plan, even though he conceded that ethnicity and vengeance could have been important factors in the killing of the Dioulas and Ouattara's supporters:

> Indeed, it is telling that out of all crimes in the Prosecutor's narrative, those pertaining to the 12 April 2011 incident were the least likely to contribute to achieving the purpose of the alleged policy to keep Mr. Gbagbo in power at all costs. At that point in time, Mr. Gbagbo had already been arrested and the struggle for power was effectively over. To the extent that the available information allows any conclusions in this regard, it appears that the crimes committed in Yopougon on 12 April 2011 were mainly driven by vengeance.[49]

For the majority, the pillaging, the checking of identity, and the burning of some supporters of Alassane Ouattara could not be imputed to the accused. They rebutted the narrative of the prosecutor about the pattern of crimes committed as the 24 uncharged incidents did not obey the same mode of operations as that of the five or four representative criminal incidents. If the number of the victims (528) were accepted in the city of Abidjan—estimated at four million inhabitants, out of which one million are Muslims and ethnically, religiously, and politically close to Alassane Ouattara—the percentage of the victims would represent 0.052% of the victim population.[50] The judges made this estimation in order to conclude that the pro-Gbagbo militants had not conceived a strategy to kill civilians known as close to Ouattara.

---

[48] Prosecutor v. Gbagbo, The Reasons, ¶ 1819.

[49] Prosecutor v. Gbagbo, The Reasons, ¶ 1861.

[50] Prosecutor v. Gbagbo, The Reasons, ¶ 1892.

Moreover, the commission of random crimes cannot sustain the implementation of a Common Plan. Even though the majority acknowledged that the accused should have been more careful in some of their political actions, and should have been more forceful in controlling some of their supporters, they could not bear any criminal responsibility for the alleged crimes that were perpetrated in the context of war. They decided to reject the suggestion of the prosecutor, who wanted to recharacterize the crimes, even though they considered that the crimes the defendants were accused of could be renamed war crimes instead of crimes against humanity.[51]

In closing, Judge Henderson contended that the trial needed to be stopped not only because the prosecutor's charges did not meet the minimum standards of admissibility but also because of the inconsistencies in her narrative, and because of the unreliability and the untrustworthiness of the witnesses. He stated in his preamble that it was not his responsibility to take a position on the moral or political responsibility of the two acquitted defendants. The dissenting position emanated from Judge Herrera Carbuccia.

Dissenting opinion

The dissenting judge Herrera Carbuccia expressed her disagreement with the decision of the majority in her 307-page document (Annex C). In her dissenting opinion, she asserted that there was enough evidence that, if admitted, would allow a reasonable Trial Chamber to declare Laurent Gbagbo and Charles Blé Goudé guilty of crimes against humanity and of crimes committed against the civilian population in the context of post-election violence in Ivory Coast (murder, attempted murder, rape, inhumane acts, and persecution).

Judge Herrera Carbuccia launched an appeal to the court inviting it to convict the former president thus demonstrating that it upholds the values of the Rome Statute:

> Establishing the truth behind events and preventing all forms of revisionism have always been the underlying objectives of all international criminal justice systems. If we allow a president in a democratic society who refuses to step down in the aftermath of a contested election to target citizens of that society and commit crimes against humanity with impunity, we fail to comply with the values and purposes enshrined in the Rome Statute ("Statute") and espoused by the international community.[52]

---

[51] Prosecutor v. Gbagbo, The Reasons, ¶ 2037.

[52] Prosecutor v. Gbagbo, ICC-02/11-01/15, The Decision: Dissenting Opinion by Judge Herrera Carbuccia, ¶ 6 (July 16, 2019).

She opposed the No Case to Answer ruling, stating that the trial should not have been abruptly terminated and argued that a reasonable trial chamber should convict the accused. She used the expression "reasonable trial" emphatically and anaphorically. The phrase is repeated throughout her dissenting opinion. She laid the ground for her dissenting opinion by giving a series of definitions of terms such as state policy, systematic attack, and civilian population. Her narrative was similar to that of the prosecutor, who had been disavowed by the majority of Trial Chamber I. She acknowledged that the former Ivorian president's criminal responsibility cannot be established in the April 12 incident, which occurred a day after his downfall, but yet she devoted several paragraphs to this incident as she built her rationale for his conviction. Similarly, she agreed with the prosecutor who dropped the March 3 and the March 17 incidents from the list of charges against Blé Goudé but still held the April 12 incident against him, even though he was in hiding in the last weeks of Gbagbo regime. [53]

In light of the inconsistencies and the discrepancy between the witnesses' recorded statements before the trial and their testimonies in the courtroom, as underlined by the defense and reiterated by the majority opinion, Herrera Carbuccia advised the court to consider the relevant part of the testimonies as elements of conviction and to ignore the nonreliable part.[54] She defended the same approach for the forensic evidence, which was not all conclusive. In the same vein, she added that hearsay should not be refuted and rebutted, as it can have probative value. She downplayed the role of the Invisible Commando, ignored the actions of pro-Ouattara forces, namely the Dozos, but briefly alluded to them when she attempted to define the concept of "civilian population." She added that the inconsistencies could be the result of several factors, namely post-traumatic stress disorder. Rejecting the opinion of the defense, who argued that several witnesses could not be credible because they were Alassane Ouattara's supporters, Judge Herrera Carbuccia instead contended that the dual state of a witness does not negate the reliability, the validity, and the credibility emanating from that witness.

She claimed to have conducted an evaluation that led to the expression of her dissenting voice, but in her more than 307-page document, she did not dedicate even a single page to the *modus operandi* of the rebel groups and failed to link them to Alassane Ouattara; she acknowledged them only to say that the prosecutor should prosecute them as well; words which resonate like another wishful thinking. She added that the existence of evidence of the

---

[53] Prosecutor v. Gbagbo, Dissenting Opinion by Carbuccia, ¶18.

[54] Prosecutor v. Gbagbo, Dissenting Opinion by Carbuccia, ¶ 29.

rebels' crimes did not exculpate the state of Ivory Coast, which failed to honor one of its obligations, which was to protect the civilian population.

In her narrative to sustain the former president having committed crimes against humanity, she deconstructed the meaning of the term "civilian population," inferring that it was not because the armed rebel forces operated in the midst of civilians that the latter ceased to be civilians: "Most importantly, the presence of armed persons within a population does not, of itself, alter the civilian nature of that population."[55] Regarding the crimes attributed to the former president, she specifically stressed that they were committed in places that were essentially civilian, such as "homes, mosques, markets, and headquarters of political parties."[56] She claimed the state apparatus was aware of the pro-Gbagbo criminal activities, did not deter and condemn them, and had the obligation to protect the civilians even in a context of urban guerrilla warfare, that she denied was the situation.

She added to her list of criminal acts and words the instruction of Laurent Gbagbo, who did not declare Abobo a war zone and who urged the chief of the army who just reported to him that the place they needed to attack in Abobo was full of civilians. The former president instructed that they should make sure to keep the number of casualties and death down. She concluded that his intention was to use heavy weaponry, which he did. She added that the former Ivorian president's decision to requisition the army, and his instructions to his officers to do everything possible to keep Abobo, were an authorization given to the soldiers to use every heavy weapon at their disposal, namely the 120 mm mortars. Consequently, the crimes committed during the use of the weapons established the criminal responsibility of Laurent Gbagbo.[57]

Blé Goudé, the leader of the *Galaxie Patriotique*, who viewed himself as a leader of a revolution against neo-colonialism, gave multiple peaceful instructions. Herrera Carbuccia gave herself the mission, alongside the prosecutor, to attempt to detect any word or act that would destroy that image. She acknowledged that he had power over several state security officials,[58] leaders of the agoras, youth activists, and all the grassroots organizations, including the militia groups. She added that substantive proof revealed, besides the in-court testimonies of the head of the police Brédou M'Bia, that Blé Goudé had provided funds to finance militia groups such as the GPP.[59]

---

[55] Prosecutor v. Gbagbo, Dissenting Opinion by Carbuccia, ¶ 58.

[56] Prosecutor v. Gbagbo, Dissenting Opinion by Carbuccia, ¶ 216.

[57] Prosecutor v. Gbagbo, Dissenting Opinion by Carbuccia, ¶ 530–531.

[58] Prosecutor v. Gbagbo, Dissenting Opinion by Carbuccia, ¶ 235.

[59] Prosecutor v. Gbagbo, Dissenting Opinion by Carbuccia, ¶ 236.

Regarding the hateful speech that she accused Blé Goudé of, she recalled the following words of Laurent Gbagbo's co-accused, who, exasperated during the electoral crisis, once declared: "I do not want war. But when I say I do not want war, it does not mean that I am weak." For Herrera Carbuccia this meant that he did not rule out the necessity of war, and she saw the above-mentioned words as having a criminal intent.[60]

In her attempt to consolidate her narrative about the hate speech pattern she accused Blé Goudé of, she alluded to the one he delivered at a rally at *Place de la République* on March 26, 2011, after which the Mauritanian community accused of being pro-Ouattara became the target of his followers. Herrera Carbuccia recalled the following words of Laurent-Gbagbo co-accused: "Who leaves Abidjan?…Mauritanians have left their shops. They are gone, when they come back, they will find new shopkeepers in Ivory Coast."[61] She claimed that after the speech, Blé Goudé sympathizers attacked the Mauritanians' shops and pillaged many of them in Yopougon Siporex. She added other words pronounced by Blé Goudé, who once declared that he was conducting a revolution and there would be collateral damage. Carbuccia reiterated that the damage Blé Goudé was alluding to was criminal, not financial or economic.[62]

Judge Herrera Carbuccia was adamant in her blatant and blunt claim that Yopougon was still under the pro-Gbagbo forces on April 12 after the fall of the Ivorian president. Regarding the inner circle, the dissenting judge devoted pages to Simone Gbagbo who, alongside Blé Goudé and some senior military and political officials of the former regime, remained an important player of the Common Plan who used the state apparatus to oppress and repress the pro–Ouattara people. She argued that Simone Gbagbo's aide de camp, Séka Séka, who had at his disposal powerful and heavy weapons supposedly stationed in the basement of the presidential palace, was known as being an overseer of several contingents of Liberian mercenaries. She claimed her assertion stood on several in-court testimonies. Her assessment of the incriminating incidents particularly the March 3, 2011 one is a reprise of the prosecutor's narrative and the propaganda of various international players. She analyzed Gbagbo's refusal to step down after being recognized by the international community as the loser of the election as an escalating factor for the commission of crimes. In her eyes, this was a crime for which he needed to be punished:

> Finally, Mr Gbagbo's actions during the post-election violence must be evaluated with regard to the manner in which the situation evolved. He

---

[60] Prosecutor v. Gbagbo, Dissenting Opinion by Carbuccia, ¶ 160.

[61] Prosecutor v. Gbagbo, Dissenting Opinion by Carbuccia, ¶ 633.

[62] Prosecutor v. Gbagbo, Dissenting Opinion by Carbuccia, ¶ 632.

had several opportunities to step down or to negotiate an agreement that could have prevented the commission of crimes, in particular after the consequences of the incident at the March on RTI. At all times during the post-election violence, it was open to Mr Gbagbo to consider his actions or omissions and to desist from them. For example, he could have done so when the international community—specifically the African Union—recognised Mr Ouattara as the winner of the election and the democratically-elected President (first at a meeting in Ethiopia on 9 December 2010 and then at another meeting on 10 March 2011). After the latter meeting, Philippe Mangou proposed that Mr Gbagbo resign on 11 March 2011. As noted in Philippe Mangou's evidence, he suggested this to Mr Gbagbo not only because of the international community's decision, but also because, simply put, too many people had lost their lives. Another opportunity came when, at a meeting in March 2011, the FDS hierarchy again suggested that a political solution for peace should be reached. Again, Mr Gbagbo rejected this suggestion. Mr Gbagbo thus had available to him reasonable measures which, as advised by his subordinates, could have prevented the commission of crimes and in particular the shelling of Abobo on 17 March 2011.[63]

After taking notice of the position of the majority and that of the minority, the diseenting voice, the ICC Chief Prosecutor, Fatou Bensouda, who disagreed with the verdict appealed. I discuss in the next section the grounds of her appeal.

The prosecutor's appeal

The reaction of the prosecutor was made public in mid-October 2019. She asserted that the trial chamber committed legal and procedural errors and therefore called for a mistrial. Her goal was to reverse the verdict that acquitted the accused, arguing that it was misinformed by an erroneous assessment by the majority judges. She declared that they made a partial assessment of the evidence she presented. If her claim was granted by the Appeals Chamber, the trial was set to restart. The two grounds of her appeal were as follows:

1. The acquittal violated the requirements of article 74(5).

2. The Trial Chamber failed to define a clear standard of proof it used to assess the evidence and it should have notified it before, during the proceedings or on the lead up to January 25, 2019 hearing which acquitted the accused.

The prosecution's appeal two grounds stood on four major points:

---

[63] *Prosecutor v. Gbagbo*, Dissenting Opinion by Carbuccia, ¶ 552.

1.   The nature of the announcement and of the pronouncement of the decision of January 15, 2019;

2.   The noncompliance of the decision of January 15 with any of the requirements of Article 74;

3.   The lack of a consistent and predictable legal procedure informing the decision of acquittal;

4.   The erroneous assessment of the evidence presented by the prosecutor which informed the decision of acquittal.

From the prosecutor's point of view, when the majority judges opted to announce the acquittal through an oral decision, they did not provide the foundations of their decision. It delayed the written and expansive rationale of the verdict, which was finally made public six months, or 182 days, after the verbal pronouncement. In light of the above, Fatou Bensouda felt justified to reject the acquittal which was in her eyes unlawful, as it was not in conformity with any of the four requirements of article 74(5) which stipulates: "The decision shall be in writing and shall contain a full and reasoned statement of the Trial Chamber's findings on the evidence and conclusions. The Trial Chamber shall issue one decision. When there is no unanimity, the Trial Chamber's decision shall contain the views of the majority and the minority. The decision or a summary thereof shall be delivered in open court." [64]

For the sake of clarity, it is imperative to sum up the four conditions of a lawful decision as stated in Article 74(5), which are as follows:

1.   The decision shall be in a written format.

2.   It shall present a comprehensive analysis of the findings and conclusions of the majority.

3.   The decision shall be one and indivisible and should reflect both the views of the majority and the dissenting opinion.

4.   The pronouncement of the verdict shall be in open court.[65]

As already mentioned, the acquittal was an oral decision whose written version was made public in October (point number 1). In her appeal, Fatou Bensouda maintained that the majority took the decision of acquittal without fully assessing each item of evidence (point number 2). Regarding point number 3 of article 74(5), Fatou Bensouda started her argument with Judge Henderson's own admission: "What follows are my own written reasons for

---

[64] International Criminal Court, *Rome Statute*, 36.

[65] Prosecutor v. Gbagbo, ICC-02/11-01/15, Prosecution Document in Support of Appeal, ¶ 29 (October 17, 2019).

joining Judge Tarfusser in deciding to end the case..."[66] For the prosecutor there was no indication that the presiding Judge (Tarfusser) participated in the drafting of the written version of the decision.[67] Also, Judge Tarfusser has expressed his disagreements with Judge Henderson on the legal procedure that had informed the supposedly common decision. She therefore concluded that the written format of the verdict was the position of one judge (Henderson) supported by the other (Tarfusser) and that the document "The Reasons" did not represent the undivided and harmonious views of the majority. She therefore summed up her opinion, stating that this was a violation of point number 3 of Article 74(5), which required the decision be one. The fact that the oral decision and the reasons were not pronounced in open court violated, according to the prosecutor, point number 4 of Article 74(5).

The lack of consensus about the legal procedure and the standard of proof upon which the decision of acquittal was pronounced was extensively debated by the prosecutor. Fatou Bensouda also added that the majority had already taken the decision of acquittal even before receiving the No Case to Answer motion of the defendants' legal defense teams. Consequently, she argued, the Reasons of Judge Henderson and the Opinion of Judge Tarfusser came later as written rationalizations of an already-taken decision not informed by a full assessment of the evidence.[68]

She noted that Tarfusser had expressed disagreements about the legal procedure that informed the decision.[69] The judges of the majority opinion did not agree on the standard of proof or the legal procedure that sustained the decision of acquittal. Judge Henderson was in favor of and applied the No Case to Answer standard, and Judge Tarfusser opted for that of "beyond reasonable doubt."

For the prosecutor, the lack of transparency shed a shadow of doubt on the verdict, as it left the court stakeholders in the dark. She claimed therefore that for a legal decision to be legitimate, it must be based or informed by a qualitative legal procedure. She added that a decision that was made from a legal procedure tainted with irregularities should be null and void.

She recalled that on June 13, 2018 the presiding judge had rejected her request to seek some clarifications about the No Case to Answer proceedings. The prosecutor recalled that the No Case to Answer standard was used only once in the Ruto and Sang case and is not a common standard of proof, not even

---

[66] *Prosecutor v. Gbagbo,* Prosecution Document in Support of Appeal, ¶ 53.

[67] *Prosecutor v. Gbagbo,* Prosecution Document in Support of Appeal, ¶ 54.

[68] *Prosecutor v. Gbagbo,* Prosecution Document in Support of Appeal, ¶ 75.

[69] *Prosecutor v. Gbagbo,* Opinion of Tarfusser, ¶ 2.

prescribed by the Rome Statute. In addition, she argued, in that particular case, the Trial Chamber should have stated just from the start it would give the opportunity to the defense to submit the No Case to Answer motion.[70]

When the prosecutor discussed what she saw as the inconsistencies and the irregularities in the legal procedure that informed the decision, she built her argument on another admission by Judge Henderson, who acknowledged that Article 74 did not provide the framework for opting for the No Case to Answer[71] and who therefore relied on Article 66(2) in order to be able to accept the No Case to Answer legal procedure.[72]For the prosecution, the majority misapplied rule 144, which was used to justify the delaying of the dissemination of the copies of the written decision.[73]Rule 144 entitled "Delivery of the Decisions of the Trial Chamber" indicates that the decisions concerning the admissibility of a case, the jurisdiction of the court, reparation, and the sentence of a trial can be pronounced in public and the copies of the decisions can be made available as soon as possible.[74]

Moreover, the prosecutor argued that, for a case to be legitimate, the rules must be clear and should not be changed in the course of the proceedings. Also, she considered that the majority did not state clearly the legal foundation of the acquittal before they assessed the evidence she had presented.[75]

In her appeal the prosecutor stated that the majority opinion did not assess thoroughly and properly the evidence she presented for the five core incriminating incidents and for the secondary ones. She mentioned that the judges ignored the five eyewitnesses' testimonies and rejected the reliability and validity of the video of the March 3 incident[76] and those of the experts.[77] They did not address the question of who shot the victims, she claimed. The application of corroboration as an evidentiary approach by Judge Henderson did not suit the prosecutor, who argued that his understanding of the approach was not in line with the praxis of international tribunals. For her, corroboration can still be relevant and valid even when testimonies are different as long as they present thematic consistencies.[78] The prosecutor disagreed with the court

---

[70] Prosecutor v. Gbagbo, Prosecution Document in Support of Appeal, ¶ 154.

[71] Prosecutor v. Gbagbo, The Reasons, ¶ 13.

[72] Prosecutor v. Gbagbo, Prosecution Document in Support of Appeal, ¶ 37.

[73] Prosecutor v. Gbagbo, Prosecution Document in Support of Appeal, ¶ 44.

[74] United Nations, *International Criminal Court: Rules of Procedure and Evidence*, 59.

[75] Prosecutor v. Gbagbo, Prosecution Document in Support of Appeal, ¶ 137.

[76] Prosecutor v. Gbagbo, Prosecution Document in Support of Appeal, ¶ 168.

[77] Prosecutor v. Gbagbo, Prosecution Document in Support of Appeal, ¶ 171.

[78] Prosecutor v. Gbagbo, Prosecution Document in Support of Appeal, ¶ 158.

when it viewed some evidence as hearsay and anonymous hearsay, and argued that it could not establish that the FDS convoy was responsible for the death of the 13 victims of the March 3 event. For her, this was an illustration of an inconsistent evidentiary approach, as the judges were believed to have discounted the eyewitness testimonies.[79]

She reiterated her line of attack: The March 3 event was essentially peaceful led by defenseless and vulnerable women who were shot at by a FDS convoy. Seven of them were murdered. The prosecutor accused the judges of having ignored the attribution of crimes. One witness's testimony, according to the prosecutor, led the majority judges to discredit and disregard the probative value of other aspects of the evidence, and she therefore exclaimed: "The presence of one possible 'counter-view' was not sufficient reason to reject the swathes of credible and reliable evidence consistently demonstrating the opposite view."[80]

Regarding the firing of the 120 mm mortar, the majority judges argued that there were several explosions, while the prosecutor considered there was only one shot fired, and that it was impossible to situate Gbagbo's responsibility in the firing of the 120 mm mortar. Some witnesses during the court hearing claimed to have overheard Captain Zadi use the word *presidency* when discussing the source of the authorization of the use of the mortar. For Bensouda, a witness inferred the president had ordered the use of the mortars even though it was not clearly stated that the order came from the president himself. For the prosecutor, such testimony should not be discounted or disregarded. It should not be refuted, for it was established that Gbagbo gave the order for the use of the weapons, including the 120 mm mortar.[81]

Gbagbo's knowledge of military affairs, having been interned in a military camp in the early years of his struggle, was emphasized by the prosecutor, who claimed he was aware of all operations and that he was the primary originator of all orders for the military operations during the crises. She added that the requisition of the army alone sufficed to establish the criminal responsibility of Gbagbo, particularly in the use of the 120 mm mortar. Regarding the clashes that occurred during the February 25 incident between the militaries of both rivals, the prosecutor again maintained that the fact that witnesses gave different testimonies should not lead the judges to invalidate the incriminating essence of the evidence.[82]

---

[79] Prosecutor v. Gbagbo, Prosecution Document in Support of Appeal, ¶ 167.

[80] Prosecutor v. Gbagbo, Prosecution Document in Support of Appeal, ¶ 177.

[81] Prosecutor v. Gbagbo, Prosecution Document in Support of Appeal, ¶ 204.

[82] Prosecutor v. Gbagbo, Prosecution Document in Support of Appeal, ¶ 214.

The prosecutor contended: "Again, it appears that the consistencies of the evidence were relegated while the inconsistencies were elevated."[83] The crime of rape during the crisis was a contentious issue. While the majority judges concluded it could have been an opportunistic crime, the prosecutor disagreed and stated that rape was not an opportunistic crime but rather a calculated criminal action by Gbagbo's forces, at times ordained by Simone Gbagbo herself during several incidents, namely, the December 16 2010 rally, which was the first charged incident, and April 12, 2011, which was the fifth charged incident. Judge Tarfusser dismissed the accusations against Simone Gbagbo, seeing them as hearsay and claimed that they were not collaborated. The prosecutor concluded that the women were raped because they were northerners and supporters of Alassane Ouattara.[84] So, in light of the above, the prosecutor asked the chamber to reverse the decision according to the provision of Article 83 (2)(a). "The proceedings in this case were unfair and unreliable, and the decision was affected by legal and procedural errors and accordingly the prosecution respectively request the Appeals Chamber to reverse the decision."[85]

The Office of the Prosecutor through one of its deputies made an announcement that baffled and puzzled the court stakeholders. Chief Prosecutor Fatou Bensouda intended to continue the proceedings against Mr. Gbagbo and Mr. Blé Goudé. She called upon the Appeals Chamber to draw on Article 83(2)(a) to nullify the verdict and call for a new trial against Mr. Gbagbo and Mr. Blé Goudé. This was the major news of the hearing. Fatou Bensouda requested a mistrial and wanted a new trial.

The Ivory Coast lawyers, who represented Alassane Ouattara's interests, led by Jean-Pierre Mignard, requested the resumption of the trial and the completion of its proceedings. They argued that this was the only way which would guarantee the legitimacy of the decision and avoid that it be questioned and questionable. They added that it was a necessity that would guarantee peace, reconciliation, and international public order. They asked the court to maintain the binding conditions on Laurent Gbagbo, whose defense played a video of Alassane Ouattara, the Ivorian president who was saying during a rally that he did not send the lawyers to the ICC, but they were there on their own initiative.

Jennifer Naouri, member of the former Ivorian president's legal team, therefore asked the Appeals Chamber not to consider their request. She added

---

[83] Prosecutor v. Gbagbo, Prosecution Document in Support of Appeal, ¶ 226.

[84] Prosecutor v. Gbagbo, Prosecution Document in Support of Appeal, ¶ 234–237.

[85] Prosecutor v. Gbagbo, Prosecution Document in Support of Appeal, ¶ 266.

that the true intention of the lawyers of the state of Ivory Coast was to oppose the return of Laurent Gbagbo to his country because President Alassane Ouattara wanted to prevent all the opponents from standing for the 2020 presidential election in the country. She alluded to the imprisonment of lawmakers close to Guillaume Soro who announced he would run for president, and who was condemned in absentia in Ivory Coast after being accused of attempting to overthrow the regime of Alassane Ouattara. The legal representative of the victims, Paolina Massida, also requested that the total freedom of the acquitted not be granted. She added that if Laurent Gbagbo could go back to Ivory Coast, he could take over state power and escape justice.

The defense lawyers requested the lifting of the restrictions of liberty imposed on their clients. A hearing presided by Judge Chile Eboe-Osuji to review the conditions of release of the acquitted was then held on February 6, 2020. On Friday, February 7, the various parties (the prosecutor, the legal representative of the victims, and the counsels of Laurent Gbagbo and Charles Blé Goudé submitted written documents to the Registry of the ICC. The awaited decision of the Appeals Chamber to the request of the prosecutor was finally made public in a court hearing of that chamber led by Judge Chile Eboe-Osuji on March 31, 2021. That court decision is called "Judgement."[86]

Appeals Chamber judgement

Like any court hearing of the ICC, there were various interpretations of the evidentiary assessment, testimonies, and of the Rome statute articles. The Appeals Chamber called upon to decide whether the Laurent Gbagbo and Blé Goudé trial should continue or not made the decision to confirm the acquittal on March 31, 2021 after a careful analysis of the prosecutor's appeal which stood on two grounds, both on the form and the content of the decision of acquittal. The majority of the Appeals Chamber judges claimed that their decision was based on the three pillar-legal practice in force in Europe and Latin America (where it is called *Sana Critica*) which informs legal decisions. According to that legal practice, a legal decision should be taken after an evaluation is done on the basis of sound reasoning, logic, and common knowledge.[87]

The legal procedure that the Trial Chamber used to shorten the trial was the No Case to Answer ruling. The prosecution, the judges of the Trial Chamber and of the Appeals Chamber all agreed that there is no article in the Rome Statute

---

[86] Prosecutor v. Gbagbo, ICC-02/11-01/15 A, Appeals Chamber's Judgement (March 31, 2021).

[87] Prosecutor v. Gbagbo, Appeals Chamber's Judgement, ¶ 68.

about the No Case to Answer procedure. The prosecutor thought that the Trial Chamber judges should not have resorted to it but the Appeal Chamber judges disagreed. Even if the No Case to Answer is not clearly expressed in the Rome Statute, the Appeals Chamber had to answer whether it was permissible by the ICC.

The Appeals Chamber from the onset bluntly stated that it did not remember if the No Case to Answer framework had ever been part of the discussions leading to the adoption of the Rome Statute and to the creation of the International Criminal Court. The Appeals Chamber, even though it conceded that there is no article in the Rome Statute that discusses the No Case to Answer, claimed that it is not incompatible with the Rome Statute and postulated that article 64 (6) (f) may provide a legal basis for it.[88] The article stipulates that "In performing its functions prior to trial or during the course of a trial, the Trial Chamber may, as necessary.... rule on any other relevant matters."[89]

The Appeals Chamber advocated that the opinion about the No Case to Answer ruling is at the discretion of the judges and it can be applied on a case-by-case basis. In light of such a statement, the Appeals Chamber thus concluded that the Trial Chamber can decide to stop the proceedings of a trial on the grounds of the No Case to Answer framework. Moreover, it contended that it is one of the three principles which constitute a trio of commonly legal principles practiced in the international justice system, the second being the presumption of innocence of the accused, and the third that the burden of proof falls on the prosecutor.[90] Arguing that a trial can continue if there is a need for the court to hear and receive the arguments of the defense, similarly, a court can decide to stop a trial if the incriminating evidence lacks a strong probative value for a conviction to be pronounced. In that case, the Appeals Chamber maintained, if the need to stop such trials arises, the No Case to Answer standard can be applied.[91] In order to support its claim, the Appeals Chamber referred to the Ntaganda trial which was halted on a No Case to Answer basis. The judges in the Ntaganda case had argued that their decision was informed by Article 64.[92]

The Appeals Chamber in the Laurent Gbagbo case made it clear that even if the decision to stop the trial was supposedly informed by Article 64, the decision of acquittal or conviction is to be provided by Article 74, which neither

---

[88] Prosecutor v. Gbagbo, Appeals Chamber's Judgement, ¶ 104.

[89] International Criminal Court, *Rome Statute*, Article 64 (6) (f).

[90] Prosecutor v. Gbagbo, Appeals Chamber's Judgement, ¶ 106.

[91] Prosecutor v. Gbagbo, Appeals Chamber's Judgement, ¶ 105.

[92] Prosecutor v. Gbagbo, Appeals Chamber's Judgement, ¶ 108.

obstructs nor precludes the No Case to Answer legal procedure.[93] In addition, the Appeals Chamber disagreed with the understanding and the interpretation that the prosecutor had of the judgement, which according to the Rome Statute "shall be based on its evaluation of the evidence and the entire proceedings." While for the prosecutor, the phrase "the entire proceedings meant the full trial (the presentation of incriminating evidence, the court hearings, the accused legal defense team presentation…), for the Appeals Chamber, that phrase implied and suggested that a decision can be made based upon the assessment of the probative value of the incriminating evidence provided by the prosecutor even before an eventual continuation of the trial. In that case, Article 74 can provide the legal basis for the decision even if that article is not a provision for a No Case to Answer.

Consequently, the Appeals Chamber's decision to reject the prosecutors appeal is also based on another international legal principle *ne bis in idem* (not twice about the same). This principle means that no defendant should be judged twice for the same crimes. Seeing the January15, 2019 decision as the final outcome of a long trial, the ultimate decision of years of legal proceedings after an assessment of the incriminating evidence which happened to be weak and insufficient for a conviction, the Appeals Chamber therefore decided that continuing the trial would be a violation of the *ne bis in idem* legal principle.[94]

The delay between the oral pronouncement and the written version of the verdict was also a matter of concern for the prosecutor. On this point, the Appeals Chamber recalled that there is jurisprudence for this case: the Zlatko Alekvoski trial before the special tribunal on Yugoslavia. The written version of the verdict came after the oral pronouncement of the sentence.[95] The majority of the Appeals Chamber dismissed the prosecutor's first ground of appeal and revealed that the prosecutor had used a selective and distorted interpretation of the R v. Teskey case in Canada to support her claim. The Supreme Court of Canada revealed that an oral pronouncement of a sentence can be made prior to the written version of that sentence.[96] Moreover, the Appeals Chamber also added that the European Commission on Human Rights condones the separation of oral and written versions of a sentence.[97] The Appeals Chamber challenged the prosecutor, who claimed that there was a six month delay

[93] Prosecutor v. Gbagbo, Appeals Chamber's Judgement, ¶ 109.

[94] Prosecutor v. Gbagbo, Appeals Chamber's Judgement, ¶ 112.

[95] Prosecutor v. Gbagbo, Appeals Chamber's Judgement, ¶ 171.

[96] Prosecutor v. Gbagbo, Appeals Chamber's Judgement, ¶ 174.

[97] Prosecutor v. Gbagbo, Appeals Chamber's Judgement, ¶ 178.

between the oral verdict and its written version, and advanced that there is no time limit set in the drafting of the verdict in the Rome Statute.

Fatou Bensouda accused the Trial Chamber of having given a hasty, premature, not fully informed decision. She added that the speedy delivery of the verdict by the Trial Chamber demonstrated that its judges had not made a profound assessment of the incriminating evidence. She argued that judges Henderson and Tarfusser provided later a result-driven reasoning to rationalize their decision which could not have been well informed. The majority of the Appeals Chamber judges rejected her claim that the Trial Chamber judges made a decision which was not fully informed. To sustain their challenge of her claim, they recalled that the trial had been in force for at least three years, which was a decent length of time during which the prosecutor submitted all kinds of incriminating documents, including the Mid-Trial Brief, which the judges analyzed during the course of the proceedings.[98] The prosecutor's premise that judges should only form their idea at the end of the proceedings was not valid and was therefore not accepted.

The second ground of the prosecutor appeal was also rejected by the Appeals Chamber. She had argued that there was no consensus on the standard of proof among the judges in their pronouncement of the verdict of acquittal. She added that they should have informed the court, her office, and the stakeholders before the pronouncement of the decision about the standard of proof to be used for the verdict. Moreover, the prosecutor argued that this procedural error should constitute a reason for the nullification of the verdict because it was a defective procedure that led to defective findings which consequently led to a defective verdict. She felt that prejudice was done to her and that the interests of justice were not preserved and that justice was not served.

For the sake of clarity, it is important to note that Judge Cuno Tarfusser had argued that the Rome Statute does not have any provision on the No Case to Answer standard. And both Judges Tarfusser and Henderson had some minor differences about the standard of proof used to assess the evidence presented to the court by the prosecutor. According to the Appeals Chamber, if the evidence does not prove beyond a reasonable doubt the guilt of a defendant, a verdict of conviction should not be pronounced.[99] This can be applied to the No case to Answer. If there is some doubt in the evidence presented, the trial can be adjourned and the acquittal can be pronounced.[100] The notion of beyond reasonable doubt is applied to the assessment of evidence presented

---

[98] Prosecutor v. Gbagbo, Appeals Chamber's Judgement, ¶ 238.

[99] Prosecutor v. Gbagbo, Appeals Chamber's Judgement, ¶ 306.

[100] Prosecutor v. Gbagbo, Appeals Chamber's Judgement, ¶ 307.

by the prosecutor. It does not mean that it ought to be extended to the supposedly exculpatory evidence to be presented by the defense team.[101]

To the argument of the prosecutor who claimed that the No Case to Answer and the legal procedure led to defective findings, the Appeals Chamber advocated that the fairness of a trial does not reside in its prolongation.[102] The trial does not need to be prolonged if the evidence cannot meet the standard of proof beyond reasonable doubt. In light of the preceding observation, there is no requirement nor obligation to bring forth the legal defense team to present evidence as the burden of proof is on the prosecutor.

Regarding the notion of credibility and reliability, the Appeals Chamber made it clear that the judges had clearly analyzed the evidence through the prism of these notions and rebutted the insinuation made by the prosecutor that the Trial Chamber judges had not shown integrity and impartiality. It challenged such a claim and saw it as mere speculation with no ground to support it.[103] The Appeals Chamber also rejected the opinion of the prosecutor who contended that there was no clarity and consensus among the judges of the majority about the standard of proof in the decision to acquit. It decided not to ignore the weaknesses of the prosecution and reiterated that both judges Henderson and Tarfusser agreed on the extreme weakness of the incriminating documents presented by the prosecution.[104]

In sum, the Appeals Chamber concluded that Fatou Bensouda could not demonstrate how the Trial Chamber was not well informed before the decision of acquittal, how the acquittal was premature, and how its judges were impartial and lacked integrity. Concurring with the verdict of January 15, 2019 the Appeals Chamber confirmed the decision to acquit Laurent Gbagbo and Blé Goudé. In other words, even though it had the power to reverse the Trial Chamber decision, and to order a new trial, according to Article 81 (1) (a),[105] as it did not see any wrongdoing in the legal procedure, the No Case to Answer ruling, used to pronounce the acquittal of Laurent Gbagbo and Blé Goudé, the Appeals Chamber decided to reject the grounds of the prosecutor's appeal, thus confirming the acquittal of the two accused, consequently ending a trial which was highly political in nature.[106]

---

[101] Prosecutor v. Gbagbo, Appeals Chamber's Judgement, ¶ 310.

[102] Prosecutor v. Gbagbo, Appeals Chamber's Judgement, ¶ 311.

[103] Prosecutor v. Gbagbo, Appeals Chamber's Judgement, ¶ 321.

[104] Prosecutor v. Gbagbo, Appeals Chamber's Judgement, ¶ 328.

[105] Prosecutor v. Gbagbo, Appeals Chamber's Judgement, ¶ 379.

[106] Prosecutor v. Gbagbo, Appeals Chamber's Judgement, ¶ 380.

Conclusion

I have analyzed the three-decade crisis in Ivory Coast through the lens of its various features; dissected its anatomy; stressed the role of diverse players, domestic and international; and I deconstructed the mainstream and the widespread Manichean view about it. Laurent Gbagbo's trial which was an outcome of the crisis has had a global resonance: It was the trial of Guillaume Soro, who assumed the rebellion; of Alassane Ouattara, who was the godfather of the rebellion; of former president of Burkina Faso, Blaise Compaoré, who trained and provided strategic support to pro–Ouattara rebels; of France, which waged a neocolonial war against Ivory Coast; of the international community; and of the International Criminal Court. The trial of Laurent Gbagbo destroyed the credibility of the ICC, whose creation was motivated by the dual need for the existence of an international arbitration institution and for the respect and protection of human rights. It will be recorded that in ten years, the prosecutors who claimed to serve justice were unable to open an investigation into the crimes committed by pro-Ouattara forces and by the forces of France and the United Nations. This victor's justice, observed since the Nuremberg trial, is not true justice.

Through the eight years of proceedings against Laurent Gbagbo and Blé Goudé, three years of trial, an unfair and partial accusation, an acquittal and a release with conditions, the ICC appeared as an instrument abused and used by France, the United Nations, and by the Ivorian regime of Alassane Ouattara. The one-sided prosecution of the court mirrored the domestic expedited justice under Alassane Ouattara, who resorted to violence to impose his candidacy and to become the effective president of Ivory Coast, and whose regime has been exclusively responsible for massive human rights violations since the fall of Laurent Gbagbo on April 11, 2011.

The ICC's tardy decision to acquit the former Ivorian president does not exculpate it nor does it dissolve its indictment before the tribunal of history. Laurent Gbagbo's trial is therefore the indictment of the International Criminal Court. It has been a historic opportunity with a multiplying effect and ramifications that exposed the scheme of neo-colonialism and contributed to the revival of Pan-Africanism in the twenty-first century.

Laurent Gbagbo's trial galvanized Ivorian nationalists, African nationalists and Pan-Africanists. Moreover, justice lovers and freedom seekers across the globe of all races, mainly in France, building on the resistance and resilience of African nationalists and Pan-Africanists joined the latter in a symphony of true brotherhood transcending ideologies and races to denounce the ICC victor's justice in Ivory Coast and the ICC bias against Africa. This contributed to placing issues of French neo-colonialism in Africa and the quest for self-determination and sovereignty of Africans into the center of world affairs. The Ivorian crisis is embedded in a renewed revival of Pan-Africanism. Even though the Pan-African credentials of the former president of Ivory Coast Laurent Gbagbo were meager, his fate, his trial, and his nationalist resistance against France contributed to energize African nationalism and the Pan-African consciousness.

The international community, including France and the ICC should understand the cry for freedom, justice, and unity of Africa and refrain from any action which could be seen or perceived as an attempt to hinder the journey of Africa's self-determination, and political and economic sovereignty. The court cannot ignore the African collective memory or the burden of history while it seeks to pursue its mission.[1] Laurent Gbagbo's trial was a historical landmark which was the hallmark of international (in)justice in the first decades of the twenty-first century. He was the first head of state to be brought before the court and was then the first head of state to be acquitted, thus shaking, shattering and rattling the foundations of the International Criminal Court.

The final months of Gbagbo's trial occurred during the hype of the Black Lives Matter Movement, which reached international heights after the killing of George Floyd on May 25, 2020 (on African Liberation Day) by a white racist police officer for a non-violent crime, when Covid-19 was ravaging lives, destroying assets and properties, and when the world economy was crumbling. This event nurtured and revived the African collective memory, filled with the despicable images of lynching. In the meantime, African leaders with a sense of collective consciousness, with a historical consciousness, and cognizant of the African collective memory filled also with the tragic fate of African and people of African descent, were more determined to fight for Laurent Gbagbo's freedom as he was viewed and perceived by a number of the ICC stakeholders as a victim of imperialism and neo-colonialism.

After April 11, 2011, West Africa experienced a series of revolutionary movements that affected Senegal, Burkina Faso, Mali, Guinea, and even the Central African Republic. Citizens in these respective countries are engaged in a series of people's power movements either against constitutional change or against terrorism. In that heightened momentous Pan African momentum,

---

[1] Solomon A. Dersso, "The ICC's Africa Problem A Spotlight on the Politics and Limits of International Criminal Justice," in *Africa and the ICC*, eds. Clarke, Knottnerus, and Volder, 71.

France's reputation was scorned because of its forceful neo-colonial engagement in Africa. Alassane Ouattara's decisions to change the constitution in 2016 and run in 2020 for a third term with the tacit approval and the complicity of the international community demonstrated that what happened in the Ivory Coast 2010-2011 electoral crisis was not about democracy but about France fighting for its survival as a hegemon.

Despite the factual findings it contains, this book does not pretend to put to rest the debate about the ICC and Africa controversy nor does it intend to end the conversation on the court involvement in the Ivorian crisis, but it rather contributes to the discussion about the effectiveness and fairness of international justice in every corner of the globe. That was the essence of this book on Laurent Gbagbo's trial.

The ICC made fool of itself trying unsuccessfully to convince the whole world of one side of the story. It found itself in the dock and got caught in the custody of the danger of a single story. Writing the other side of the story, different from the one put out by the ICC and neo-colonial forces was a duty. I had to respond to that call. This book is a tale (although unsavory) of the International Criminal Court. It is a side of the story that did not make it to the headlines of the international media. It is a voice that was overlooked or smothered and which needed to be heard. I end with the closing words of Nigerian writer Chimamanda Ngozi Adichie she pronounced during the TED Talk she gave in 2014 about the danger of a single story and about the redemptive function of a complete and unbias story: "Stories matter. Many stories matter. Stories have been used to dispossess and to malign, but stories can also be used to empower and to humanize. Stories can break the dignity of a people, but stories can also repair that broken dignity. I would like to end with this thought: That when we reject the single story, when we realize that there is never a single story about any place, we regain a kind of paradise."[2]

---

[2] Chimamanda Adichie Ngozi, "The Danger of a Single Story", Filmed March 10, 2014, TED Video, 19:16, https://www.youtube.com/watch?v=D9Ihs241zeg&t=94s.

Bibliography

Africa Forum. "An Urgent African Appeal to the Prosecutor of the International Criminal Court: Côte d'Ivoire and Africa Need Former President Laurent Koudou Gbagbo in order to achieve Peace and Justice!" September 9, 2015.

African Union. "Decision on the Abuse of the Principle of Universal Jurisdiction." Assembly of the African Union Thirteenth Ordinary Session, July 3, 2009.

AfroPlanete. "Justice: un Témoin qui ne Connait pas son Village." YouTube video, January 22, 2019. https://www.youtube.com/watch?v=L-U_HPUrAWI.

Aboa, Ange, and Joe Bavier. "Gbagbo's Trial Exposes Old Wounds," *Reuters*. Accessed June 28, 2019. https://br.reuters.com/article/us-warcrimes-ivorycoast-gbagbo-idUSKCN0V621B.

Al Jazeera. "Gambia withdraws from the International Criminal Court" Al Jazeera, October 25, 2016, https://www.aljazeera.com/news/2016/10/26/gambia-withdraws-from-international-criminal-court.

Akuetteh, Nii. "Democracy and Africa's Top Priorities Minimizing Conflict. Alleviating Poverty. Defending Sovereignty and Resources: What Has Democracy Got to Do with Any of These?" 3rd Annual Fr. Bill Dyer Lecture, Africa Faith & Justice Network, Washington, DC, November 4, 2011.

Amnesty International. "Côte d'Ivoire: A Succession of Unpunished Crimes." February 27, 2003. https://www.amnesty.org/en/wp-content/uploads/2021/06/afr310072003en.pdf.

Amnesty International. "Côte d'Ivoire: "It Looks Like Nothing Ever Happened Here": Still No Justice One Year After Nahibly Camp Attack." April 29, 2013. https://www.amnesty.org/en/documents/AFR31/009/2013/en/.

Amnesty International. "International Criminal Court: Declarations Amounting to Prohibited Reservations to the Rome Statute." November 2005. https://www.amnesty.org/en/wp-content/uploads/2021/08/ior400322005en.pdf.

Amnesty International. "They Looked at His Card and They Shot Him Dead." May 25, 2011. https://www.amnesty.org/fr/wp-content/uploads/2021/06/afr310022011en.pdf.

Andersen, Erik André. "The International Military Tribunals in Nuremberg and Tokyo: Epoch-Making and Standard-Setting, yet with Different Effectiveness." In *The Effectiveness of International Criminal Justice*, edited by Cedric Ryngaert, 1–26. Antwerp: Intersentia, 2009.

Annan, Kofi. *Interventions: A Life in War and Peace*. New York: Penguin Books, 2012.

APA News. "Le General Kassaraté révèle avoir tenté de demander à Gbagbo de rendre le pouvoir a Ouattara," March 14, 2017. https://news.abidjan.net/articles/611397/le-general-kassarate-revele-avoir-tente-de-demander-a-gbagbo-de-rendre-le-pouvoir-a-ouattara.

Assalé, Philippe. *Reconstruire les forces de défense et de securité en Côte d'Ivoire: Contribution citoyenne*. Paris: L'Harmattan, 2011.

Azikiwe, Nnamdi. *Political Blueprint of Nigeria.* African Book Co., 1943.

Azikiwe, Nnamdi. *Zik: A Selection from the Speeches of Namdi Azikiwe.* Cambridge: Cambridge University Press, 1961.

Bakari-Akin, Tessy. *Côte d'Ivoire: une succession impossible?* Paris: L'Harmattan, 1991.

Baobab News. "P1: Procès de Laurent Gbagbo et Blé Goudé du 25 septembre 2017." YouTube video. Accessed June 18, 2019. https://www.youtube.com/watch?v=jwvcYh5aWkA.

Baobab News. "P2: Procès de Laurent Gbagbo et Blé Goudé du 25 septembre 2017 avec le Général Mangou Philippe." YouTube video, September 26, 2017. https://www.youtube.com/watch?v=jwvcYh5aWkA

Barluet, Alain, "Côte d'Ivoire: Paris planche sur l'après-crise," *Le Figaro,* April 7, 2011. http://www.lefigaro.fr/international/2011/04/07/01003-20110407ART FIG00697-ci-paris-planche-sur-l-après-crise.php.

Basu, Moni. "Ouattara versus Gbagbo: Good versus evil?" CNN, April 12, 2011. http://www.cnn.com/2011/WORLD/africa/04/12/ivory.coast.atrocities/index .html.

BBC. "Ivory Coast Mutiny: Government Announces Deal with Soldiers." May 15, 2017. https://www.bbc.com/news/world-africa-39920149.

Bi, Saint-Tra. *Duékoué: La vérité interdite.* Abidjan: Nouvelles Editions Balafons, 2019.

Biddis, Michael. "From the Nuremberg Charter to the Rome Statute: A Historical Analysis of the Limits of International Criminal Accountability." In *From Sovereign Impunity to International Accountability: The Search for Justice in a World of States,* edited by Ramesh Thakur and Peter Malcontent, 42–60. New York: United Nations University Press, 2004.

Bigot, Laurent. "Côte d'Ivoire: mais qui a gagné la présidentielle de 2010?" *Le Monde,* May 19, 2016. https://www.lemonde.fr/afrique/article/2016/05/27/côte-d-ivoire-mais-qui-a-gagne-la-presidentielle-de-2010_4927642_3212.html.

Bigot, Laurent. "La faiblesse du dossier contre Laurent Gbagbo a fait un tort considérable a la crédibilité de la CPI." *Le Monde,* October 1, 2018. https://www.lemonde.fr/afrique/article/2018/10/01/la-faiblesse-du-dossier-contre-laurent-gbagbo-a-fait-un-tort-considerable-a-la-credibilite-de-la-cpi_5362813_3212.html.

Boggs, James. *The American Revolution: Pages from a Negro Workers Notebook.* New York and London: Monthly Review Press, 1963.

Brodryk, Johann. *Ubuntu Life Lessons from Africa.* Pretoria: Ubuntu School of Philosophy, 2002.

Burke, Roland. *Decolonization and the Evolution of International Human Rights.* Philadelphia: University of Pennsylvania Press, 2010.

Centre for Conflict Resolution. "Peace versus Justice: Truth and Reconciliation Commission and War Crimes Tribunals in Africa." Policy Advisory Group Seminar, Cape Town, May 17–18, 2007.

Bouquet, Christian. *Géopolitique de la Côte d'Ivoire.* 2nd ed. Paris: Armand Colin, 2008.

Busch, Gary K. "The French, the UN and Ivory Coast." Academia. Accessed February 26, 2022. https://www.academia.edu/5096960/The_French_the_UN_and_the_Ivory_Coast.

Campbell, Horace. "Côte d'Ivoire: Gbagbo and the Ivorian Test - Moving Beyond Anti-Imperialist Rhetoric." Rasta Livewire, January 17, 2011. https://www.africaresource.com/rasta/articles/cote-divoire-gbagbo-and-the-ivorian-test-moving-beyond-anti-imperialist-rhetoric.

Campbell, Horace. *Global NATO and the Catastrophic Failure in Libya.* New York: Monthly Review Press, 2013.

Carpenter, David. "Magna Carta 1215: its social and historical context." In *Magna Carta: History, context and influence,* edited by Lawrence Goldman, 17-24. London: Institute of Research Institute, 2018.

Charbonneau, Bruno. *France and the New Imperialism: Security Policy in Sub-Saharan Africa.* Farnham: Ashgate, 2008.

Chirot, Daniel. "The Debacle in Côte d'Ivoire." *Journal of Democracy* 17, no. 2 (April 2006): 63–77.

Citoyen Media. "CPI Francafrique Ecoute." YouTube video, March 14, 2017. https://www.youtube.com/watch?v=mZQAbCkMt0A.

Cotteril, Joseph. "Court rules against South Africa decision to leave ICC". *Financial Times.* February 22, 2017. https://www.ft.com/content/f7561a18-f8ee-11e6-9516-2d969e0d3b65.

Clarke, Kamari M. *Affective Justice: The International Criminal Court and the Pan-Africanist Pushback.* Durham and London: Duke University Press, 2019.

Clark, Phil (@philclark79). "In my book Distant Justice I argue the #ICC is fundamentally unable to prosecute cases of sitting govt officials." Twitter, January 15, 2019. https://twitter.com/philclark79/status/108511956115704 2176.

Clottey, Peter. "Gbagbo Aide Hails Call for 'Restraint' in Ivory Coast Crisis." VOA, December 27, 2010. https://www.voanews.com/a/gbagbo-aide-hails-call-for-restraint-in-ivory-coast-crisis—112576964/157108.html.

Cocks, Tim, and Andrew Quinn. "Exile or Sanctions: Ivory Coast's Gbagbo Told." *Reuters,* December 17, 2010. https://www.reuters.com/article/us-ivorycoast/exile-or-sanctions-ivory-coasts-gbagbo-told-idUSTRE6BG3ID20101217.

Constitution de la République de Côte d'Ivoire, Loi No 90-1529 du 6 novembre 1990.

Côte d'Ivoire Government Communiqué. "Acquittement et Liberation de Gbagbo et Blé Goudé: Le Gouvernement prend note et formule un souhait." Linfodrome, January 16, 2019. http://www.linfodrome.com/actualites-gouvernement-ivoirien/45012-acquittement-et-liberation-de-gbagbo-et-ble-goude-le-gouvernement-prend-note-et-formule-un-souhait.

Council of the European Union, General Secretariat of the Council. *The European Union and the International Criminal Court: May 2010.* Council of the European Union, 2011.

CPP Ghana Online. "Nkrumah Speech Forces against Africa." YouTube video, October 7, 2012. https://www.youtube.com/watch?v=OeozQd5cemg.

de Crete, Stephano. "Partie 3 Procès Gbagbo/Blé 10 mars 2017 Kassaraté ex cdt sup gendarmerie ntle Côte d'Ivoire." YouTube video, March 10, 2017. https://www.youtube.com/watch?v=Bl1jzR4690M.

Davenport, David. "The New Diplomacy." *Policy Review*, no. 116 (December 2002/January 2003). https://www.hoover.org/research/new-diplomacy.

Dersso, Solomon A. "The ICC's Africa Problem: A Spotlight on the Politics and Limits of International Criminal Justice." In *Africa and the ICC: Perceptions of Justice*, edited by Kamari M. Clarke, Abel S. Knottnerus, and Eefje de Volder, 61–77. Cambridge: Cambridge University Press, 2018.

Dierenfield, Bruce J. *The Civil Rights Movement*, Revised edition. London and New York: Routledge, 2013.

Dossier de Presse V8-20190514 CPI. Le Procès de Laurent Gbagbo et de Charles Blé Goudé: Jalons et Enjeux.

Du Plessis, Max. *The ICC that Africa wants*. Pretoria: Institute for Security Studies, 2010.

Du Plessis, Max. "Exploring Efforts to Resolve the Tension between the AU and the ICC over the Bashir Saga." In *The International Criminal Court and Africa: One Decade On*, edited by Evelyn A. Ankumah, 245-74. Cambridge: Intersentia, 2016.

Ellenbogen, Alice. *La Succession d'Houphouët-Boigny: entre tribalisme et democratie*. Paris: L'Harmattan, 2002.

Esedebe, P. Olisanwuche. *Pan-Africanism: The Idea and Movement 1776–1963*, 2nd ed. Washington, DC: Howard University Press, 1994.

Fairlie, Megan. "The International Criminal Court and the Community of Nations." Presented at a Conference, University of Georgia School of Law, Athens, Georgia, March 8, 2019.

Fagiolo, Nicoletta. "Laurent Gbagbo, The Right to Difference, part 1." YouTube video, September 14, 2014. https://www.youtube.com/watch?v=xwDLCb2UkXE.

Felter, Claire. "The Role of the International Criminal Court." Council on Foreign Relations, February 23, 2021. https://www.cfr.org/backgrounder/role-international-criminal-court.

Ferencz, Benjamin B. "Foreward." In *The International Criminal Court and Africa: One Decade On*, edited by Evelyn A. Ankumah. Cambridge: Intersentia, 2016.

Fletcher, George P. "The Law of War and Its Pathologies." *Columbia Human Rights Law Review* 38, no. 3 (Spring 2007): 517–545.

France 24. "Bombardement de Bouaké: Les proches des victimes en colère face à l'abandon des poursuites," May 29, 2019. https://www.france24.com/fr/20190529-bombardement-bouake-2004-colere-victimes-abandon-poursuites-jean-balan.

France 24. "Ivory Coast: ICC Chief Prosecutor Luis Moreno Ocampo." YouTube video, April 5, 2011. https://www.youtube.com/watch?v=tm83P-pBSzA

France 24. "Le Procureur de la CPI met le Camp Gbagbo en garde." YouTube video. Accessed December 4, 2014. https://www.youtube.com/watch?v=p6cA-KBHNOE.

France 24. "Video-Les internautes Ivoiriens lancent 'le bracelet electronique challenge'," December 14, 2018. https://observers.france24.com/fr/2018 1214-cote-ivoire-internautes-bracelet-electronique-challenge-gbagbo.

Fraser, Giles. "Desmond Tutu Should Not Have Snubbed Tony Blair." *The Guardian,* September 3, 2012. https://www.theguardian.com/commentis free/2012/sep/03/desmond-tutu-snubbed-tony-blair.

Fraternité Matin. December 27, 1982.

Frindéthié, K. Martial. *From Lumumba to Gbagbo: Africa in the Eddy of the Euro-American Quest for Exceptionalism.* Jefferson: McFarland & Co. Inc., 2016.

Glendon, Mary Ann. *A World Made New: Eleanor Roosevelt and the Universal Declaration of Human Rights.* New York: Random House, 2001.

Godé, Pierre Dagbo. *La Diplomatie Africaine: Theorie et Pratique.* Paris: L'Harmattan, 2014.

Grantham, Dewey W. *The United States since 1945: The Ordeal of Power.* New York: McGraw-Hill Book Company, 1976.

Guguen, Guillaume. "Les électeurs suspendus à la publication des résultats." *France 24,* December 3, 2010. http://www.france24.com/fr/20101129-cote-ivoire-election-presidentielle-taux-participation-second-tour-cei-gbagbo-ouattara.

Hamer, Magali Chelpi-den. *Militarized youths in Western Côte d'Ivoire: Local Processes of mobilization, demobilization, and related humanitarian interventions (2002-2007).* Leiden: African Studies Centre, 2007.

Harris, David B., and Aaron Eitan Meyer. "Lawfare: A Supporting Arm in Modern Conflict." *The Lawfare Project,* April 4, 2011. https://www.thelaw fareproject.org/articles/2011/4/4/ilawfare-a-supporting-arm-in-modern-conflictibrthe-lawfare-project.

Heikkilä, Mikaela. "The Balanced Scorecard of International Criminal Tribunals." In *The Effectiveness of International Criminal Justice,* edited by Cedric Ryngaert, 27-54. Antwerp: Intersentia, 2009.

Helms, Jesse. Subcommittee on International Operations of the Senate Committee on Foreign Relations of the United States Senate, 23 July 1998, 105th Congress, 2nd Session, S. Rep. No.105.

Hoile, David. *Justice Denied: The Reality of the International Criminal Court.* London: The Africa Research Centre, 2014.

Holligan, Anna. "Laurent Gbagbo Case: Ivory Coast's Leader Acquittal Rattles ICC Foundations." BBC, January 15, 2019. https://www.bbc.com/news/world-africa-46874517.

Houphouët-Boigny, Félix. *Anthologie des Discours, 1946–1978.* Abidjan: CEDA, 1978.

Hugueux, Vincent. "Côte d'Ivoire: Ouattara veut 'protéger' les minorités." *L'Express,* January 25, 2012. http://www.lexpress.fr/actualite/monde/afrique/cote-d-ivoire-ouattara-veut-proteger-les-minorites_1075076.html.

Human Rights Watch. "They Killed them like it was Nothing." October 5, 2011. https://www.hrw.org/sites/default/files/reports/cdi1011webwcover_0.pdf.

Ibhawoh, Bonny. "Testing the Atlantic Charter: linking anticolonialism, self-determination and universal human rights." *The International Journal of Human Rights*. Routledge Taylor and Francis Group, September 2014. http://dx.doi.org/10.1080/13642987.2014.951340.

United Nations. *Rome Statute of the International Criminal Court*. The Hague: International Criminal Court, 2011.

ICC. *How the International Criminal Court works*. The Hague: ICC, 2020.

James, C. L. R. *The Black Jacobins: Toussaint L'Ouverture and the San Domingo Revolution*, 2nd ed. New York: Vintage Books, 1989.

James, John. "Gbagbo transfer to The Hague shocks supporters." BBC, November 30, 2011. https://www.bbc.com/news/world-africa-15962777.

Jensen, Steven L. B. *The Making of International Human Rights: The 1960s, Decolonization and the Reconstruction of Global Values*. Cambridge: Cambridge University Press, 2016.

Jeune Afrique. No. 112, December 1984.

Joselow, Gabe. "US Official Says Kenya's Elections Have 'Consequences." VOA, February 7, 2013. https://www.voanews.com/a/us-official-says-kenya-elections-have-consequences/1599063.html.

Juppé, Alain. "France/UN/Côte d'Ivoire – Libya/French role/NATO role." Interview given by Alain Juppé, Ministre d'Etat, Minister of Foreign and European Affairs, to "France Info," Paris, April 12, 2011.

Kadet, Bertin. *La Politique de défense et de sécurité de la Côte d'Ivoire*. Paris: L'Harmattan, 2011.

Kamruzzaman, Md, and Sashi Kanto Das. "The Evaluation of Human Rights: An Overview in Historical Perspective." *American Journal of Service Science and Management* 3, no. 2 (2016): 5–12.

Kemp, Gerard. "Taking Stock of International Criminal Justice in Africa: Three Inventories Considered." In *International Criminal Justice in Africa: Challenges and Opportunities*, edited by Beitel Van der Merwe, 7–32. Nairobi, Kenya: Friedrich Ebert Stiftung, 2014.

Kessié, Raymond Koudou. "Pourquoi le Président Laurent Gbagbo doit être libéré." In *Le President Laurent Gbagbo à la Cour Pénale Internationale: Justice ou Imposture?*, edited by Raymond Koudou Kessié and Hubert Oulaye, 217-225. Paris: L'Harmattan, 2013.

Kessié, Raymond Koudou. "Quand le Président Laurent Gbagbo porte sa croix." In *Le Président Laurent Gbagbo à la Cour Pénale Internationale: Justice ou Imposture?*, edited by Raymond Koudou Kessié and Hubert Oulaye, 57-62. Paris: L'Harmattan, 2013.

Khan, Akbar. "Ten Years of International Criminal Court Practice -Trials, Achievements and Tribulations: Is the ICC Today What Africa Expects or Wants?" In *The International Criminal Court and Africa: One Decade On*, edited by Evelyn A. Ankumah, 433-40. Cambridge: Intersentia, 2016.

Kielsgard, Mark D. *Reluctant Engagement: US Policy and the International Criminal Court*. Leiden: Martinus Nijhoff Publishers, 2010.

King, Jr., Martin Luther. *The Autobiography of Martin Luther King, Jr*. Edited by Clayborne Carson. New York: Warner Books, Inc., 1998.

Kokutse, Francis. "Ghana President Says 'no' to Troops in Ivory Coast." *The San Diego Union Tribune*, January 7, 2011. https://www.sandiegouniontribune.com/sdut-ghana-president-says-no-to-troops-in-ivory-coast-2011jan07-story.html.

Konaté, Yacouba. "Le Destin Tragique d'Alassane Ouattara." In *Côte d'Ivoire l'Année Terrible 1999–2000*, edited by Marc Le Pape and Claudine Vidal, 253-309. Paris: Karthala, 2003.

Koulibaly, Mamadou. *Sur la Route de la Liberté*. Abidjan: Presses des Universites de Côte d'Ivoire, 2004.

Kouassi, Abraham. "Mangou Asked Gbagbo to Resign." International Justice Monitor, September 26, 2017. https://www.ijmonitor.org/2017/09/philippe-mangou-asked-gbagbo-to-resign/.

Kouassi, Abraham. "Philippe Mangou: 'Gbagbo Accidentally Financed the Invisible Commando'." International Justice Monitor, October 2, 2017. https://www.ijmonitor.org/2017/10/philippe-mangou-gbagbo-accidentally-financed-the-invisible-commando.

Laffont, Michèle. "Le General Guiai Bi Poin révèle "Comment j'ai été obligé de témoigner contre Laurent Gbagbo à la CPI." *Ivoire Business*, April 2, 2017. https://www.ivoirebusiness.net/articles/cpi-le-g%C3%A9n%C3%A9ral-guiai-bi-poin-r%C3%A9v%C3%A8le-%C2%AB-comment-j%E2%80%99ai-%C3%A9t%C3%A9-oblig%C3%A9-de-t%C3%A9moigner-contre-laurent.

Gnaka, Lagoké. "Le Film de la Démission d'Alassane Ouattara." *Le Nouvel Horizon*, no. 171 (December 24, 1993).

Lamony, Stephen. "African Court Not Ready for International Crimes." African Arguments, December 10, 2012. https://africanarguments.org/2012/12/african-court-not-ready-for-international-crimes-by-steven-lamony.

Le Monde. "La Pression Internationale contre Laurent Gbagbo s'accentue." *Le Monde*, December 17, 2010. https://www.lemonde.fr/afrique/article/2010/12/17/sarkozy-enjoint-a-gbagbo-de-quitter-le-pouvoir-avant-la-fin-de-la-semaine_1454779_3212.html.

Las Casas, Bartolomé de. *A Brief Account of the Destruction of the Indies*. London: R. Hewson, 1689.

Lauren, Paul G. "From Impunity to Accountability: Forces of Transformation and the Changing International Human Rights." In *From Sovereign Impunity to International Accountability: The Search for Justice in a World of States*, edited by Ramesh Thakur and Peter Malcontent, 15–41. New York: United Nations University Press, 2004.

Loucou, Jean Noel. "De l'Ivoirité." In *L'Ivoirité, ou, l'esprit du nouveau contrat social du Président Henri Konan Bédié*, edited by Saliou Touré. Abidjan: Presses Universitaires de Côte d'Ivoire, 1996.

Luyet. Nakouty. "Procès de Laurent Gbagbo et de Charles Blé Goudé: il faut sauver le temoin P 100000 Degamage." YouTube video, February 2, 2016. https://www.youtube.com/watch?v=WSu1dzsQQ28.

Madsen, Deborah L. *American Exceptionalism*. Edinburgh: Edinburgh University Press, 1998.

Maisonneuve, Charles. *Le Bourbier Ivoirien*. Paris: Editions Privat, 2005.

Mandela, Nelson. *Long Walk to Freedom: The Autobiography of Nelson Mandela*. Boston, MA: Little, Brown, 1995.

Mandela, Nelson. "I am prepared to die" https://africanlegends.files. wordpress.com/2013/11/nelson-mandela-1964-speech_i-am-prepared-to-die.pdf.

Maupas, Stéphanie. "Victoire pour le Kenya à la Cour pénale internationale." *Le Monde*, December 9, 2014. http://www.lemonde.fr/idees/article/2014/ 12/09/victoire-pour-le-kenya-a-la-cour-penale-internationale_4537601_32 32.html.

Maupas, Stéphanie. *Le Joker des Puissants: Le Grand Roman de la Cour Pénale Internationale*. Paris: Don Quichotte Editions, 2016.

Manirakiza, Eric. "La CPI, 'un instrument politique'." VOA, January 16, 2019. https://www.voaafrique.com/a/la-cpi-un-instrument-politique-analyste/47 46165.html.

Mazrui, Ali A. *Towards a Pax Africana: A Study of Ideology and Ambition*. Chicago and London: The University of Chicago Press, 1967.

Mbeki, Thabo. "Prologue." In *African Renaissance*, edited by Malegapuru William Makgoba. Cape Town: Tafelberg Publishers, 1999.

Mbeki, Thabo. "What the World got Wrong in Côte d'Ivoire." *Foreign Policy*, April 29, 2011. https://foreignpolicy.com/2011/04/29/what-the-world-got-wrong-in-cote-divoire.

McGoldrick, Dominic, and Eric Donnelly. "Criminal Trials before International Tribunals: Legality and Legitimacy." In *The Permanent International Criminal Court: Legal and Policy Issues*, edited by Dominic McGoldrick, Peter Rowe, and Eric Donnell, 9–46. Oxford: Hart Publishing, 2004.

Meacham, Jon. *The Soul of America: The Battle for our Better Angels*. New York: Random House, 2019.

Mearsheimer, John J. *The Tragedy of Great Power Politics*. New York: W. W. Norton & Company, 2003.

Memel-Fotê, Harris. "Un Mythe Politique des Akan en Côte d'Ivoire: Le sens de l'État." In *Mondes Akan: Identité et Pouvoir en Afrique Occidentale*, edited by Pierluigi Valsecchi and Fabio Viti, 21–42. Paris: L'Harmattan, 1999.

Monga, Célestin, and Jean-Claude Tchathouang. *Sortir du Piège Monétaire*. Paris: Economica, 1996.

Moyn, Samuel. *The Last Utopia: Human Rights in History*. Cambridge and London: The Belknap Press of Harvard University Press, 2010.

Musila, Godfrey M., "The Role of the African Union in International Criminal Justice: For Good or Bad?" In *The International Criminal Court and Africa: One Decade On*, edited by Evelyn A. Ankumah, 299–346. Cambridge: Intersentia, 2016.

Mutua, Makau W. "Africans and the ICC: Hypocrisy, Impunity, and Perversion." In *Africa and the ICC: Perceptions of Justice*, edited by Kamari M. Clarke, Abel S. Knottnerus, and Eefje de Volder, 47–60. Cambridge: Cambridge University Press, 2018.

Adichie, Chimamanda Ngozi. "The Danger of a Single Story." Filmed March 10, 2014. TED Video, 19:16, https://www.youtube.com/watch?v=D9Ihs241zeg &t=94s.

Nguessan, Kouamé. "Le Forum pour la réconciliation nationale. 9 octobre–18 décembre 2001." In *Côte d'Ivoire l'Année Terrible 1999–2000*, edited by Marc Le Pape and Claudine Vidal, 325-351. Paris: Karthala, 2003.

Nill, David A. "National Sovereignty: Must It Be Sacrificed to the International Criminal Court?" *Brigham Young University Journal of Public Law* 14, no. 1 (1999): 119-50.

Nkrumah, Kwame. *Neo-Colonialism: The Last Stage of Imperialism*. London: Thomas and Nelson & Sons, Ltd., 1965.

Nossiter, Adam. "Women Said to Be Killed at Ivory Coast Protest." *The New York Times*, March 4, 2011. https://www.nytimes.com/2011/03/04/world/africa/04ivory-coast.html.

Nwoya, Leo C. "Transitional Justice and the ICC: Lessons from Rwanda." In *The International Criminal Court and Africa: One Decade On*, edited by Evelyn A. Ankumah, 549–91. Cambridge: Intersentia, 2016.

Ochs, Sara L. "The United States, the International Criminal Court, and the Situation in Afghanistan" *Notre Dame Law Review Reflection* 95, no. 2 (December 2019).

Office of the Prosecutor. "Strategic Plan 2019–2021." International Criminal Court, July 17, 2019. https://www.icc-cpi.int/itemsDocuments/20190726-strategic-plan-eng.pdf.

Olasolo, Hector. *The Role of the International Criminal Court in Preventing Atrocity Crimes through Timely Intervention*. The Hague: Eleven International Publishing, 2011.

Onana, Charles. *Côte d'Ivoire: Le Coup d'État*. Paris: Editions Duboiris, 2011.

O'Toole, Marisa. "Africa and the International Criminal Court: Behind the Backlash and Toward Future Solutions" PhD Diss. *Honors Projects*. 64. Bowdoin College, 2017.

Peter, Chris Maina. "Fighting Impunity: African States and the International Criminal Court." In *The International Criminal Court and Africa: One Decade On*, edited by Evelyn A. Ankumah, 1-62. Cambridge: Intersentia, 2016.

Pigeaud, Fanny. "The Devious Manoeuvres behind ex-Ivorian Leader Laurent Gbagbo's Trial at ICC," *Mediapart*, October 8, 2017. https://www.mediapart.fr/en/journal/international/081017/devious-manoeuvres-behind-ex-ivorian-leader-laurent-gbagbos-trial-icc?_locale=en&onglet=full.

Pigeaud, Fanny. *France Côte d'Ivoire: Une histoire tronquée*. Paris: Vents d'ailleurs, 2015.

Pigeaud, Fanny and Ndongo Samba Sylla. *L'Arme Invisible de la Francafrique: Une histoire du Franc CFA*. Paris: La Découverte, 2018.

Plesch, Dan. *Human Rights after Hitler: The Lost History of Prosecuting the Axis War*. Washington: Georgetown University Press, 2017.

Poe, Zizwe. *Kwame Nkrumah's Contribution to Pan-Africanism: An Afrocentric Analysis*. Los Angeles: University Press of Sankore, 2010.

Prosecutor v. Gbagbo, ICC-02/11-01/11-1, Decision on Warrant Arrest, November 23, 2011.

Prosecutor v. Gbagbo, ICC-02/11-01/15, Request for Authorization of an Investigation Pursuant to Article 15, June 23, 2011.

Prosecutor v. Gbagbo, ICC-02/11-01/11-432, Decision adjourning the hearing on the confirmation of charges pursuant to Article 61(7)(c)(i) of the Rome Statute, June 3, 2013.

Prosecutor v. Gbagbo, ICC-02/11-01/11-572, Judgment on the appeal of the Prosecutor, December 16, 2013.

Prosecutor v. Gbagbo, ICC-02/11-01/11-637-Conf-Anx2-Corr2, 2014.

Prosecutor v. Gbagbo, ICC-02/11-01/11-656-Red, Decision on the confirmation of charges against Laurent Gbagbo, June 12, 2014.

Prosecutor v. Gbagbo, CIV-OTP-0049-0048, p.0050, June 12, 2014.

Prosecutor v. Gbagbo, ICC-02/11-01/15-T-138-Red2-FRA, Witness P-0010, Transcript of the Hearing, March 28, 2017.

Prosecutor v. Gbagbo, ICC-02/11-01/15, Office of the Prosecutor, The Mid-Trial Brief, March 29, 2018.

Prosecutor v. Gbagbo, ICC-02/11-01/15-1136-Conf-Anx1-Corr, June 13, 2018.

Prosecutor v. Gbagbo, ICC-02/11-01/15, Annex 3, September 28, 2018.

Prosecutor v. Gbagbo, ICC-02/11-01/15-T-221-Red2-ENG, Transcript of the Hearing, October 1, 2018.

Prosecutor v. Gbagbo, Defense Motion on No Case to Answer, ICC-02/11-01/15-1199-Anx4-Corr-Red 28-09-2018 1/57 RH T Annex 4 (September 28, 2018).

Prosecutor v. Gbagbo, Defense Motion on No Case to Answer, ICC-02/11-01/15-1199-Anx4-Corr-Red 28-09-2018 1/57 RH T Annex 5, (September 28, 2018).

Prosecutor v. Gbagbo, ICC-02/11-01/15, Office of the Prosecutor, January 15, 2019.

Prosecutor v. Gbagbo, ICC-02/11-01/15, Trial Chamber Oral Decision, January 15, 2019.

Prosecutor v. Gbagbo, ICC-02/11-01/15, Judgment on the Prosecutor's appeal, February 1, 2019. https://www.icc-cpi.int/CourtRecords/CR2019_00611.PDF

Prosecutor v. Gbagbo, ICC-02/11-01/15, The Decision: The Reasons by Judge Geoffrey Henderson, July 16, 2019.

Prosecutor v. Gbagbo, Case No. ICC-02/11-01/15, The Decision: Opinion of Judge Cuno Tarfusser, July 16, 2019.

Prosecutor v. Gbagbo, ICC-02/11-01/15, The Decision: Dissenting Opinion by Judge Herrera Carbuccia, July 16 2019.

Prosecutor v. Gbagbo, ICC-02/11-01/15-T-200-Red2-FRA P-0009, Transcript of the Hearing, October 5, 2019.

Prosecutor v. Gbagbo, ICC-02/11-01/15, Prosecution Document in Support of Appeal, October 17, 2019.

Prosecutor v. Gbagbo, ICC-02/11-01/15 A, Appeals Chamber's Judgement, March 31, 2021.

Quist-Adade, Charles. "From Neo-Colonialism to Neoliberal Globalization: Lessons from Nkrumah's Neo-Colonialism: The Last Stage of Imperialism." In *Re-Engaging the African Diasporas Pan-Africanism in the Age of Globalization*, edited by Charles Quist-Adade and Wendy Royal, 103-37. London: Cambridge Scholars Publishing, 2016.

Radio Television Ivoirienne. YouTube video. Accessed March 30, 2011. http://www.youtube.com/watch?v=EF-ScWulSaM.

Reus-Smit, Christian. "International Crises of Legitimacy," *International Politics* vol. 44 (2007): 157–174.

RFI. "Choi Young-jin: L'ONUCI est toujours en contact avec Laurent Gbagbo." April 4, 2011. https://www.rfi.fr/fr/afrique/20110411-yong-jin-choi.

RFI. Interview de Choi sur RFI. "La Majorité des Militaires ne sont pas prêts à Combattre pour Gbagbo." March 3, 2011. https://www.connectionivoirienne.net/2011/03/14/interview-choi-sur-rfi-la-majorite-des-militaires-ne-sont-pas-prets-a-combattre-pour-gbagbo/.

Reus-Smit, Christian. *Individual Rights and the Making of the International System*. Cambridge: Cambridge University Press, 2013.

Robertson, Geoffrey. *Crimes Against Humanity: The Struggle for Global Justice*, 4th ed. London: Penguin Books, 2012.

Rothe, Dawn, and Christopher W. Mullins. *Symbolic Gestures and the Generation of Global Social Control*. Lanham: Lexington Books, 2006.

RTI. YouTube video. Accessed June 10, 2013. https://www.youtube.com/watch?v=d3zO4euzF7Q#t=98

RTI. "Côte d'Ivoire: Document RTI sur la marche du 16/12/2010 et les combats qui ont suivi." YouTube video, December 31, 2010. https://www.youtube.com/watch?v=Hy3aj3zUniw.

RTI Bengue. "(2e Partie) Procès: Gbagbo et Blé Goudé: 29 Mai 2017, Ate Kloosterman." YouTube video, May 29, 2017. https://www.youtube.com/watch?v=LZG7_aiySt4RTI.

Rueff, Judith. *Côte d'Ivoire: Le feu au pré carre*. Paris: Editions Autrement Frontieres, 2004.

Ryngaert, Cedric, ed. *The Effectiveness of International Criminal Justice*. Antwerp: Intersentia, 2009.

Ryngaert, Cedric. "The Principle of Complementarity as a Means of Ensuring Effective International Criminal Justice." In *The Effectiveness of International Criminal Justice*, edited by Cedric Ryngaert, 143–173. Antwerp: Intersentia, 2009.

Sander, Barrie (@Barrie_Sander). "Emerging narratives in the lead up to and aftermath of today's #ICC majority decision to grant the defence's "no case to answer" motion to acquit #Gbagbo & #BleGoudé." Twitter, January 15, 2019. https://twitter.com/Barrie_Sander/status/1085140840199213057.

Sands, Philippe. "International justice is needed—even if it takes 100 more years to perfect it." *The Guardian*, May 16, 2012. https://www.theguardian.com/law/2012/may/16/international-justice-needed-expert-view.

Schmitt, Paul D. "France, Africa, and the ICC: The Neo-colonialist Critique and the Crisis of Institutional Legitimacy." In *Africa and the ICC: Perceptions of Justice*, edited by Kamari M. Clarke, Abel S. Knottnerus, and Eefje de Volder, 127–151. Cambridge: Cambridge University Press, 2016.

Sikkink, Kathryn. *The Justice Cascade: How Human Rights Prosecutions are Changing World Politics*. New York: W.W. Norton & Co., 2011.

Smith, David. "New Chief Prosecutor Defends International Criminal Court." *The Guardian*, May 23, 2012. https://www.theguardian.com/law/2012/may/23/chief-prosecutor-international-criminal-court.

Smith, Stephen, Damien Glez, and Vincent Rigoulet. "Le Vrai Visage de la Rebellion. *Le Monde*, October 11, 2002. https://www.lemonde.fr/archives/article/2002/10/11/cote-d-ivoire-le-visage-de-la-rebellion_4260860_181921 8.html.

Soro, Guillaume. *Pourquoi je suis devenu un rebelle: La Côte d'Ivoire au bord du gouffre*. Paris: Hachette Littérature, 2005.

Stone, Oliver, and Peter Kuznick. "Chapter Four: The Bomb." In *The Untold History of the United States*, 131-80. New York: Gallery Books, 2019.

Taiwo, Olufemi. "The African Union and the Moral Abdication." *Pambazuka News*, November 20, 2013. https://www.pambazuka.org/governance/african-union-and-moral-abdication.

Tano, Félix. "L'Ajournement d'Audience pour Insuffisance de Preuves de la Cour Pénale Internationale: Un Acharnement Judiciaire." In *Cour pénale internationale: l'introuvable preuve contre le président Laurent Gbagbo*, edited by Raymond Koudou Kessié, Hubert Oulaye, and Félix Tano, 67-114. Paris: L'Harmattan, 2013.

Tawa, Netton Prince, and Alexandra Engelsdorfer. "Acceptance of the International Criminal Court in Côte d'Ivoire: Between the Hope for Justice and the Concern of 'Victor's Justice." In *After Nuremberg. Exploring Multiple Dimensions of the Acceptance of International Criminal Justice*, edited by Susanne Buckley-Zistel, Friederike Mieth, and Marjana Papa. Nuremberg: International Nuremberg Principles Academy, 2017. https://www.nuremberg academy.org/fileadmin/user_upload/Cote_d_Ivoire.pdf.

The Avalon Project. The Versailles Treaty June 28, 1919: Part VII. Penalties. Article 227. Accessed February 27, 2022. https://avalon.law.yale.edu/imt/partvii.asp.

Thompson, Vincent Bakpetu. *Africa and Unity: The Evolution of Pan-Africanism*. New York: Humanities Press, 1969.

United Nations. *International Criminal Court: Rules of Procedure and Evidence*.

United Nations. Operations in Côte d'Ivoire, Communiqué 937, November 29, 2011.

United Nations. "Press Conference by Prosecutor of International Criminal Court," December 15, 2011. https://www.un.org/press/en/2011/111215_ICC.doc.htm.

United Nations Security Council Report of May 13, 2004.

UNWCC. *History of the United Nations War Crimes Commission and the Development of the Laws of War*. London: Her Majesty's Stationery Office, 1948.

Verschave, Francois-Xavier. *La Françafrique, le plus long scandale de la République*. Paris: Editions Stock, 1998.

War Crimes Research Office. *The Confirmation of Charges at the International Criminal Court: A Critical Assessment and Recommendations for Change*. Washington, DC: American University Washington College of Law, 2015.

X, Malcolm. *By Any Means Necessary*. New York: Pathfinder, 1970.

Zartman, William. *Politics of Trade Negotiations between Africa and the European Economic Community: The Weak Confront the Strong.* Princeton: Princeton University, 1971.

Zolberg, Aristide R. *One Party Government in the Ivory Coast.* Princeton: Princeton University Press, 1964.

Glossary

UNOCI	United Nations Operations in Côte d'Ivoire
NATO	North Atlantic Treaty Organization
GIMPA	Ghana Institute of Management and Public Administration
WAEMU	West African Economic Monetary Union
PANA	*Parti Nationaliste*
SAA	*Syndicat Agricole Agricole*
RDA	*Rassemblement Démocratique Africain*
PDCI	*Parti Démocratique de Côte d'Ivoire*
SYNARES	*Syndicat National pour la Recherche et l'Enseignement Superieur*
MEECI	*Mouvement des Etudiants et Elèves de Côte d'Ivoire*
FESCI	*Fédération Estudiantine et Scolaire de Côte d'Ivoire*
FPI	*Front Populaire Ivoirien*
GPP	*Groupement Patriotique pour la Paix*
FLGO	*Front de Libération du Grand Ouest*
NFI	Netherlands Forensic Institute
ECOWAS	Economic Community of West African States
ECOMOG	the Economic Community of West African Monitoring Group
AU	African Union
FRCI	*Forces Républicaines de Côte d'Ivoire*
BCEAO	Banque Centrale des États de l'Afrique de l'Ouest
FDS	Forces de Défense de Sécurité
IMT	International Military Tribunals
NCNC	National Council for Nigeria and the Cameroons
NEPAD	New Economic Partnership for Africa's Development
PIDE	*Polícia Internacional e de Defesa do Estado*
AfCFTA	African Continental Free Trade
OAU	Organization of African Unity
UNIA	Universal Negro Improvement Association
ASPA	American Servicemembers' Protection Act
UNWCC	United Nations War Crimes Commission
COJEP	*Congrès Panafricain des Jeunes Patriotes*
CFA	*Communauté Financière Française*

Index

Y

Z